D0705407

Student Workbook

INTRODUCTORY STATISTICS FOR BUSINESS AND ECONOMICS FOURTH EDITION

and

INTRODUCTORY STATISTICS FIFTH EDITION

Thomas H. Wonnacott
Ronald J. Wonnacott

Prepared by
Thomas H. Wonnacott
Clayton D. Block
University of Western Ontario

*Containing Complete Solutions
for Odd-Numbered Problems,
Plus 250 Review Problems with Answers*

John Wiley & Sons
New York Chichester Brisbane Toronto Singapore

Copyright © 1990 by John Wiley & Sons, Inc.

All rights reserved.

Reproduction or translation of any part of
this work beyond that permitted by Section
107 or 108 of the 1976 United States Copyright
Act without the permission of the copyright
owner is unlawful. Requests for permission or
further information should be addressed to the
Permissions Department, John Wiley & Sons, Inc.

0-471-50899-3

Printed in the United States of America

10 9

Printed and bound by the Courier Companies, Inc.

PREFACE

This workbook contains the complete solutions to all the odd-numbered problems in <u>Introductory Statistics for Business and Economics</u>, 4th edition. The purpose of a complete solution is to let you see how we arrived at an answer. In comparing this to your own, however, keep in mind that our solution can often be improved. We would be sorry indeed if these published solutions were held as an absolute standard.

Remember that reading a solution before attempting it yourself is just like reading a crossword puzzle solution before you try it yourself. It kills the enjoyment, as well as the learning. If time is your limitation, it would be far better to do just half as many problems properly.

This workbook also contains over 250 new review problems, in increasing order of difficulty within each chapter. Major illustrations of important themes are included -- similar to the Final Challenges in the text. Brief answers to all these problems are finally provided, both odd and even.

Tom Wonnacott
Clayton Block
The University of Western Ontario
London, Canada, 1989

CONTENTS

LIST OF THEMES WITHIN PART B -- LIKE FINAL CHALLENGES

WARNING

The purpose of a complete solution is to let you see how we arrived at an answer. In comparing this to your own, however, keep in mind that our solution can often be improved. We would be sorry indeed if these published solutions were held as an absolute standard.

Remember that reading a solution before attempting it yourself is just like reading a crossword puzzle solution before you try the puzzle itself. It kills the enjoyment, as well as the learning. If time is your limitation, it would be far better to do just half as many problems properly.

1-1　a.
$$\pi = P \pm 1.96 \sqrt{\frac{P(1-P)}{n}} \qquad (1\text{-}2)$$

in 1968,　$\pi = .50 \pm 1.96 \sqrt{\dfrac{(.50)(.50)}{1500}} = .50 \pm .0253$

$\simeq 50\% \pm 3\%$

in 1972,　$\pi = .38 \pm .0246$　$\simeq 38\% \pm 2\%$
in 1976,　$\pi = .51 \pm .0253$　$\simeq 51\% \pm 3\%$
in 1980,　$\pi = .48 \pm .0253$　$\simeq 48\% \pm 3\%$
in 1984,　$\pi = .41 \pm .0249$　$\simeq 41\% \pm 2\%$
in 1988,　$\pi = .44 \pm .0251$　$\simeq 44\% \pm 3\%$

b.　Most intervals are correct. For example, in 1968 the interval may be written

$$47\% < \pi < 53\%$$

This does indeed cover the given true value $\pi = 49.7\%$.
　One interval is wrong: The 1980 interval is wrong, because it fails to cover the true value $\pi = 44.7\%$.

Remarks The chance of each confidence interval being wrong is more than 5 %, because there are problems in addition to sampling uncertainty. For example, between the pre-election poll and the actual election, some voters may change their mind.

1-3　In each case, bias can be eliminated by taking a random sample. Then every member of the population has a known chance to be drawn.
　Without this randomness, bias is introduced -- so much bias, in fact, that the sample may be worse than useless. Specifically:

a.　Constituents with extreme views are likeliest to write, including members of organized lobbies like the National Rifle Association. People with moderate views may be vastly under-represented.

b.　Many of the people who would benefit most from the subsidy to day-care centers -- the working couples with small children -- would not be represented at all in this sample.

c.　The alumni who don't return to their reunion may be the ones most distant, most busy, least anxious to meet their classmates, and so on. They may well have a different income pattern from the alumni who do return. And the alumni who are willing to disclose their income are probably vastly different from those who are not.

1-5　Here is one of many possible examples: the "treatment" of very young children in day-care centers. The government, through subsidies and tax policy, encourages it without much real evidence of what it does to the child. (The potential benefits and harms are easy enough to guess: For example, it is better than parents who are incompetent and bored. Yet can it give children the same sense of belonging and love as average parents? Let's sketch how we might begin to evaluate day-care experimentally (recognizing that a fuller evaluation would require many more experiments and studies):

a. As subjects, we might start with families who applied for subsidized day-care out of economic necessity, and would be willing to take either day-care or the alternative control sketched below.

b. Families would be randomly assigned to treatment or control. The treatment might consist of subsidized day-care, and to be realistic, we could select several day-care centers randomly to make them representative. As well, we might investigate a second treatment: very expensive day care, that included a generous amount of well-paid help.

For the control families, we could pay them the equivalent amount as a family allowance that helped one of the parents to stay home with the children.

c. Of course, it would be impossible to keep the parents or children blind. But it would still be important to keep the evaluators blind, as described below.

d. The evaluation would be the most difficult step. The point of good child-care is to raise happy, loving kids, but how do you <u>measure</u> that? Here are some possible proxies:

(i) When the children start school, have their teachers evaluate them on how well they behaved, how well they interacted with other children, and in general, how happy they seemed. This evaluation could be repeated in later years to look for longer-term effects, and average out some of the evaluation error. It would be very difficult, but very important, to keep the evaluators from finding out who was in the treatment group and who was not.

(ii) Perhaps a thorough psychological interview, including an IQ test, and test for depression.

(iii) More objective differences might be interesting to look at in later years: progress through school including total number of years of schooling, marriage and divorce rates, kind of occupation, and even crime rates. (Since crime is rare, however, it would take a large number of subjects to get meaningful statistics.)

One of the great difficulties of such a study would be the long time required to get answers. Not only would it be hard to keep adequate followup, it would also require patience for the answers to come in. And of course it would cost millions of dollars. Yet its cost might be trivial compared to the possible benefits. For example, reducing crime and unemployment just the tiniest fraction would pay for it many times over.

Large scale and long range studies on <u>physical</u> health have been shown to be feasible and very worthwhile. Perhaps the same thing could be done for <u>emotional</u> health, as we have suggested.

1-7 When the variable of interest is changing in an <u>observational study</u>, a lot of other variables are also changing and confound the answer. The effect of that one variable alone can be best understood by conducting an <u>experiment</u>, where the variable of interest is deliberately changed - making sure that the subjects or experimental units are assigned at <u>random</u> to the various levels of that variable, so that every confounding variable is kept constant on average.

1-9 **a.** Death rates from respiratory disease are unusually high in Arizona. A foreigner might guess that this is caused by Arizona's terrible air. But any American knows that, on the contrary, Arizona's air is so dry and clean that it attracts people who suffer from respiratory disease. We therefore conclude that: Arizona has a lot of people dying from respiratory disease [because Arizona causes the disease, because the disease causes these people to move to Arizona.]

The high death rate from respiratory disease in Arizona occurs because the effect of people with respiratory disease entering Arizona [overwhelms, is overwhelmed by] the good effects of the climate.

b. In Sri Lanka, a negative relation has been observed between population density and malaria; that is, low density is associated with a high malaria rate (Gourou, 1966). Two possible reasons for this are:

1. High malaria rates [drive out, attract] people, thus producing a relatively [low, high] population density in a district, or

2. A high population density might help [maintain, destroy] drainage and consequently [reduce, increase] the breeding grounds of malaria-carrying mosquitoes.

From the negative relation alone, it is [impossible, possible but difficult, quite easy] to tell which of these explanations are true.

c. Some studies have shown that states with capital punishment have *higher* murder rates.[4] Again, two possible reasons for this are:

1. Capital punishment [works, is counterproductive], causing the murder rate to be [lower, higher], or

2. States with [low, high] murder rates tend to be the most anxious to reduce them, by resorting to drastic measures such as capital punishment.

From the positive relation alone, it is [impossible, possible but difficult, easy] to tell which explanation is true.

1-11 **a.** Some confounding factors that might explain much of the crime are age, poverty, racial tension, lack of social and family support, etc.

b. **i.** This illustrates how [double-blindedness, observational studies, randomized experiments] can often be deceptive when analyzed naively.

ii. Specifically, the [confounding factors, confidence intervals, sociological theories] may be what produce some— or all—of the effects.

iii. We therefore say the effect of population density is [biased by, interchangeable with, multiplied by] the effect of the confounding factors.

1-13 The statement claims far too much, that the MBA doubles income. Causation is never proved by an observational study. For example, it may be that people with the MBA tend to have high intelligence and ambition, and it may be these qualities that partly (or even completely) increase income.

To reduce the bias, the data should be analyzed by multiple regression. This could hold constant the measurable confounding factors, such as IQ and social class.

A final subtlety: Even if there were no bias from confounding factors, the statement would not be correct. This is because lifetime earnings are found by multiplying average annual salary x number of years. And high school graduates have about 6 more years of earning just after high school. If interest is considered, those early 6 years look even more attractive.

1-15 a. The 95 % CI for the rate of moderate injury:

<u>for those wearing lap-and-shoulder belts</u>, we use the third line of the given table. The number of occupants was n = 7.8% of 100,000 = 7,800 and their injury rate was .005. Thus the population injury rate was:

$$\pi_1 = .005 \pm 1.96 \sqrt{\frac{.005(.995)}{7,800}} = .005 \pm .0016 \qquad (1\text{-}2)$$

$$\simeq .005 \pm .002$$

<u>for those wearing no belt</u>, we use the first line of the table:

$$\pi_2 = .023 \pm 1.96 \sqrt{\frac{.023(.977)}{85,950}} = .023 \pm .001$$

b.

$$\pi_1 = .004 \pm 1.96 \sqrt{\frac{.004(.996)}{7,800}} = .004 \pm .001$$

$$\pi_2 = .013 \pm 1.96 \sqrt{\frac{.013(.987)}{85,900}} = .013 \pm .001$$

c. As parts (a) and (b) showed, the sample size n is large enough so that the sample error is relatively small and unimportant. For simplicity, we therefore shall ignore it in this discussion.

We see that lap-and-shoulder belts seem to greatly reduce the number of injuries: belted passengers have about 1/4 or 1/3 as many injuries as unbelted passengers. Since this is an observational study, these figures cannot be regarded as proved. Nevertheless, as we saw in Problem 1-14, many confounding factors have been eliminated so that these figures are probably not terribly biased.

In simple English: It is foolhardy not to buckle up.

1-17 a. In the sample of n = 100,000, the number participating is 62,690 + 4,080 = 66,770, that is, a proportion or rate of:

$$P = 66,770/100,000 \simeq .668$$

Thus the 95% CI is:

$$\pi = .668 \pm 1.96 \sqrt{\frac{.668(.332)}{100,000}} = .668 \pm .003$$

b. The unemployment rate of course ignores those outside the labor force, that is, uses just those 66,770 people participating. Thus the sample unemployment rate is:

$$\frac{4,080}{66,770} = .061$$

Thus the 95% CI is:

4

$$\pi = .061 \pm 1.96 \sqrt{\frac{.061(.939)}{66,770}} \qquad (1\text{-}2)$$

$$= .061 \pm .002$$

That is, the unemployment rate was about 6%.

c. As part (b) showed, the third decimal place is very uncertain (± .002), so the drop from .058 to .057 may be just sampling fluctuation. (In fact, the real unemployment rate could easily have gone up a little.)

2-1 a. The clue is the sharp peak at X = 65, followed by a complete blank. It therefore looks as if the maximum acceptable hardness was 65, and anything over that was obligingly reported as 65, or 64 or 63 occasionally.

This failure to report honestly caused great difficulty later on, of course. And this simple histogram easily cleared up the reporting trouble.

b. The outlier on the extreme right, or possibly, the outlier on the left.

2-3 a. Using the 5 dots in Problem 2-2(a), we obtain the following box plot. Note that for such a small sample, the 5 dots turn out to be the 5 crucial values of the box (the median, the two quartiles, and the two extremes):

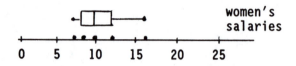

b. Using the 25 dots in Problem 2-2(b), turned 90°, we obtain the following box plot.

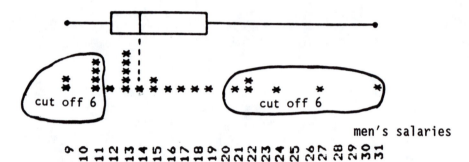

Alternatively, it can be graphed by MINITAB (with a little editing). For comparison, we also show the women's salaries:

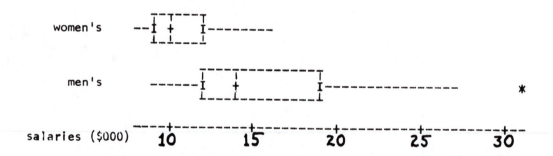

2-5 On the graph from Problem 2-2(b), it is easy to pick out how many dots (at 4% each) lie below the specified salary of 10 thousand:

6

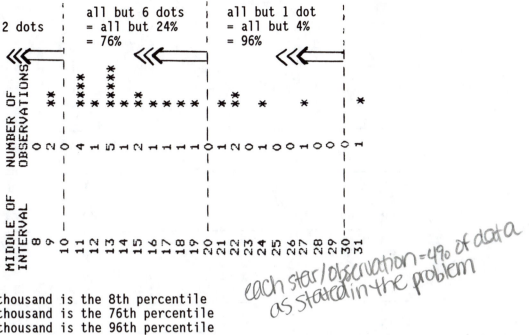

Thus 10 thousand is the 8th percentile
20 thousand is the 76th percentile
30 thousand is the 96th percentile

each star/observation = 4% of data as stated in the problem

2-7

$$\text{total} = 200 \times \underline{\text{mean}}$$

Formal justification:

$$\bar{X} \equiv \frac{1}{n} \Sigma X \qquad\qquad (2\text{-}4)$$

i.e., $\quad \bar{X} \equiv \frac{1}{n} (\text{total})$

Solve: $\quad \text{total} = n\bar{X}$

2-9 a.

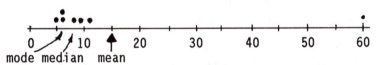

mode median mean

b. Total = 6 + 8 + ... + 60 = 105 thousand

$$\text{Mean} = \frac{\Sigma X}{n} = \frac{\text{total}}{n} = \frac{105}{7} = 15 \text{ thousand}$$

To find the median and mode, we use the observations in the graph above. The median is the middle observation, that is, 8 thousand. The mode is the most frequent value, 6 thousand.

Note that the order is what we also found in the skewed distribution of Figure 2-4b:

$$\text{mode} < \text{median} < \text{mean}$$

c. If production averages 7.8 per country, and if there are 10 countries, then the total production must be 10 x 7.8 = 78. (Information about the median or mode was irrelevant, of course.)

Here is the formal justification:

7

$$\bar{X} \equiv \frac{1}{n} \Sigma X \qquad\qquad (2-4)$$

$$\text{i.e.,} \quad \bar{X} \equiv \frac{1}{n} \text{(total)}$$

Solve: total $= n\bar{X} = (10)(7.8) = 78$

2-11

Cell Boundaries	Cell Mid-point X	Freq. f	(a) Relative Freq. f/n	(b) Xf
55.00-65.00	60	5	.25	300
65.00-75.00	70	7	.35	490
75.00-85.00	80	8	.40	640
		20 √	1.00 √	$\frac{1430}{20}$

$$\bar{X} = 71.5$$

a.

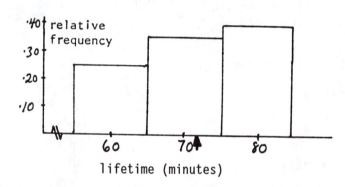

lifetime (minutes)

Alternatively, we could use MINITAB:

```
MIDDLE OF      NUMBER OF
INTERVAL       OBSERVATIONS
   60.0            5    *****
   70.0            7    *******
   80.0            8    ********
```

b. From the table, $\bar{X} \approx 71.5$. And the mode is the most frequent value, X = 80.

2-13 The total profit is just n times the mean or average, which we calculate from the given table:

Speed	n = Weekly Production	$\bar{X}$ = Average Profit	irrelevant Median Profit	total profit = nX
Standard	10,000	$ .50		$5,000
20% slower	8,000	$ .80		$6,400 max
40% slower	6,000	$1.00		$6,000
50% slower	5,000	$1.10		$5,500

So the most profitable speed is 20% slower.

8

2-15

a. X	b. $(X-\bar{X})$		c. An example: X	$(X-\bar{X})$
3	-6		10	2.5
7	-2		3	-4.5
8	-1		4	-3.5
12	3		13	5.5
15	6			
ave $= \dfrac{45}{5}$	ave $= \dfrac{0}{5}$		ave $= \dfrac{30}{4}$	ave $= \dfrac{0}{4}$
$= 9$	$= 0$		$= 7.5$	$= 0$

It will <u>always</u> turn out that the total deviation is zero (and hence the average deviation is zero too). In other words, the + and - deviations exactly cancel. In terms of balancing point, it means that the weight on the right exactly balances the weight on the left.

d. The proof is given in equation (2-9) in footnote 4 of the text.
   Is it equally true that deviations from the median have a zero average? Let us just try an example. For the 5 numbers in (a):

X	$X - \overset{\shortmid}{X}$
3	-5
7	-1
8	0
12	4
15	7
$\overset{\shortmid}{X} = 8$	ave $= \dfrac{5}{5}$
	$= 1$

So the average deviation from the median is <u>not</u> zero. But the median deviation is zero, of course.

2-17 a. From the box plot in Problem 2-3, we can read off the range from the ends of the whiskers:

$$\text{Range} = 16 - 8 = 8$$

We can also read off the IQR from the ends of the box:

$$\text{IQR} = 12 - 9 = 3$$

9

b.

X	X-X̄	|X-X̄|	(X-X̄)²
8	-3	3	9
9	-2	2	4
10	-1	1	1
12	1	1	1
16	5	5	25

$$\bar{X} = 11 \qquad 0 \checkmark \quad MAD = \frac{12}{5} \quad MSD = \frac{40}{5}$$

$$= 2.4 \qquad = 8.0$$

$$\text{variance } s^2 = \frac{40}{4} = 10.0$$

$$\text{standard deviation } s = \sqrt{10.0} = 3.2$$

2-19 a.

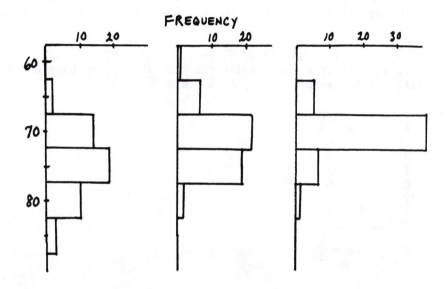

We note that the distributions are changing in two ways:
- **(i)** The central value is becoming smaller.
- **(ii)** The spread is getting less--as we might expect, if his measurement error decreases as he learns from experience.

b.   For the first 50 measurements:

x	f	xf	x-X̄	(x-X̄)²	(x-X̄)²f
65	2	130	-10	100	200
70	15	1050	- 5	25	375
75	19	1425	0	0	0
80	11	880	5	25	275
85	3	255	10	100	300

$$\bar{X} = \frac{3740}{50} \qquad\qquad s^2 = \frac{1150}{49}$$

$$= 74.8 \qquad\qquad\qquad = 23.47$$

$$\approx 75 \qquad\qquad\qquad s = 4.84$$

Similarly, for the next 50 measurements, $\bar{X} = 71.3$, $s = 4.14$. And for the last 50, $\bar{X} = 70.3$, $s = 2.75$. This shows the same two phenomena as noted in part a: $\bar{X}$ is decreasing, and so is s.

c.

x	given f		total f	xf	x-$\bar{X}$	(x-$\bar{X}$)^2	(x-$\bar{X}$)^{2}f
60	0 1 0		1	60	-12	144	144
65	2 7 5		14	910	- 7	49	686
70	15 22 38		75	5250	- 2	4	300
75	19 18 6		43	3225	3	9	387
80	11 2 1		14	1120	8	64	896
85	3 0 0		3	255	13	169	507

$$150 \qquad \bar{X} = \frac{10,820}{150} \qquad\qquad s^2 = \frac{2920}{149} = 19.60$$

$$= 72.1 \approx 72 \qquad\qquad s = 4.43$$

Alternatively, we could have used the three sums already calculated in part b to easily get the overall sum for the numerator of $\bar{X}$:

$$\bar{X} = \frac{3,740 + 3,565 + 3,515}{150} = \frac{10,820}{150} = 72.1$$

Or, we could get a better understanding by writing it as:

$$\bar{X} = \frac{n_1\bar{X}_1 + n_2\bar{X}_2 + n_3\bar{X}_3}{n_1 + n_2 + n_3} \qquad\qquad \text{like (2-7)}$$

$$= \frac{50\ (74.8) + 50\ (71.3) + 50\ (70.3)}{50 + 50 + 50}$$

$$\bar{X} = \frac{74.8 + 71.3 + 70.3}{3} = 72.1$$

This shows that when all n_i are equal, the overall mean is just the average of the component means.

For the standard deviations, there is no such simple relation. We note that the overall s of 4.43 is <u>greater</u> than the average of the components:

$$4.43 > \frac{4.84 + 4.14 + 2.75}{3}$$

The reason is intuitively clear: the overall sample is spread out not only because of the three individual spreads, but also because the three individual means are spread out too (which makes the overall s larger).

2-21 a. $\bar{X} = 230$, $s = 8.1$ (by calculator)

b.   Since $C = (F - 32) \times 5/9$

11

By (2-19), $\bar{C} - (\bar{F} - 32) \times 5/9$

$$= (230 - 32) \times 5/9 = 110$$

and $\qquad s_C = 5/9 \; s_F$

$$= 5/9 \; (8.1) = 4.5$$

2-23 Since the plots are <u>square</u>, the area of the first plot, for example, is just 10 ft. x 10 ft. = 100 ft.^{2} Thus we have:

a.	b.
length	area
X	$A = X^2$
10	100
20	400
30	900
50	2500
90	8100

$\bar{X} = \dfrac{200}{5}$ Total = 12,000

$\qquad = 40$ Average $= \dfrac{12,000}{5} = 2400$

Since $A = X^2$ is not a linear transformation, we could not use a simple formula like (2-19) to find the average area. It would give just a very crude approximation as follows:

$$\bar{A} \approx \bar{X}^2 = 40^2 = 1600$$

This is pretty far off the correct value of 2400 found in b.

2-25

x	f/n	x f/n	$x - \bar{X}$	$(x-\bar{X})^2$	$(x-\bar{X})^2 f/n$
10	.28	2.8	-6	36	10.08
15	.40	6.0	-1	1	.40
20	.20	4.0	4	16	3.20
25	.08	2.0	9	81	6.48
30	.04	1.2	14	196	7.84
		$\bar{X}$ = 16.0			MSD = 28.00

$$s^2 = \left(\frac{n}{n-1}\right) MSD = \frac{25}{24} \; 28.00 = 29.2$$

$$s = \sqrt{29.2} = 5.4$$

2-27 Compared to the base dollar in 1958, the final dollar in 1978 is 44% as long AND 44% as wide, so that its area is only $.44^2$ = 19% as much. This is a "lie" factor of .44, corresponding to the one extra dimension (not as bad as the lie factor of 6^2 that occurred in the three dimensional oil drums in Figure 2-11).

One solution is to keep the width constant, and just show more and more of the length cut off, like this:

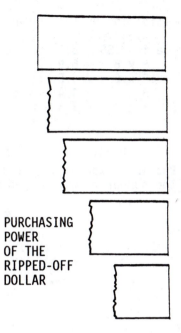

PURCHASING
POWER
OF THE
RIPPED-OFF
DOLLAR

2-29 a. Crossing the River Berezina, at about -20°C (-4° Fahrenheit) on Nov. 28. cost Napoleon half his remaining men.

b. The others came from two salients split off early in the campaign.

c. Each of the two salients in (b) was as big as the remnant force of Napoleon that it rejoined. Since this happened twice, we would estimate that only ½ x ½ of the 10,000 returning soldiers were from Moscow with Napoleon. (Assuming all troops had the same attrition rate.) Thus the chances of a soldier successfully returning from Moscow would be about 2,500/100,000 ≈ 2.5%.

   The earlier chance of a soldier making it to Moscow is easier -- 100,000/422,000 ≈ 24%.

   <u>Remark</u> To motivate Chapter 3, we would calculate the overall chance of a soldier making it to Moscow <u>and</u> returning: 250/422,000 ≈ 0.6%. Less than 1 in a hundred!

   We could get this same answer by multiplying the two answers of part (c):

   $$.025 \times .24 = .006 = 0.6\%$$

2-31 a. b. generation 1, about 5.5 million
generation 2, about 11.0 million
generation 3, about 8.6 million

} growth factor = 11.0/5.5 = 2.0
} growth factor = 8.6/11.0 = 0.8

The bars in (a) were estimated roughly, and the decimal place is uncertain. This makes the factors in (b) also uncertain. For anyone who wants them, the exact figures are available from the original source (Statistical Abstract of the United States, 1987, p. 18):

first growth factor = $\dfrac{10.865 \text{ million}}{5.660 \text{ million}}$ = 1.92

later growth factor = $\dfrac{8.806 \text{ million}}{10.865 \text{ million}}$ = .81

c. Projections are obtained by multiplying by the "growth" factor of 0.8:

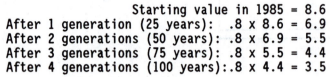

Starting value in 1985 = 8.6
After 1 generation (25 years): .8 x 8.6 = 6.9
After 2 generations (50 years): .8 x 6.9 = 5.5
After 3 generations (75 years): .8 x 5.5 = 4.4
After 4 generations (100 years):.8 x 4.4 = 3.5

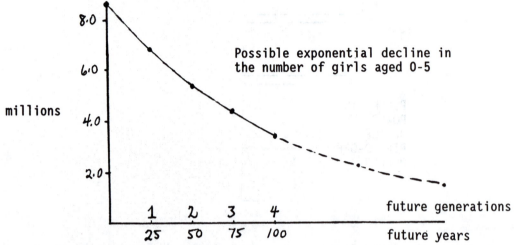

Just to emphasize the nature of this exponential decline, we have projected another hundred years (dashed).

d. This projection is more useful to suggest what will happen __if__ present trends continue.

It would be rash indeed to regard it as a prediction. If anything is certain, it is the universality of change. The present pattern of family size won't continue. But will it go up or down? This is a terribly difficult question to answer. In fact, demographers have been fooled so often in the past that they now often admit it's anybody's guess.

A more fruitful question, perhaps, is the policy question: __Should__ family size go up or down? And for this question, projections are indeed useful. They help to focus the consequences of our decision. We could draw several alternative projections, depending on the possible changes contemplated in family size:

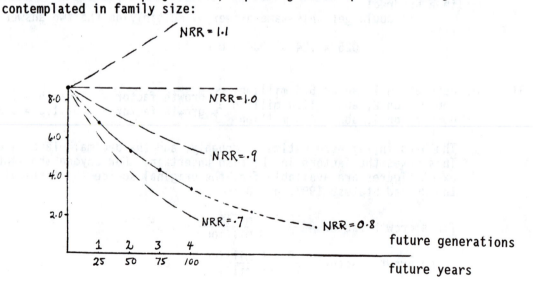

2-33 The mean is 34 4/16, and the standard deviation is 2.65/16 ≈ 3/16. These provide one possible answer to the question.

2-35 **a.**

Price x	Number f	Amount invested A = xf
$ 8	100	$ 800
$ 8	100	$ 800
$10	100	$1000
$ 5	100	$ 500
n = 400		$\bar{X} = \dfrac{\$3100}{400} = \$7.75$

b.

Amount invested A	Price x	Number bought f = A/x
$800	$ 8	100
$800	$ 8	100
$800	$10	80
$800	$ 5	160
total = $3200		n = 440

$$\text{average price} = \frac{\text{total}}{n} = \frac{\$3200}{440} = \$7.27$$

c. The "dollar cost" average is lower. And it will <u>always</u> be lower, because it buys more when the price is low (last quarter, in this example).

d. In (c) we showed that the dollar-cost average is <u>always</u> lower. So when she wants a <u>high</u> average price in selling, she should get the straight average, that is, sell off 20 shares per quarter.

2-37 **a.** median ≈ 2.9

b. The mean can be found from the total, which was stated in the first line to be 222 million. Thus:

$$\bar{X} = \frac{222}{50} = 4.44$$

c.

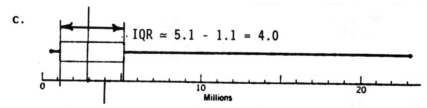

IQR ≈ 5.1 - 1.1 = 4.0

d. At 4.0 million, Louisiana is about halfway between the 50th and 75th percentile. It is therefore about the 60th or 65th percentile.

It is interesting to compare these approximate values with the exact values obtainable from the original data (in the 1981 Statistical Abstract of the United States): X̄ = 3.0, IQR = 3.9, and Louisiana is the 60th percentile.

2-39 a. Use the $\bar{X}$ and s function on your calculator, or else by hand:

X	X-$\bar{X}$	$(X-\bar{X})^2$
11	-33	1089
41	- 3	9
77	33	1089
84	40	1600
8	-36	1296

$$\bar{X} = \frac{221}{5} \qquad s^2 = \frac{5083}{4}$$

$$= 44.2 \qquad = 1271$$

$$\simeq 44 \qquad s = 35.6$$

b. total = $n\bar{X}$ = 50(44.2) like (2-4)

= 2210 thousand square miles

Compare this to the true value (given as 3620 thousand square miles, or 36.2 million). We see the a sample of size n = 5 from a population of so widely varying states is not very reliable.

2-41 a.

X
8
12
120

$$\bar{X} = \frac{140}{3} = 47$$

b. The possible class sizes are still 8, 12, and 120. However, they are no longer equally frequent from the _students'_ point of view. There are _many_ more students who have to take to large class of 120 students -- 120 of course, which we duly record as the last frequency f in the table below. This will raise the overall average, as calculation will verify:

class size	number of students	
x	f	xf
8	8	64
12	12	144
120	120	14,440

$$n = 140 \qquad \bar{X} = \frac{14,608}{140} = 104$$

3-1 **a.**   We define probability or chance as long-run relative frequency (proportion).

    b.   To estimate the chance that a loaded die comes up 1, we could throw it many times. If 1 came up 105 times in 500 throws, for example, then
$Pr \simeq 105/500 = .21$

    c.   To estimate the chance that it will snow in Boston next Christmas day, we could look at a large number of similar days.
        Since there have been perceptible trends in temperature over the past hundred years, it would be wise to select recent years, say the past decade.
        If we further selected just Christmas days, there would be too few (only 10) days. On the other hand, if we included all of the winter days, from December to March, say, we would have lots of days, but those February and March days might not be similar enough.
        As a compromise, we might select the week before and the week after Christmas in the past decade, for a total of 140 days. Then, if it snowed 43 of those days, $Pr(snow) \simeq 43/140 = .31$.

    d.   Referring to the data in Problem 2-1, suppose a coil was randomly sampled from the same production run. Then the chance that its hardness would be 50 or less is approximately the relative frequency, found from the graph to be 7/100 = .07.

3-3 **a.**   In 50 tosses we got 29 heads, or a relative frequency of .58. For the long-run, we can make a better guess from the .50-.50 symmetry of the coin:

$$probability = .50$$

    b.   In 50 tosses, we got 23 points up, or a relative frequency of .46. Since a tack has no obvious symmetry between point up and point down, this empirical relative frequency remains our best guess for the probability:

$$probability \quad .46$$

    c.   Starting at the beginning of Appendix Table I, we happened to obtain the following simulation:

3̸9̸	65	7̸6	45	45	1̸9̸	9̸0̸	6̸9̸	...

Thus,	3,6/	5,6/	4,5/	4,5/	1,6/	...
E occurs	no	yes	no	no	yes	...

After 50 rolls, "7 or 11" came up 12 times, for a relative frequency of .24--a rough empirical estimate of the probability.
    Alternatively, we could use the symmetry of the dice along with some systematic reasoning (as in Problem 3-8c) to obtain an exact answer:

$$probability = \frac{8}{36} = .222$$

    In a very simple way, this illustrates the "Monte Carlo" (experimental sampling) research that is currently very popular: Certain probabilities that are too difficult to work out theoretically may nevertheless be approximated by "playing the game" over and over, thus generating a relative frequency that approximates the desired probability. High-speed computers generate the random numbers and carry out the subsequent calculations so fast that good accuracy is now feasible.

3-5 a. Let F = failure, S = success. Since Pr(F) = .40, Pr(S) = .60. Then for 2 attempts, we have the following tree:

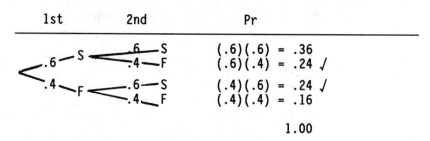

	1st	2nd		Pr
	.6—S	.6—S	(.6)(.6) = .36
		.4—F	(.6)(.4) = .24 ✓
	.4—F	.6—S	(.4)(.6) = .24 ✓
		.4—F	(.4)(.4) = .16
			1.00

Pr(exactly one failure) = .24 + .24 = .48

b. For 3 attempts, we have a three-fold tree:

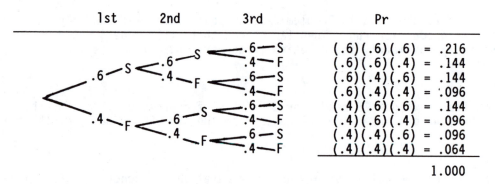

1st	2nd	3rd	Pr
		.6—S	(.6)(.6)(.6) = .216
	.6—S	.4—F	(.6)(.6)(.4) = .144
.6—S	.4—F	.6—S	(.6)(.4)(.6) = .144
		.4—F	(.6)(.4)(.4) = .096
	.6—S	.6—S	(.4)(.6)(.6) = .144
.4—F		.4—F	(.4)(.6)(.4) = .096
	.4—F	.6—S	(.4)(.4)(.6) = .096
		.4—F	(.4)(.4)(.4) = .064
			1.000

Pr (exactly one failure) = .144 + .144 + .144 = .432

3-7 a. Let A denote an acceptable clock
U denote an unacceptable clock

It makes no difference to the answer, whether the 3 clocks are all drawn at once, or one by one. The simplest way to lay out the calculations, however, is to imagine them drawn one by one:
The chance of the first clock being acceptable is 8/12. Then, in the carton there would remain only 7 acceptable clocks in a total of 11, so that the chance of the second clock being acceptable would be 7/11. Similarly, the chance of the third clock then being acceptable would be 6/10. Thus the probability tree branches as follows:

FIRST CLOCK	SECOND CLOCK	THIRD CLOCK	OUTCOME	PROBABILITY
		6/10 —A	Accept lot	$\frac{8}{12} \cdot \frac{7}{11} \cdot \frac{6}{10}$
	7/11 —A	—U	Reject	= .255
8/12 —A	—U		Reject	
—U			Reject	

Thus Pr(accepting shipment) = .255 ≈ 25%

b. $\dfrac{6}{12} \; \dfrac{5}{11} \; \dfrac{4}{10}$ = .091 ≈ 9%

18

3-9 a. <u>Intuitive Solution:</u> Just imagine what is actually going on. "At least one will work" means that there will be some help given. How often does this happen?

   Well, we are told that both fail only 4% of the time. So the remaining 96% of the time we get help.

<u>Venn Diagram Solution:</u> A Venn Diagram is a simple routine procedure that helps in many problems like this.

   Let S denote the sprinkler failing and A the alarm failing. We first fill in the diagram with the central lens probability of .04. Then we work gradually outwards using the other given probabilities listed on the top, to eventually fill in the probabilities in all four sections:

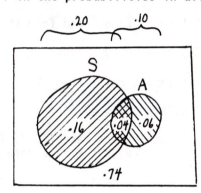

"At least one will work" is everything but the lens at the center, so its probability is 1.00 - .04 = .96.

b. "Both will work" is just the clear area of the Venn Diagram, and its probability has already been found:

   Pr = 1 - (.16 + .04 + .06) = 1 - .26 = .74

3-11 a. $Pr(G_1 \text{ and } G_2 \text{ and } ..) = \frac{1}{2} \times \frac{1}{2} \times ... = \left(\frac{1}{2}\right)^{10} \simeq .001$

   So Pr(at least 1 boy) = 1 - Pr(all girls) = 1 - .001 = .999

b. From part (a), we found Pr (all girls) = $(1/2)^{10}$. Similarly, Pr (all boys) = $(1/2)^{10}$. The complement is what we want:

   Pr (boys and girls both occurring) = $1 - (1/2)^{10} - (1/2)^{10}$
   $$= .998$$

3-13 The Venn diagram is filled in first at the center: Pr (all 3 sports) = .02. Then we work our way outwards to fill in the rest of the diagram. When this is done we can answer the questions, as follows:

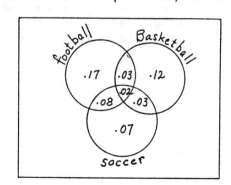

a. sum all the probabilities:
   .17 + .03 + ... = .52

b. .17

c. .40

d. $\dfrac{.17}{.52}$ = .33

e. $\dfrac{.40}{.52}$ = .77

To answer (d) and (e), it might help to imagine 100 actual students, 52 of whom are athletes, 17 of whom play football only, etc. Then we would get the same answers as before:

d. $\frac{17}{52}$ = .33   e. $\frac{40}{52}$ = .77

3-15 a. We read the unemployment rate directly from the right-hand (totals) column:

$$Pr(U) = 7.2\%/100\% = 7.2\%$$

b. Pr(U|M) is the male unemployment rate, read from the first (male) column:

$$Pr(U|M) = 3.9\%/55.8\% = .0699 \simeq 7.0\%$$

c. Similarly, Pr(U|F) is the female rate, read from the second (female) column:

$$Pr(U|F) = 3.3\%/44.2\% = .0747 \simeq 7.5\%$$

<u>Remarks</u>: Note that the <u>overall</u> unemployment rate (7.2%) is the average of the male rate (7.0%) and female rate (7.5%), -- with the male rate weighted more heavily, since most of the workers are male.

3-17

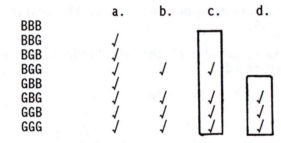

	a.	b.	c.	d.
BBB				
BBG	√			
BGB	√			
BGG	√	√	√	
GBB	√			
GBG	√	√	√	√
GGB	√	√	√	√
GGG	√	√	√	√

a. 7/8 = .875

b. 4/8 = .50

c. 4/7 or .50/.875 = .57

d. 3/4 or .375/.50 = .75

3-19 A preposterous argument of course, but not very different from similar fallacies perpetrated every day. The key to the fallacy is this: We are quoted the unconditional probability of two bombs: one in a million million.
   But what is really relevant is the conditional probability that somebody else will have a bomb: This of course is one in a million, because of the uncertainty of the other passengers -- regardless of whether or not he himself carries a bomb.
   Another way of saying it is this: Once he knowingly carries on a bomb himself, then ordinary probability calculations (which are based on uncertainty) are not relevant.

3-21

	F	F̄	totals
E	7.8 %	22.2 %	30.0 %
Ē	18.2 %	51.8 %	70.0 %
totals	26.0 %	74.0 %	100.0 %

20

a. From the total in the F column,

$$Pr(F) = 26.0\ \%$$

b. From the total in the E row, $Pr(E) = 30.0\ \%$ and hence

$$Pr(F|E) = \frac{Pr(F \text{ and } E)}{Pr(E)}$$

$$= \frac{7.8\ \%}{30.0\ \%} = 26.0\ \%$$

c. Because $Pr(F|E) = Pr(F)$, F is indeed independent of E, according to (3-20).

3-23 a. From the last column:

$$Pr(U) = 8.3/115.5 = 7.2\%$$

This agrees with Problem 3-15(a), of course.

b. From the first column:

$$Pr(U|Y) = 3.2/23.6 = 13.6\%$$

c. Not independent, since $Pr(U|Y) \neq Pr(U)$ like (3-20)

3-25 This can be solved either with a tree, or with a Venn diagram like Figure 3-10 as follows:

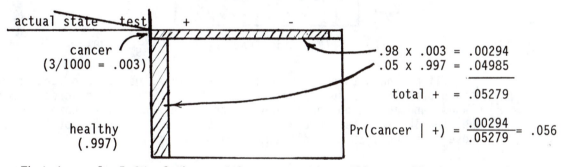

.98 x .003 = .00294
.05 x .997 = .04985
_____
total + = .05279

$$Pr(cancer \mid +) = \frac{.00294}{.05279} = .056$$

That is, only 5.6% of those with a + reaction will actually have cancer!

<u>Remarks</u> When asked to guess the answer before doing any calculating, many students guess somewhere between 95% and 98%. The correct answer is astoundingly low, and it is important to understand why: Most of the + reaction comes from that huge majority of healthy people.

3-27

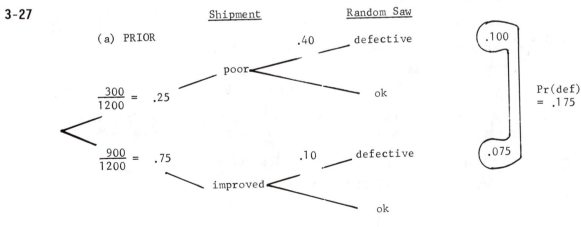

21

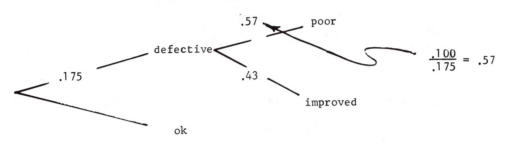

Random Saw   Shipment

(b) POSTERIOR

$$\frac{.100}{.175} = .57$$

3-29 a.   The prior chance is just .50 (first number in the table)

   c.   We will do part (c) first, since it is a standard Bayesian problem. We can do it with trees, or with a Venn diagram like Figure 3-10 as follows:

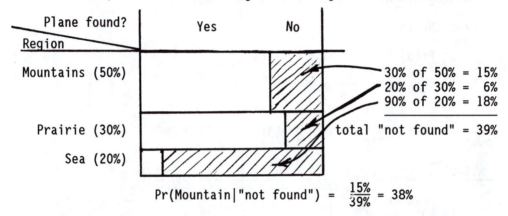

30% of 50% = 15%
20% of 30% = 6%
90% of 20% = 18%
_____
total "not found" = 39%

$$Pr(\text{Mountain}|\text{"not found"}) = \frac{15\%}{39\%} = 38\%$$

   It may help to envision millions of planes going down, and interpret each probability as just a proportion. Or to be really concrete, imagine 100 planes, and just drop the % sign. Then to interpret the answer, we see that when the 100 searches were over, only 39 planes remained "not found". Of those 39 planes, 15 are in the mountains, and therefore

$$Pr(\text{Mountain}|\text{"not found"}) = \frac{15}{39} = 38\%$$

   b.   This part is so simple it can be tricky. It works best if you continue to imagine just 100 planes crashing. After the initial search in the mountains, and nothing found, how many does this leave? A lot more than in part (c), as calculation will show:

Not found in mountains 30% of 50%	=	15%
somewhere in prairie		30%
somewhere in sea		20%
	total =	65%

haven't searched these areas at all yet

   Or, another way to get the total is to note that the initial search in the mountains <u>found</u> 70% of 50% = 35%. With these eliminated, 65% are left.

   Finally, we do our conditional calculation:

$$Pr(\text{Mountain}|\text{"not found in mountain"}) = \frac{15\%}{65\%} = 23\%$$

d. This is how the chance of the plane being in the mountains changes:

    a. Initially, the chance was 50%

    b. If not <u>found</u> in the mountains, its chance of <u>being</u> in the mountains has to go down. It does go down, to 23%.

    c. Now the plane isn't <u>found</u> elsewhere either. So it looks as if it may be in the mountains after all, that is, its chance of being in the mountains must go up. It does go up, to 38%
        This 38% is not as high as the initial 50%, however, because there is a relatively high chance the plane went down at sea, where it would almost certainly disappear (90% chance).

3-33 All seems valid to us.

3-35 a. For independent events, by (3-20),

$$Pr(A|B) = Pr(A)$$
$$= 0.6$$

    b. For independent events, by (3-21),

$$Pr(A \text{ and } B) = Pr(A)Pr(B)$$
$$= .6 \times .2 = .12$$

    c. For any events, by (3-12),

$$Pr(A \text{ or } B) = Pr(A) + Pr(B) - Pr(A \text{ and } B)$$
$$= .6 + .2 - (.6)(.2) = .68$$

3-37 a. Let us convert the first column to <u>relative</u> frequencies (probabilities):

Response R	(1) Probability Pr(R)	(2) Conditional Prob. of buying Pr(B|R)	(1) x (2) Pr(B and R)
definitely buy	12%	40%	4.80%
probably buy	23%	20%	4.60%
maybe buy	17%	8%	1.36%
not buy	48%	1%	0.48%
	1.00%		total buyers = 11.24%

Where do the buyers come from? Of the 12% who said they would definitely buy it, 40% actually do. Now 40% of 12% = 4.8%, so that nearly 5% of the survey are buyers who said they would "definitely buy". We show this in the last column, along with similar buyers who came from the other responses. The total number of buyers is then found to be 11.24%

b. $\dfrac{4.80\%}{11.24\%} = 43\%$

This is just a Bayesian problem, and it may help to show it with a tree or Venn diagram.

3-39 a. Pr(W and H) = Pr(W)Pr(H|W)
          = .30(.60) = .18   like (3-18)

Now that we know the intersection or "lens" of the Venn diagram, we can fill out the various sections -- as in Problem 3-10 : We start with the intersection and work our way outwards, thereby filling in the probabilities of each of the four sections:

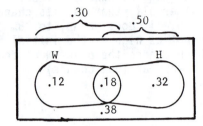

From this Venn diagram, we can easily read the rest of the answers:

b.   .12 + .18 + .32 = .62

          or, Pr(W or H) = .30 + .50 - .18 = .62   like (3-12)

c.   .38

          or 1 - .62 = .38   like (3-15)

d. $Pr(W|H) = \frac{Pr(W \text{ and } H)}{Pr(H)} = \frac{.18}{.50} = .36$ like (3-17)

e. $Pr(W|\bar{H}) = \frac{Pr(W \text{ and } \bar{H})}{Pr(\bar{H})} = \frac{.12}{.12 + .38} = .24$ like (3-17)

f.   True: .24 < .30 < .36

         Incidentally, this is generally true, and can be expressed with a general formula, as the following argument shows:

         A Venn diagram verifies that:

             Pr(W) = Pr(W and H) + Pr(W and $\bar{H}$).

These two probabilities can each be re-expressed using (3-18):

             Pr(W) = Pr(H)Pr(W|H) + Pr($\bar{H}$)PR(W|$\bar{H}$).

That is, the probability of <u>any</u> event W can be written as a weighted average of the conditional probabilities Pr(W|H) and PR(W|$\bar{H}$) -- with the weights being Pr(H) and Pr($\bar{H}$). For our specific example, we verify this:

             Pr(W) = Pr(H)Pr(W|H) + Pr($\bar{H}$)Pr(W|$\bar{H}$)
             .30 = .50(.36) + .50(.24)

24

3-41 This sounds a little like Bayes' theorem, but with the added twist of drawing a second tape. Successive draws are easily modelled with a tree. We denote B_1 as "first tape Bad", and we only fill in the necessary branches:

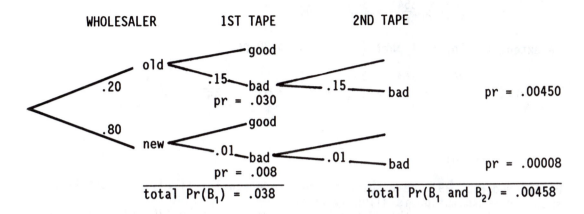

a. $Pr(B_1) = .030 + .008 = .038$, as shown above

b.
$$Pr(B_2|B_1) = \frac{Pr(B_1 \text{ and } B_2)}{Pr(B_1)} \qquad (3\text{-}17)$$

$$= \frac{.00458}{.038} = .12$$

This answer is intuitively correct as well: the first tape being defective meant that it was very likely a packet from the old bankrupt wholesaler, so that the chance of the next tape being defective is close to 15%.

3-43 a. Let us look at the 3 people one at a time (in alphabetical order, for example). Then let us denote:

B_i = ith person "chooses" a new birthday, not yet "chosen" by an earlier person.

Then $Pr(B_1) = \frac{365}{365}$ (= 1, of course)

$Pr(B_2|B_1) = \frac{364}{365}$

$Pr(B_3|B_1 \text{ and } B_2) = \frac{363}{365}$

To explain this last probability, for example, we are given that the first two people have chosen different birthdays, for example, Nov. 29 and Sept. 8. Then there remains 363 of the 365 days for the third person to choose from.

Now we put it all together:

$$Pr(E) = Pr(B_1)Pr(B_2|B_1)Pr(B_3|B_1 \text{ and } B_2) \qquad \text{like (3-18)}$$

$$= \frac{365}{365} \times \frac{364}{365} \times \frac{363}{365} \simeq .992$$

b. We extend the logic of part (a) from 3 to 30 people:

$$Pr(E) = \frac{365}{365} \times \frac{364}{365} \times \frac{363}{365} \times \frac{362}{365} \times \ldots \times \frac{336}{365} \simeq .294$$

c. 1 - answer to (b) $\simeq .706$

d. We ignored Feb. 29, and assumed all days are equally likely. Figure 17-1 shows this assumption is slightly wrong.

We also assumed the 30 people are a random sample (30 relatives gathered together for a family reunion, for example, would have a chance of twins).

All of these assumptions were reasonable, because they allowed us to get an answer very close to the true answer (which would require horrendous complications to calculate exactly).

3-45 a. True, by the definition (3-20).

b. True, by definition.

c. False: A and B are <u>statistically independent</u> if Pr (A and B) = Pr(A) Pr(B).

Or, A and B are mutually exclusive if Pr(A and B) = 0.

d. False:...the conditional probability of tails will be <u>1/2, of course</u>.

Or, the chance of 6 heads, at the start, would be 1/64.

4-1

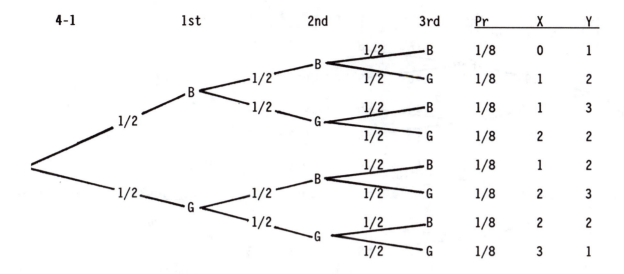

	1st	2nd	3rd	Pr	X	Y
			1/2 → B	1/8	0	1
	B 1/2 → B		1/2 → G	1/8	1	2
		1/2 → G	1/2 → B	1/8	1	3
1/2 → B			1/2 → G	1/8	2	2
		1/2 → B	1/2 → B	1/8	1	2
	G 1/2 → B		1/2 → G	1/8	2	3
1/2 → G		1/2 → G	1/2 → B	1/8	2	2
			1/2 → G	1/8	3	1

Then we condense the X and Y values into a table:

a.

x	p(x)
0	1/8
1	3/8
2	3/8
3	1/8

b.

y	p(y)
1	2/8
2	4/8
3	2/8

4-3 According to (3-1), the relative frequencies would tend to the probabilities, thus:

	a.	**b.**	**c.**
x	$(\frac{f}{n}) \rightarrow p(x)$	$x(\frac{f}{n}) \rightarrow xp(x)$	$(x-\bar{X})^2(\frac{f}{n}) \rightarrow (x-1.5)^2 p(x)$
0	1/8	0	(9/4) (1/8)
1	3/8	3/8	(1/4) (3/8)
2	3/8	6/8	(1/4) (3/8)
3	1/8	3/8	(9/4) (1/8)

$$\bar{X} \rightarrow 12/8 \qquad\qquad MSD \rightarrow 6/8$$

$$= 1.50 \qquad\qquad = .75$$

From (2-23), $s^2 = (\frac{n}{n-1})MSD \simeq MSD$

Thus $s^2 \rightarrow .75$ too

This problem motivates definitions (4-4) and (4-5) in the next section.

4-5 a.   The tree is like Problem 4-4, with the probabilities of the various branchings changed as follows (where S = sale or success, while F = no sale or failure):

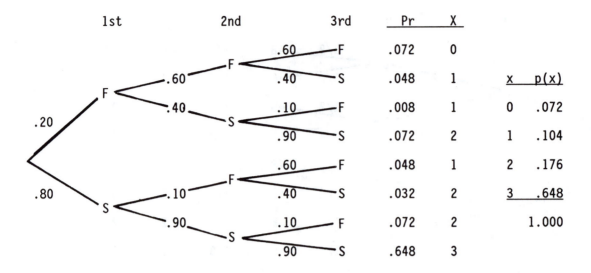

1st	2nd	3rd	Pr	X		x	p(x)
		.60 → F	.072	0			
	.60 → F	.40 → S	.048	1		0	.072
.60 → F	.40 → S	.10 → F	.008	1		1	.104
.20		.90 → S	.072	2		2	.176
	.10 → F	.60 → F	.048	1		3	.648
.80 → S		.40 → S	.032	2			1.000
	.90 → S	.10 → F	.072	2			
		.90 → S	.648	3			

b. For Pr(X ≥ 2), we add up the last two probabilities in the table of p(x):

Pr(X ≥ 2) = .176 + .648 = .824

4-7 a.

x	p(x)	xp(x)	x-μ	(x-μ)²	(x-μ)²p(x)
40	.05	2.00	-22	484	24.20
50	.15	7.50	-12	144	21.60
60	.41	24.60	- 2	4	1.64
70	.34	23.80	- 8	64	21.76
80	.04	3.20	18	324	12.96
90	.01	.90	28	784	7.84

$$\mu = 62.00 \qquad \sigma^2 = 90.00$$

$$\sigma = \sqrt{90} = 9.49$$

b. All 60 will be sold if demand is 60 or more. We find this from the last 4 probabilities in the table of p(x) above:

Pr(X ≥ 60) = .41 + .34 + .04 + .01 = .80

There will be some left over if demand is less than 60, which we similarly find:

Pr(X < 60) = .05 + .15 = .20

As a check, since these two events are complementary, their probabilities should sum to 1.00:

.80 + .20 = 1.00   √

c. To be almost sure of having enough bicycles, we need to order a lot. Let's try ordering 80. Then the chance of running out would be only:

Pr(X > 80) = .01

But it was specified this chance can be as large as 1-.95 = .05. So we need not shoot quite so high; let's try ordering 70:

Pr(X > 70) = .04 + .01 = .05   √

Thus   Pr(X ≤ 70) = .95 as required.

4-9 Let us first see what he gets if he goes ahead. His expected attendance will be found as follows:

x	p(x)	xp(x)
5,000	.30	1,500
20,000	.20	4,000
30,000	.20	6,000
50,000	.30	15,000

$$\mu = 26,500$$

After paying $2 per person for cleaning and crowd control, the $9 ticket nets $7. For an average of $26,500 people, this gives

average net = $7 x 26,500 = $185,500

From this, he must pay the fixed costs of $150,000 + $60,000 = $210,000, which leaves

profit = $185,500 - $210,000 = -$24,500

This loss of $24,500 is unattractive.

But the alternative may be worse: If he cancels, he would get nothing from ticket sales, and still have to pay half of the $60,000 administrative cost and a $15,000 cancellation penalty for the band, which leaves

profit = 0 - ($30,000 + $15,000) = -$45,000

This is indeed worse--a loss of $45,000 rather than $24,500. So if he doesn't mind taking risks, he should go ahead and hold the concert.

Incidentally, this subject of risk and decision making is covered thoroughly in Chapter 21.

4-11 The number of successful wells S is binomial, with n = 12 and π = .20. From Table III(c),

$$Pr(S \geq 3) = .442 \simeq 44\%$$

4-13 a. n = 6 and π = .50. Thus (4-13) gives

$$\mu = n\pi = 6(.50) = 3.00$$

$$\sigma = \sqrt{n\pi(1-\pi)} = \sqrt{6(.50)(.50)} = \sqrt{1.50} = 1.22$$

b. n = 12 and π = .20. Thus

$$\mu = n\pi = 12(.20) = 2.40$$

$$\sigma = \sqrt{n\pi(1-\pi)} = \sqrt{12(.20)(.80)} = \sqrt{1.92} = 1.39$$

4-15 a. The number of hits X is binomial, with n = 10, and π = .20. From Table III(c),

$$Pr(S \geq 4) = .121$$

b. We assumed that shots were independent, with constant probability of success. But after the first shot or two, gunners can make adjustments so that later shots are more accurate.

c. In view of part (b), we would fear that the chance of the next shot hitting is now much higher. Apparently the captain of the Prince of Wales thought so, too.

4-17 a.

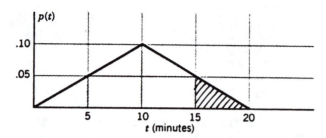

The shaded area is

$$\frac{\text{base x height}}{2} = \frac{5 \times .05}{2} = .125$$

b. By symmetry, mean = 10 minutes.

4-19 Although we could write out these solutions algebraically, it is easier to work graphically. We look up tail areas in Table IV, and so find;

a.

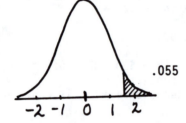

.055

b.

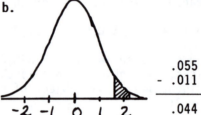

```
  .055
- .011
_____
  .044
```

c.

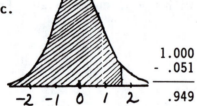

```
  1.000
-  .051
_____
  .949
```

d.

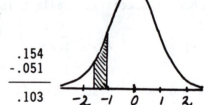

```
  .154
- .051
_____
  .103
```

e.

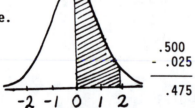

```
  .500
-  .025
_____
  .475
```

f.

```
  1.000
-  .025
-  .025
_____
  .950
```

g.

```
  1.000
- .067
- .251
_____
  .682
```

h.

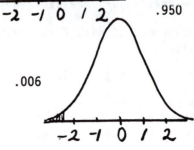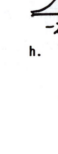

.006

30

4-21 a. $Z = \dfrac{X - \mu}{\sigma} = \dfrac{25 - 8}{10} = 1.70$

$Pr(X > 25) = Pr(Z > 1.70)$

$\qquad\qquad\quad = .045$

b. $Z = \dfrac{0 - 8}{10} = -.80$

$Pr(X < 0) = Pr(Z < -.80)$

by symmetry, $= Pr(Z > .80) = .212$

4-23 a.   This could be illustrated with a graph like Figure 4-8. We first calculate the standardized Z value:

$$Z = \dfrac{X - \mu}{\sigma} = \dfrac{50,000 - 56,000}{8,000} = -.75$$

$Pr(X > 50,000) = Pr(Z > -.75)$

$\qquad\qquad\qquad\quad = 1 - .227 = .773$

b.
and
c.   This is a messy problem; there are many possible assumptions, and therefore many possible answers. We included it precisely <u>because</u> its messiness reflects the conditions of statistical consulting.
Let us start with some simple assumptions:

(i)   Since all four tires are on the same car, they are subjected to the same kind of driving, turning, braking, etc. Then they will all wear out at the same time, approximately. (If the tires are rotated from position to position periodically, this assumption is impeccable.) That is, when the first tire wears out, they all will -- a case of perfect dependence.
Assume further that I am a driver drawn at random. Then the answer is .773, as in (a).

(ii)   More realistically, the front tires are subjected to more wear, from braking, propelling the car, hitting curbs, misalignment, etc., and so they wear out sooner. So the chance of all 4 tires, including the front tires, lasting 50,000 miles is <u>less</u> than .773.

(iii) The least realistic (but most tempting) assumption is that the tires are statistically independent, so that we can use the standard formula:

$$\text{Pr}(T_1 \text{ and } T_2 \text{ and } T_3 \text{ and } T_4) = \text{Pr}(T_1)\text{Pr}(T_2)\text{Pr}(T_3)\text{Pr}(T_4) \qquad \text{like (3-21)}$$

$$= (.773)(.773) \ldots = (.773)^4 = .357$$

where T_1 denotes the first tire lasting 50,000 miles, etc.

Strangely enough, however, this mistaken assumption works in the same direction as the adjustment in (ii) above, and therefore might bring us closer to the correct answer.

4-25

x	given p(x)	t(x)	a. xp(x)	b. t(x)p(x)	c.(i) for disp.inc. d(x) d(x)=x-t(x)	d(x)p(x)
20	.10	4	2.0	.4	16	1.6
30	.30	6	9.0	1.8	24	7.2
40	.40	9	16.0	3.6	31	12.4
50	.20	13	10.0	2.6	37	7.4

$$E(X) = 37.0 \quad E(T) = 8.4 \qquad\qquad E(D) = 28.6$$

c.(ii) Easier alternative: If her expected income is 37.0 and expected tax is 8.4, this leaves 37.0 - 8.4 = 28.6 as disposable income.

The reason this intuitive argument works is because subtracting is a <u>linear</u> transformation.

4-27 a. E(X) is the same as in Problem 4-26:

$$E(X) = n\pi = 6(.4) = 2.4$$

b. <u>Solution 1</u> The straightforward way is to tabulate p(x) from the binomial table III(b), with n = 6 and π = .40. Then tabulate g(x), and use the formula (4-32):

x	copy from Table IIIb p(x)	calculate g(x) = 200x -300-20x^2	product g(x)p(x)
0	.047	-300	-14.10
1	.187	-120	-22.44
2	.311	20	6.22
3	.276	120	33.12
4	.138	180	24.84
5	.037	200	7.40
6	.004	180	.72
	1.000		E(g(X)) = 35.76 $\approx$ 36

<u>Solution 2</u> A more theoretical alternative has easier arithmetic. We start with the profit formula:

$$g(X) = 200X - 300 - 20X^2$$

We can take the expectation term by term:

$$E[g(X)] = 200\,E(X) - 300 - 20\,E(X^2) \qquad (1)$$

Note that we can't claim the last term is $[E(X)]^2$ -- because squaring is nonlinear. Instead, we use (4-36):

$$E(X^2) = \sigma^2 + \mu^2$$

Since X is binomial, with n = 6 and π = .40, we can use (4-13):

$$E(X^2) = n\pi(1-\pi) + [n\pi]^2$$

$$= 6(.40)(.60) + [6(.40)]^2 = 7.20$$

Finally, we substitute this value of $E(X^2)$ into (1):

$$E[g(x)] = 200[6(.40)] - 300 - 20(7.20)$$

$$= 36.0$$

c. When is profit positive? The easiest solution is to scan the third column of the table in part (b) above; we find a positive profit when X ≥ 2, with total probability .776.
Finally, Pr(- profit) = 1 - .766 = .234

4-29 We shall first give the easiest answer, by appealing to a general theorem: a, b, and e are all true, because they are linear transformations.
Parts c and d are untrue because they are not linear transformations. In fact, when graphed, g(x) is seen to be concave up rather than linear. This upward warp makes the values of g(x) unusually large, so that

$$E[g(X)] > g[E(X)]$$

This can be prove generally true for <u>any</u> function g(x) that is concave up. And we will also show it by calculator below.
Now we shall give an alternative answer by calculating both sides of the equation using (4-32):

x	p(x)	xp(x)	a. g(x) = x+10	g(x)p(x)	b. g(x) = x/10	g(x)p(x)
2	.5	1.0	12	6.0	.2	.10
4	.5	2.0	14	7.0	.4	.20
		E(X) = 3.0	E(X + 10) = 13.0 E(X) + 10 = 3.0 + 10 = 13.0 ✓		E(X/10) = .30 E(X)/10 = 3.0/10 = .30 ✓	

c. g(x) = 10/x	g(x)p(x)	d. g(x) = x²	g(x)p(x)	e. g(x)=(5X+2)/10	g(x)p(x)
5	2.5	4	2.0	1.2	0.6
2.5	1.25	16	8.0	2.2	1.1
E(10/X) = 3.75 10/E(X) = 10/3.0 = 3.33		E(X²) = 10.0 [E(X)]² = 3² = 9		E(5X+2)/10 = 1.7 (5E(X)+2)/10 = (15+2)/10 = 1.7	

4-31 a. Knowing L = \$4200 is not nearly enough information. Before making a bid, you must decide what it is worth to you (V). It might also help perhaps to know how much would clinch the deal (H).

b. In (b) and (c), it is simple and workable to assume the model for (4-39), in particular, that the probability of a bid succeeding shows a <u>linear</u> rise from L to H. So now we substitute into (4-39), V = \$5600, L = \$4200, H = \$4800

$$B_o = \frac{\$4200 + \$5600}{2} = \$4900$$

BUT H = $4800 is smaller.

So B_o = $4800 (no need to go higher, since this bid is sure to succeed).

c. Now $B_o = \frac{\$4200 + \$4600}{2} = \$4400$

(H = $4800 is not smaller.)

4-33 a.

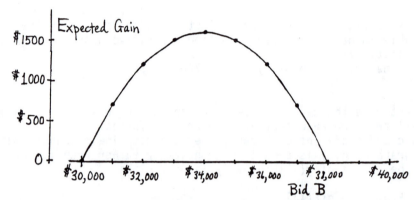

b. The graph is a parabola over the interval from L to V, and here is a rigorous proof: Expected gain in the last column of Table 4-7 is the product of gain × probability. Each factor is a first-degree polynomial (linear), so their product is a second degree polynomial (parabola).

c. True.

4-35 This is an example of the binomial distribution, each voter constituting a "trial" with π = .60.

a. If one voter is drawn, his chance of voting Republican is of course 60%, the population proportion.

b. n = 3, π = .6, and from Table IIIc:

$$Pr(S \geq 2) = .648 \simeq 65\%$$

c. n = 9, π = .60, and from Table IIIc:

$$Pr(S \geq 5) = .733 \simeq 73\%$$

4-37 a.

x	p(x)	xp(x)	$(x-\mu)^2 p(x)$
0	.17	0	.6137
1	.19	.19	.
2	.36	.72	.
3	.17	.51	.
4	.07	.28	by calculator
5	.04	.20	
	1.00	μ = 1.90	σ^2 = 1.67
			$\sigma = \sqrt{1.67} = 1.29$

The median cell is X = 2, with 36% below and 28% above. This is a discrete distribution, so we do not interpolate within a wide cell. Instead, the median is just X = 2.

The mode is the most frequent cell, also X = 2.

To determine population growth, it is the <u>total</u> number of children in the next generation that counts, which is obtainable from the <u>average</u> (mean).

b. Since this is a discrete distribution, it should be graphed with lines (like Figure 2-1), not bars.

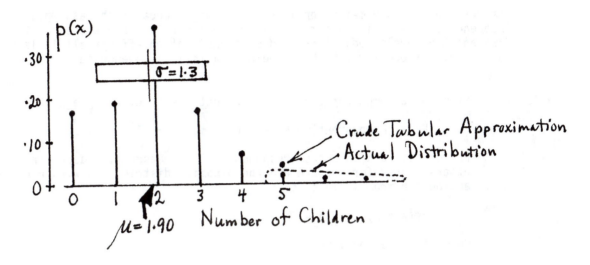

4-39 a. Binomial with   n = sample size = 7
                          π = population proportion of Asians = .60
                          S = number of Asians in the sample

From Table IIIc,

$$P(S \geq 4) = .710 \approx 71\%$$

b. Binomial with   n = 7
                    π = population proportion of Blacks = .01
                    S = number of Blacks in the sample

Since π = .01 is not in Table IIIb, we shall use the formula:

$$p(s) = \binom{n}{s} \pi^s (1-\pi)^{n-s} \qquad\qquad (4\text{-}8)$$

$$= \binom{7}{0}(.01)^0 (1-.01)^{7-0}$$

$$= (.99)^7 = .932 \approx 93\%$$

c. As in (a), n = 7, π = .60

Thus $\mu = n\pi = 7(.60) = 4.20$ $\qquad\qquad (4\text{-}13)$

$$\sigma = \sqrt{n\pi(1-\pi)} = \sqrt{7(.6)(.4)} = 1.30$$

4-41 Although we could use the binomial formula, it is simple to work from first principles. "<u>At least one</u> will work" suggests the complement

35

E = none will work, that is, all four will fail

$$Pr(E) = Pr(F_1 \text{ and } F_2 \text{ and } F_3 \text{ and } F_4)$$

Since independent, $= Pr(F_1)Pr(F_2)Pr(F_3)Pr(F_4)$ like (3-21)

$$= (.10)(.10)(.10)(.10) = .10^4 = .0001$$

Thus $Pr(E) = 1 - .0001 = .9999$

<u>Remarks</u> This figure may be optimistically high, because the assumption of independence may fail. After all, alarms often fail because their battery has run down and been neglected. This kind of trouble often affects all 4 alarms at the same time, introducing a high degree of statistical dependence.

4-43   a.   From the assumptions that the treatment has no effect, we have

$$Pr(+ \text{ improvement}) = Pr(- \text{ improvement}) = .5$$

Presumably each volunteer responds, and is measured, independently of the others. Therefore we can use the binomial distribution with $n = 8$ and $\pi = .5$, and obtain from Table IIIc,

$$Pr(X \geq 7) = .035 \simeq 4\%$$

b.   We must either believe

(1)   that the hypothesis is true and a rare event has occurred with probability 4%, or

(2)   the hypothesis is false.

We doubt (1), because we are skeptical; when events become "too rare," we look for alternate explanations.

<u>Remarks</u>: This is an example of <u>hypothesis testing</u>, and it would not hurt to introduce some of the standard terminology:

The hypothesis that the treatment has no effect whatever is called the <u>null hypothesis</u>, H_0.

The probability of 4% is called the <u>p-value</u> for H_0. When it is very low, it shows how little credibility H_0 has.

A person may decide to <u>reject</u> H_0 if the p-value sinks below an arbitrary level of skepticism, such as <u>5%</u> -- which is commonly called the <u>level of significance</u>, or just the <u>level of the test</u>.

4-45   a.   (i)   When no overtime is possible, let us see how much extra revenue the sixth plumber would generate.

            After the first five plumbers are worked to capacity, that is, after 5 x 40 hours = 200 hours, then the sixth plumber starts working. Let us denote his hours by Y, and tabulate them from the given table:

Hours X	Hours of 6th plumber Y	Midpoint y	Relative Frequency p(y)	yp(y)
180-190	0	0	.03	0
190-200	0	0	.09	0
200-210	0-10	5	.12	.60
210-220	10-20	15	.15	2.25
220-230	20-30	25	.22	5.50
230-240	30-40	35	.21	7.35
240-250	40	40	.13	5.20
250-260	40	40	.05	2.00
				22.90

At \$30/hr, these 22.90 hours would bring in \$687. Since this does not cover his cost of \$800, this sixth plumber should not be hired.

(ii)   If the sixth plumber were hired, there would only be a few possible hours of overtime, and the other five plumbers could easily cover them. So the sixth plumber would remain uneconomic. (In fact, he would be <u>particularly</u> uneconomic now; if he were not there, the first five plumbers would have a lot more overtime available, netting \$5/hour.)

b.   Now we calculate the overtime hours, in much the same way as we calculated the hours of the sixth plumber. But now the upper limit is 5 × 5 hours = 25 hours.

Hours X	Overtime Hours Y	Midpoint y	Relative Frequency p(y)		yp(y)
180-190	0	0	.03 ⎱	.12	0
190-200	0	0	.09 ⎰		
200-210	0-10	5	.12		.60
210-220	10-20	15	.15		2.25
220-230	20-30	25	.22		5.50
230-240	25	25	.21 ⎰		9.75
240-250	25	25	.13 ⎱	.39	
250-260	25	25	.05 ⎰		
					18.10

Since overtime nets \$5/hour (\$30 - \$25), 18.10 hours are worth:

18.10 hrs. × \$5/hr. = \$90.50

<u>Remarks</u>   For a slightly better answer, the Y cell covering 20-30 hours could be split in half, according to whether or not the crucial 25 hours was exceeded. That would produce the following 2 lines in place of the original single line:

X	Y	y	p(y)	yp(y)
220-225	20-25	22.5	.11	2.475
225-230	25	25	.11	2.75

This contribution is now a little less than before, specifically less by 5.5 - (2.475 + 2.75) = .275 hours, worth .275 × $5 = $1.38. This leaves the weekly value:

$90.50 - $1.38 = $89.12

5-1   **a.**   The probabilities are just the relative frequencies, obtained by dividing by N = 100,000,000, that is, just inserting an initial decimal point:

		y		**b.**	**d.**	
x	30	45	70	p(x)	xp(x)	$(x-\mu)^2 p(x)$
0	.01	.02	.05	.08	0	.271
1	.03	.06	.10	.19	.19	
2	.18	.21	.15	.54	1.08	or, by
3	.07	.08	.04	.19	.57	calculator

b.   p(y)   .29   .37   .34   1.00   1.84 $\sigma_x^2 = .674$

$\mu_x = 1.84$ $\sigma_x = .82$

c.   In real life, two variables practically never are perfectly independent, because independence requires it to be <u>exactly</u> true that

$$p(x,y) = p(x)p(y)$$
for all x and y   (5-6)

Let us try the first cell:

    L.S. = .01
    R.S. = (.08)(.29) = .023 ≠ L.S.

This one exception to (5-6) rules out independence. We need go no further. X and Y are dependent.

e.   Here is an example of what the computer can do (Harvard Graphics):

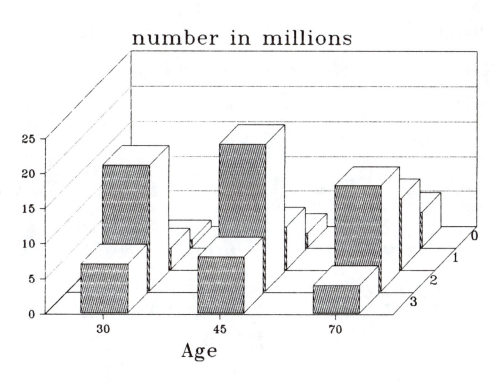

number in millions

Age

For comparison, here is another example of computer graphics, as an alternative to Figure 5-2 in the text:

Joint Distribution

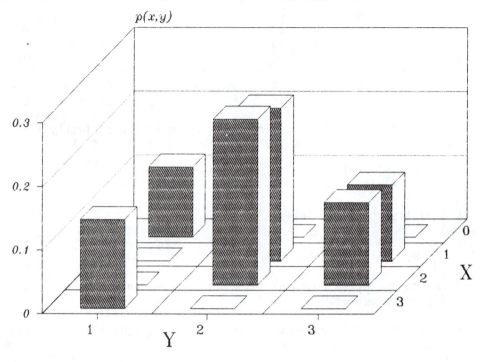

5-3   Into the given formula, we substitute y = 30 and x = 0,1,2, and 3 successively:

$$p(x|y) = \frac{p(x,y)}{p(y)} = \frac{p(0,30)}{p(30)} = \frac{.01}{.29} = .034 \quad \checkmark$$

Similarly, for x = 1,   = .03/.29 = .103   √

x = 2,   = .18/.29 = .621   √

x = 3,   = .07/.29 = .241   √

These are the same calculations we did in Problem 5-2a, except for the decimal point (using <u>relative</u> frequencies or probabilities).

5-5   We select out the middle column of the bivariate table, where Y = 1:

x	p(x,1)	p(x|Y = 1) = p(x,1)/p(1)	Compare to p(x)
1	.1	.1/.6 = .17	.20
2	.4	.4/.6 = .66	.60
3	.1	.1/.6 = .17	.20

p(1) = .6

The last two columns above show that the conditional distribution is not equal to the unconditional distribution. Thus X and Y are not independent. This agrees with the earlier conclusion in Problem 5-4.

5-7 a. We have to list the original sample space in order to get the bivariate distribution (as in Figure 5-1). Letting S = sale and F = no sale, then a tree would yield the following sample space (outcome set, as in Problem 4-4):

e	Pr(e)		X value	Y value
(SSS)	$.8^3$	=.512	3	$400
(SSF)	$.8^2(.2)$	=.128	2	200
(SFS)		.128	2	300
(SFF)		.032	1	100
(FSS)		.128	2	300
(FSF)		.032	1	100
(FFS)		.032	1	200
(FFF)		.008	0	0

			y		
x	0	100	200	300	400
0	.008				
1		.064	.032		
2			.128	.256	
3					.512

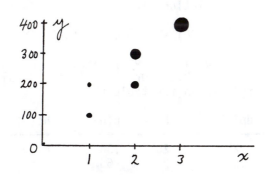

b.

			y				
x	0	100	200	300	400		p(x)
0	.008						.008
1		.064	.032				.096
2			.128	.256			.384
3					.512		.512
p(y)	.008	.064	.160	.256	.512		1.000 √

This gives the same p(x) as Problem 4-4, of course.

c.

x	p(x)	x p(x)	y	p(y)	y p(y)
0	.008	.000	0	.008	0
1	.096	.096	100	.064	6.4
2	.384	.768	200	.160	32.0
3	.512	1.536	300	.256	76.8
			400	.512	204.8
		$\mu_x = 2.400$			$\mu_Y = 320.0$

d. Not independent, because the rows of the bivariate table are not proportional.

5-9 For part (b) we will need the distribution of V anyhow (to calculate its standard deviation), so we might as well calculate it from the beginning. For part (d), we also derive the marginal distribution of D and of H:

		h					a.

d	20	25	p(d)
1.00	.16	.09	.25
1.25	.15	.30	.45
1.50	.03	.17	.20
1.75	.00	.10	.10
p(h)	.34	.66	1.00

v	p(v)	vp(v)
8.00	.16	1.28
10.00	.09	.90
12.50	.15	1.88
15.62	.30	4.69
18.00	.032	.54
22.50	.17	3.82
30.63	.10	3.06

$$\mu = 16.17$$

a.b. Using the distribution of V above, our calculator gives $\mu = 16.17$, $\sigma = 6.63$.

c. Since $\mu = \dfrac{\text{population total}}{\text{population size}}$ like (2-4)

Thus population total = μ (population size)

$$= 16.17 \, (380) = 6145 \text{ cubic feet}$$

d. From the marginal distribution in the very first table above, our calculator gives E(D) = 1.288 and E(H) = 23.3. Or, here is the detail by hand: We start by copying down the marginals in the table above:

d	p(d)	dp(d)	h	p(h)	hp(h)
1.00	.25	.25	20	.34	6.80
1.25	.45	.563	25	.66	16.50
1.50	.20	.30			
1.75	.10	.175		E(H) =	23.30
	E(D)=	1.288			

Will E(V) = .4[E(D)]²E(H)? Since volume is a nonlinear function, we wouldn't expect it to be true. Calculation bears this out:

From part (a), E(V) = 16.17
From part (d), .4 [E(D)]² = .4 (1.288)²(23.30) = 15.46

5-11 a. From the given table of X, our calculator gives

$$\mu_X = 2.33, \qquad \sigma_X = .75, \qquad \text{hence} \quad \sigma_X^2 = .56$$

b. Again, from the given table of Y, our calculator gives

$$\mu_Y = 1.83, \qquad \sigma_Y = .90, \qquad \text{hence} \quad \sigma_Y^2 = .81$$

c. If we needed only the mean of S, we would get it directly using (5-9). But we need the standard deviation of S as well, which we get from tabulating its distribution first, as follows:

For the distribution of S, first we list the joint distribution of X and Y, which we get by the multiplication rule (5-6):

x	y 1	2	3	p(x)
1	3/36	1/36	2/36	1/6
2	6/36	2/36	4/36	2/6
3	9/36	3/36	6/36	3/6
p(y)	3/6	1/6	2/6	

s	p(s)
2	3/36
3	7/36
4	13/36
5	7/36
6	6/36
	36/36

Our calculator gives

$$\mu_s = 4.17, \qquad \sigma_s = 1.17, \qquad \text{hence} \quad \sigma_s^2 = 1.36$$

d. Do the means sum?

$$E(X + Y) \stackrel{?}{=} E(X) + E(Y)$$
$$4.17 \stackrel{\checkmark}{=} 2.33 + 1.83$$

This is indeed true, allowing for rounding error.

Similarly, $\text{var}(X + Y) \stackrel{?}{=} \text{var}(X) + \text{var}(Y)$
$$1.36 \stackrel{\checkmark}{=} .56 + .81$$

Again true, allowing for rounding error.

Finally, $SD(X + Y) \stackrel{?}{=} SD(X) + SD(Y)$
$$1.17 \neq .75 + .90$$

5-13 a. In part (c) of Problem 5-12, $\rho = 0$, and X and Y are independent. In part (d), $\rho = 0$, yet X and Y are not independent.

b. Statement (1) is true, in fact is just the statement (5-12). It is illustrated by part (c) of Problem 5-12, where X and Y were independent. Then $\rho = 0$, as promised.

Statement (2) is false, as part (d) of Problem 5-12 shows: $\rho = 0$, yet it did not follow that X and Y were independent.

5-15 a. To get $E(H|X)$, we first need the conditional distribution. For X = 1, for example, we have:

	h 0	1	2	
joint distribution	.02	.08	.05	/ .15
conditional distribution	$\frac{.02}{.15}$ = .133	$\frac{.08}{.15}$ = .533	$\frac{.05}{.15}$ = .333	
for mean, h p(h)	0	.533	.666	/ 1.20

Thus $E(H|X = 1) = 1.20$

Similarly, we would find

$$E(H|X=2) = 1.42$$
$$E(H|X=3) = 1.50$$

As X increases, note that H slightly increases on average, as the graph will illustrate:

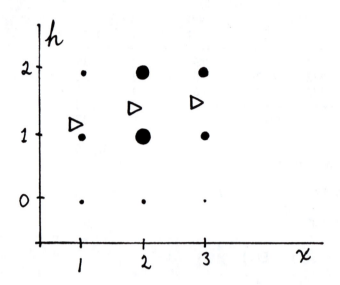

b.

x	h 0	1	2	p(x)
1	.02	.08	.05	.15
2	.02	.28	.25	.55
3	.01	.13	.16	.30
p(h)	.05	.49	.46	1.00 √

From the marginal distribution our calculator gives:

$$\mu_X = 2.15, \quad \sigma_X = .654, \quad \mu_H = 1.41, \quad \sigma_H = .585$$

For σ_{XH}, we likewise calculate E(XH) from the table of xhp(x,h):

x	h 0	1	2
1	0	.08	.10
2	0	.56	1.00
3	0	.39	.96
		E(XY) = 3.09	

Thus $\sigma_{XH} = E(XH) - \mu_X \mu_H$ like (5-11)

$$= 3.09 - (2.15)(1.41) = .0585$$

Finally $\rho = \dfrac{\sigma_{XH}}{\sigma_X \sigma_H} = \dfrac{.0585}{(.654)(.585)} = .153$

c. (i) True

44

(ii) True. In fact, the tendency is seen to be weak on the graph, so ρ is much less than 1.

(iii) Partly true. This does indeed show that the more educated people tend to be happier than the less educated (if the Gallup poll with its self-evaluation can be believed).

However, this data does not show that the <u>cause</u> of this greater happiness is the education. As we emphasized in Chapter 1, correlation does not prove causation in an observational study. There may be some other factor causing the happiness. For example, it might be that people who are raised in happy homes tend to be happier, and also tend to be better motivated to persevere in their education (or in their jobs, thus obtaining more money as in Problem 5-14).

5-17 a.   Tally of the frequency:

	y		
x	15	25	35
20	/	//	
30	/	//	/
40		//	/

This yields the following relative frequency (probability) distribution, **and** marginal distributions for part b:

	y			
x	15	25	35	p(x)
20	.1	.2	0	.3
30	.1	.2	.1	.4
40	0	.2	.1	.3
p(y)	.2	.6	.2	

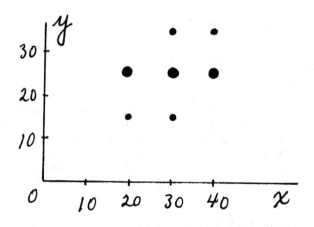

b.   From the margins of the bivariate distribution in part (a), our calculator gives:

$$\mu_X = 30.0, \qquad \sigma_X = 7.75, \qquad \text{hence} \quad \sigma_X^2 = 60$$

$$\mu_Y = 25.0, \qquad \sigma_Y = 6.32, \qquad \text{hence} \quad \sigma_Y^2 = 40$$

c. Since the means are such easy numbers, we will use the definition
$\sigma_{XY} = E(X-\mu_X)(Y-\mu_Y)$:

Table of $(X-\mu_X)(Y-\mu_Y)p(x,y)$

		y	
x	15	25	35
20	10	0	0
30	0	0	0
40	0	0	10

σ_{XY} = sum = 20

d. First we shall do it the hard way (so we can appreciate the easy way later). We begin by deriving the distribution of S from the bivariate distribution:

		y				
x	15	25	35		s	p(s)
20	.1	.2			35	.1
30	.1	.2	.1		45	.3
40		.2	.1		55	.2
					65	.3
					75	.1

hence $\mu_S = 55$, $\sigma_S = 11.8$

By contrast, the easy way is to use the individual means and variances:

$E(X + Y) = E(X) + E(Y) = 30 + 25 = 55$	(5-16)
var $(X + Y)$ = var X + var Y + 2 cov (X, Y)	(5-18)
$= 60 + 40 + 2 (20) = 140$	

e.

$E(.6X + .8Y) = .6\ E(X) + .8\ E(Y)$	like (5-17)
$= .6\ (30) + .8\ (25) = 38$	
var $(.6X + .8Y) = .6^2$ var X $+ .8^2$ var Y $+ 2\ (.6)(.8)$ cov (X,Y)	(5-19)
$= .36\ (60) + .64\ (40) + .96\ (20) = 66.4$	

f.

$E(X-Y) = E(X) - E(Y) = 30 - 25 = 5.0$	like (5-17)
var $(X-Y) = 1^2$ var X $+ (-1)^2$ var Y $+ 2(1)(-1)$ cov (X,Y)	(5-19)
$= 60 + 40 - 2\ (20) = 60$	

g. Although it is incontestable that wives earn less (by 5 thousand dollars) than husbands on the average, there is no evidence given that this is _because_ of sex discrimination. There are many other possible explanations for wives having a lower average income in an observational study like this. For example, wives may be younger on average (and people tend to earn more as they gain experience).

5-19 (i) Since the total government revenue is N times the mean, we just have to look at the mean value of T. It was greatest for scheme b, (at 20.0), next for scheme c (11.8), and a close third for scheme a (11.0).

(ii) The net income after taxes is given by the formula N = S - T, of course. We then calculate its standard deviation as we did for S in Problem 5-18. Here are the details:

46

a. $N = S - T = S - .20S = .80 \ S$
    Thus $SD(N) = .80 \ SD(S) = .80(11.8) = 9.5$

b. $N = S - T = S - .5(S - 15) = .5S + 7.5$
    Thus $SD(N) = .5 \ SD(S) = .5(11.8) = 5.9$

c. This nonlinear function requires working through the table:

s	t	n=s-t	p(n)=p(s)
35	5	30	.1
45	7	38	.3
55	11	44	.2
65	16	49	.3
75	22	53	.1

$\mu = 43.2, \quad \sigma = 6.7$

5-21 a. Basic Solution: Since we are considering the subpopulation of males, we select the first column of the given table:

x	male f	p(x) = f/N	c. x p(x)
0	4,000,000	.085	0
1	10,000,000	.213	.213
2	23,000,000	.489	.978
3	10,000,000	.213	.639
N = 47,000,000		1.000 ✓	1.83 = E(X|Z=0)

Equivalent Solution can be obtained by using the conditional probability formulas:

$$p(x|z) = \frac{p(x,z)}{p(z)} \qquad \qquad \text{like (3-17)}$$

first $= \dfrac{.04}{.47} = .085$

second $= \dfrac{.10}{.47} = .213,$ etc.

b. Since the conditional distribution is different from the unconditional distribution in Problem 5-20, X is therefore statistically dependent on Z. As shown above, this makes the conditional mean different, too.

d. We first find the conditional distribution, as in (a):

x	male f	p(x) = f/N	c. x p(x)
0	5,000,000	.094	0
1	12,000,000	.227	.227
2	29,000,000	.547	1.094
3	7,000,000	.132	.396
N = 53,000,000		1.000 ✓	1.72 = E(X|Z=1)

This mean educational level for females (1.72) is lower than for males (1.83).

47

e. The overall mean education for all adults (1.77) is about halfway between the male and female means: It is just a little closer to the female mean, since females are a little more than half of the population. To be precise, we find:

overall mean = .53 female mean + .47 male mean

$$1.77 \overset{\checkmark}{=} .53 \ (1.717) + .47 \ (1.830)$$

5-23 A linear function of X and Z has the form $aX + bZ + c$, and so includes part (b) and (c). For part (a) and (d), we tabulate the distribution of S instead, to get E(S).

a. Here is the probability distribution repeated from Problem 5-22, with the values of S = 10 + 10XZ added in brackets:

x	z 0	1
0	.04 (s=10)	.05 (s=10)
1	.10 (s=10)	.12 (s=20)
2	.23 (s=10)	.29 (s=30)
3	.10 (s=10)	.07 (s=40)

Now we list the values of s in increasing order, with their corresponding probabilities:

s	p(s)	sp(s)
10	.52	5.2
20	.12	2.4
30	.29	8.7
40	.07	2.8
	1.00 $\checkmark$	19.1 = E(S)

Note that transforming the expected values the same way as the individual combination of X and Z would give the wrong answer, in this nonlinear case:

$$10 + 10 \ E(X) \ E(Z) = 10 + 10 \ (1.77) \ (.53)$$
$$= 19.38 \neq E(S)$$

b. Since S is linear, we **can** transform the expected values with the same formula:

$$E(S) = E(10 + 3X - 2Z) = 10 + 3E(X) - 2E(Z)$$
$$= 10 + 3(1.77) - 2(.53) = 14.25$$

c. Just to be sure that S is linear, we write it in the standard form:

$$S = \frac{2X + 40}{5} = \frac{2}{5} X + 8 = .4X + 0Z + 8$$

Thus $E(S) = .4E(X) + 0E(Z) + 8$

$$= .4(1.77) + 0 + 8 \approx 8.7$$

d.

	z	
x	0	1
0	.04 (s=10)	.05 (s=10)
1	.10 (s=11)	.12 (s=11)
2	.23 (s=14)	.29 (s=14)
3	.10 (s=19)	.07 (s=19)

s	p(s)	sp(s)
10	.09	0.90
11	.22	2.42
14	.52	7.28
19	.17	3.23
	1.00	13.83 = E(10 + X^2)

5-25 a. To calculate the conditional distribution of education for males aged 30, we start with the first column in the table given in Problem 5-24. Then we finally go on to calculate the expected mean:

sex Z = 1 (female) and Age Y = 30

education x	freq.	rel. freq. = p(x)	x p(x)
0	400,000	.028	0
1	1,600,000	.114	.114
2	8,400,000	.596	1.192
3	3,700,000	.262	.786
N = 14,100,000		1.000 √	2.09 = E(X|Y=30 and Z = 0)

To repeat this calculation now for <u>females</u>, we start with the <u>fourth</u> column in the table given in Problem 5-24, and so continue:

sex Z = 1 (female) and Age Y = 30

education x	freq.	rel. freq. = p(x)	x p(x)
0	400,000	.028	0
1	1,700,000	.118	.118
2	9,300,000	.646	1.292
3	3,000,000	.208	.624
N = 14,400,000		1.000 √	2.03

So the females have slightly less education on average (2.03 compared to 2.09).

b. **(i) AGE 45**

x	sex Z = 0 (male) freq.	p(x)	xp(x)	x	sex Z = 1 (female) freq.	p(x)	xp(x)
0	1,200,000	.067	0	0	1,100,000	.058	0
1	3,300,000	.186	.186	1	3,600,000	.189	.189
2	9,100,000	.511	1.022	2	11,500,000	.606	1.212
3	4,200,000	.236	.708	3	2,800,000	.147	.441
	17,800,000	1.000	1.92		19,000,000	1.000	1.84

About the same gap between female and male education (1.84 compared to 1.92).

(ii) AGE 70

x	sex Z = 0 (male) freq.	p(x)	xp(x)	x	sex Z = 1 (female) freq.	p(x)	xp(x)
0	2,700,000	.179	0	0	3,300,000	.168	0
1	4,700,000	.311	.311	1	6,300,000	.322	.322
2	5,600,000	.371	.742	2	8,600,000	.439	.878
3	2,100,000	.139	.417	3	1,400,000	.071	.213
	15,100,000	1.000	1.47 ✓		19,600,000	1.000	1.41

Still the same gap between female and male education (1.41 compared to 1.47)

c.   We plot first the overall difference between men's and women's average education (from Problem 5-21(d)):

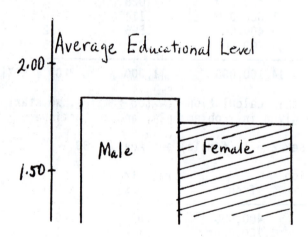

We note the gap is small (1.83 - 1.72 = .11 schools completed, on average. At about 4 years per school, this amounts to .44 years -- less than half a year of education.)

    To determine why this gap occurs, it helps to plot the average education of males and females <u>for each age level</u> (from parts b and c). And to clarify later issues, we let the width of each bar be proportional to the number of people in that category:

50

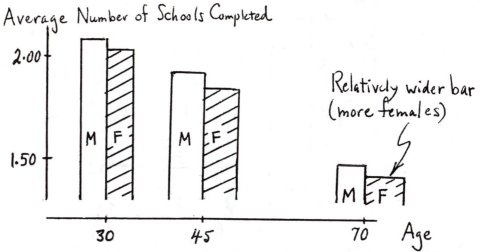

Average Number of Schools Completed

Relatively wider bar (more females)

There is about the same small gap at each age -- about .06 schools completed. To explain the overall gap of .11, there is still .05 missing. How come? What is the source of the confounding?

As the graphs show, there are more older women than men, and it is the older people who tend to have less education.

Remarks We must always remember that these averages that we have plotted and discussed do not tell the whole story. The distributions before averaging provide some interesting detail that was lost in averaging. For example, we might look for the detailed reason why females have less schooling at every age, age 70 for instance. We therefore compare the conditional distributions given in part (b)(ii) above. The major difference is that males show more college graduates (.139 vs. .071), and correspondingly fewer graduates who stopped after high school (.371 vs. .439). That is, males who graduated from high school had more opportunity to go on to college. But the histories before high school were very similar.

d.   See part (c) for explanations of this answer:

In part (c) we found females had about .06 units of education less than males, at each age level. Earlier in Problem 5-21(d) the analysis that ignored age showed an overall difference that was [the same of course, surprisingly larger]. This confounding occurs because there are [more, fewer] older women than men, and it is the older people who tend to have [more, less] education.

To restate this point, suppose at each age women achieved the same education as men. Then women's average education overall would [still be somewhat less than men's, now be equal to men's].

Routinely and easily controlling for confounding factors—not just age, but any others as well—is what [multiple regressions, confidence intervals] do, and we will accordingly analyze this data again in Problem 14-8.

5-27   To really find out how effective a treatment is, a [RCE, OS] is better than a [RCE, OS], where feasible. This is because a [RCE, OS] actually makes the treatment and control groups equal on average in every respect—except for the treatment itself, of course; whereas a [RCE, OS] is usually cluttered up with confounding factors that bias the answer. To the extent these confounding factors can be measured and analyzed with a [multiple regression, confidence interval], however, bias can be reduced.

5-29   a.

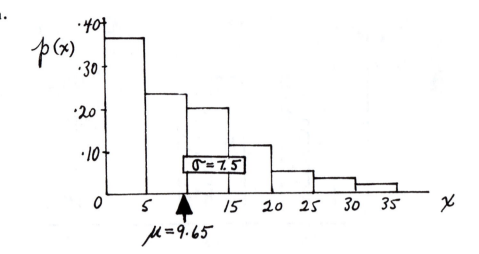

b.

midpoint x	p(x)	x p(x)
2.5	.36	.900
7.5	.23	1.725
12.5	.20	
17.5	.11	Better to use a
22.5	.05	calculator or
27.5	.03	computer to find
32.5	.02	μ and σ

$$\mu = 9.65$$
$$\sigma = 7.5$$

c.   Mode = 2.5 (or 0, if you imagine the finer detail that could have been given). Since the distribution is skewed to the right, the median will be between the mode and mean.

<u>Remarks</u>   This is the same distribution as Figure 2-5, except the cell width is now 5 instead of 2 thousand. Note that the mean and median are therefore about the same.

5-31   The CBS poll is much smaller. Because it is random, however, it gives an <u>unbiased</u> estimate of the various proportions of the population of registered voters (who can be reached by telephones, which includes nearly everybody now.) To allow for the sampling variability, a 95% confidence interval could be constructed. For the proportion who believed Carter had won, for example, we obtain

$$\pi = P \pm 1.96 \sqrt{\frac{P(1-P)}{n}}$$

$$= .36 \pm 1.96 \sqrt{\frac{.36\,(.64)}{1019}}$$

$$= .36 \pm .03$$

Although it was very large, the ABC poll may have been seriously biased by choosing only people who volunteered. In view of this, it would be misleading to quote a confidence interval. (The interval would be based on a proportion P = 244,000/967,000 = 25%) who voted for Carter. In having n = 967,000, it would be very precise, and of course disagree with the 36% ± 3% quoted for the CBS poll.)

x	n(x)	a. L(x)	b. m(x)
0-10	26	1,000	.026
10-20	9	974	.009
20-30	18	965	.019
30-40	21	947	.022
40-50	49	926	.053
50-60	117	877	.133
60-70	219	760	.288
70-80	282	541	.521
80-90	208	259	.803
90-100	51	51	1.000

b. **(i)** Correct version: The mortality rate is lowest during the <u>second</u> decade.

(ii) Improved version: Roughly speaking, <u>from age 30 until age 90</u>, the mortality rate about doubles every decade.

c. **(i)** The probability of a man dying is taken from the mortality rate column. For a man in his 20's, this is .019.

We shall assume that if he dies, on average he dies about halfway through the decade, so that about half of his premium x will have been paid (in monthly instalments). Then the table of net payments to the man or his estate will be:

outcome	prob.	net payment
dies	.019	$1000 - x/2
lives	.981	- x

For a "fair bet", by definition the expected net payment is zero:

$$.019(\$1000 - x/2) + .981 (-x) = 0$$

$$(.981 + .019/2) x = .019(\$1000)$$

$$x = \frac{\$19}{.9905} \approx \$19$$

(ii) For a man in his 40's, the mortality rate increases to .053, and the "fair premium" x correspondingly increases as follows:

$$(.947 + .053/2) x = .053 (\$1000)$$

$$= \frac{\$53}{.9735} \approx \$54$$

d. **(i)** The relative number dying in their 40's is found from the n(x) column.

$$49/1000 = .049$$

(ii) The relative number living to forty is found from the L(x) column:

$$926/1000 = .926$$

(iii) The answer is the mortality rate found in the m(x) column:

$$.053$$

Incidentally, if we let A and B denote the events in (i) and (ii), note that (iii) can be written as Pr(A|B). So we could alternatively use our conditional probability formulas to obtain an answer:

$$Pr(A|B) = \frac{Pr(A \text{ and } B)}{Pr(B)} = \frac{Pr(A)}{Pr(B)} = \frac{.049}{.926} = .053$$

5-35 a.   We assume the 3 refrigerators are statistically independent. (Thus, for example, we rule out the possibility of them being defective because of a faulty shipping procedure that all 3 refrigerators might share.) We can therefore use the binomial distribution with n = 3, π = .20, and so obtain from Table IIIb,

	a.		c.
x	p(x)	c(x)	c(x)p(x)
0	.512	0	0
1	.384	25	9.60
2	.096	40	3.84
3	.008	55	.44

average cost = $13.88

b. $\mu = n\pi = 3 (.2) = .60$ (4-13)

$\sigma^2 = n\pi(1-\pi) = 3(.2)(.8) = .48$

Or, using a calculator on the distribution in part (a) would be almost as easy.

c.   This is not a linear transformation, because the formula for c(x) is defined in 2 pieces. [Or, geometrically, the graph of c(x) would turn out to be a <u>broken</u> line, broken at x = 0.] We therefore have to compute E[c(X)] the hard way, using $\Sigma c(x)p(x)$, as in (4-32) as shown above in the last 2 columns.

5-37 A tree will show our work nicely, and also be easily reversed to give the Bayesian answer in part (c). Letting D represent diabetes, and +/- represent the possibly incorrect <u>test</u> for diabetes, we have:

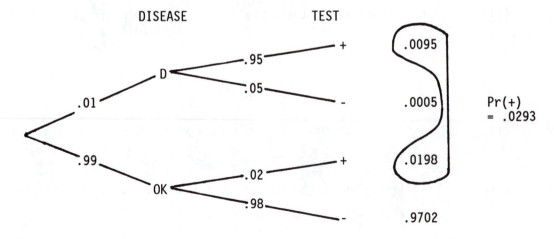

54

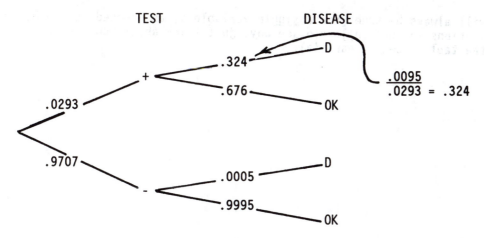

TEST   DISEASE

$\frac{.0095}{.0293} = .324$

a.   In the second line of the first tree, we see the probability of diabetes and a - diagnosis is .0005. Among 10,000 patients, this represents just 5.

b.   To the right of the first tree, we circle the probability of a + diagnosis, .0293 Among 10,000 patients, this represents about 293 people.

c.   The second tree is the reversed tree, and gives us the posterior probability: $Pr(D|+) = .324 \simeq 32\%$.

d.   There are so many non diabetics (99%) that even the small 2% error rate produces more "false alarms" than there are "true alarms"--the true alarms being produced by the relatively few (1%) true diabetics.

5-39   a.

x	c = 200x + 300	p(x) = p(c)	
1	500	.4	
2	700	.2	◄— Median X = 2
3	900	0	Median C = 700
4	1100	.4	

The median is where half the probability is below, half above, roughly speaking. Since the distributions are discrete, however, there is a lump of probability right at the median. This leaves less than half the probability strictly below, and less than half the probability strictly above. This is shown above for the distribution of X and C, and is equally true for all the other distributions.
     The given distribution of Y likewise shows median Y = 1 (with 40% of the probability below, and 40% above).
     Since X and Y were given to be independent, their joint distribution can be found by multiplying: p (x,y) = p(x)p(y). Then the distribution of the sum T can be obtained as in Problem 5-17(d). When you finish tabulating the distribution of T, you will find median T = 4 (with 36% of the probability below and 48% above).

b.   M(X+Y) = M(X) + M(Y)
        4   ≠ 2 + 1

Thus the median is <u>not</u> a linear operator like the expectation operator. This is one more reason why statisticians prefer the mean over the median.

c.   M(200X + 300) = 200 M(X) + 300
        700   = 200 (2) + 300   √

This will always be true [for a <u>single</u> variable X, as opposed to the bivariate complications in part (b)]. To see why, just think about how c corresponds to x in the table shown in part (a).

6-1 **a.** In the sample, the proportion of dollars that were for resale was

$$\frac{\$\ 8,030}{\$38,160} = 21\%$$

Assuming the sample is representative of the whole population, the value of all resale orders is therefore estimated as

21% of $7,010,000 = $1,475,000

b. We assumed the sample was representative of the whole population. But there are two reasons to doubt this:

(i) Nonresponse bias would occur if the nonrespondents tended to be different from the respondents. Perhaps the nonrespondents were more likely to move or to have poor records. Or maybe they tended to be the individuals who order for personal use rather than the retailers who order for resale. Then the $1,475,000 resale estimate would be too high.

(ii) There is also uncertainty due to random sampling. This is about as likely to be in one direction as the other, and its possible magnitude is also <u>known</u> (as we shall see from the formulas we develop in this chapter). So it is not nearly so serious or contentious an issue as the bias.

c. The $1,475,000 of resale orders, at 6½%, would give a tax refund of $96,000.

<u>Epilogue</u> The firm (the plaintiff) had to take the California tax board to court to try to get this refund of $96,000. Using some subtle information not included in this Problem, the plaintiff made an ingenious argument as to why the nonresponse bias would likely be small. The court ruled for the plaintiff on constitutional grounds, and did not make specific findings on the statistical issues.

6-3 **a.**

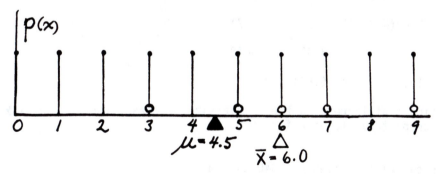

b. The first 5 digits from Table I are 3, 9, 6, 5, 7, and are graphed as hollow dots in the figure above.

c. By symmetry, μ is the midpoint between 0 and 9, that is, $\mu = 4.5$.

d. $X = \dfrac{3 + 9 + 6 + 5 + 7}{5} = \dfrac{30}{5} = 6.0$

This is graphed as the hollow triangle, and is indeed closer to μ than many of the observations, which illustrates equation (6-2).

6-5 **a.** True

b. Correction: SE of only $\sigma/\sqrt{n}$

6-7 a. $SE = \dfrac{\sigma}{\sqrt{n}} = \dfrac{8}{\sqrt{780,000}} = .009$ thousand $= \$9$

b. $SE = \dfrac{\sigma}{\sqrt{n}} = \dfrac{8}{\sqrt{78,000}} = .029$ thousand $= \$29$

Note that it is n that makes the difference, not the sampling fraction (1% in both cases.)

6-9 a. ... an expected value of $\underline{\mu = \$30,000}$ with a standard error of $\underline{\sigma/\sqrt{n} = \$9000/\sqrt{25}}$ $\underline{= \$1800}$, and with a distribution shape that is <u>normal</u>.

b. "10% high" is an income of: $30,000 + 30,000 \times .10 = \$33,000$

To calculate the chance of exceeding this, we standardize it:

$$Z = \frac{X - \mu}{SE} = \frac{33,000 - 30,000}{9,000/\sqrt{25}} = 1.67 \qquad (6\text{-}11)$$

$$Pr(X > 33,000) = Pr(Z > 1.67) = .047$$

6-11 X has an approximately normal distribution, with mean $\mu = 16.20$ and standard error $= \sigma/\sqrt{n} = .12/\sqrt{n}$. We use these to standardize the critical value $\overline{X} = 16$:

$$Z = \frac{\overline{X} - \mu}{SE} \qquad (6\text{-}11)$$

$$= \frac{16 - 16.20}{.12/\sqrt{n}} = -1.67 \sqrt{n}$$

a. $n = 1$, and so $Z = -1.67$. Thus

$$Pr(\overline{X} < 16) = Pr(Z < -1.67) = .047$$

b. $n = 4$, $Pr(Z < -3.33) < .00048$

c. $n = 16$, $Pr(Z < -6.67) \approx 0$

Notice that increasing the sample size decreases the probability of drawing a discrepant sample with $\overline{X} < 16.0$.

6-13 a. Our calculator gives $\mu = 34.0$, $\sigma = 8.0$

b. From 9 to 5 pm is 8 hours. The number of minutes available for 4 men is therefore:

$$8 \times 60 \times 4 = 1920 \text{ minutes.}$$

For 50 jobs, this is an average of:

$$\overline{X} = \frac{1920}{50} = 38.4 \text{ minutes per job}$$

To find the chance of exceeding this critical average, we first standardize:
$$Z = \frac{\overline{X} - \mu}{SE} = \frac{38.4 - 34.0}{8.00/\sqrt{50}} = 3.9$$

Thus $Pr(Total > 1920) = Pr(\bar{X} > 38.4)$

$$= Pr(Z > 3.9)$$

$$= .000048$$

c. We assumed the 50 mufflers were a <u>random</u> sample from the year's given record. But some cold and wet winter days, for example, may be very time consuming days for mufflers; then the chance of not finishing on time would be much higher.
    Also, some workers tend to be slower. On the days when slow workers are scheduled, watch out again.
    Of course, we assumed myriad other things, such as no time off for coffee or lunch, etc.

6-15 The population size doesn't matter when it is large. Only the sample size counts, in $SE = \sigma/\sqrt{n}$. Since n is 4 times as large in LA (1000 vs. 250), its accuracy will increase $\sqrt{4} = 2$ times.

6-17 We express the total as a proportion: $P = 5/50 = .10$. To standardize, we use $\pi = .20$:

$$Z = \frac{P - \pi}{SE} = \frac{.10 - .20}{\sqrt{\frac{.20(.80)}{50}}} = -1.77$$

$$Pr(P < .10) = Pr(Z < -1.77) = .038$$

For the continuity correction, we can re-express "no more than 5" as "fewer than 6". Taking 5 1/2 as our compromise, we finally get:

$$Pr(P < 5.5/50) = Pr(Z < -1.59) = .056$$

6-19 An erroneous prediction occurs if the proportion of Republicans is less than a majority: $P < .50$. To find the chance of this, we standardize using $\pi = .539$:

$$Z = \frac{P - \pi}{SE} = \frac{.50 - .539}{\sqrt{\frac{.539(.461)}{1000}}} = -2.47$$

$$Pr(P < .50) = Pr(Z < -2.47) = .007$$

For such a large n, the continuity correction is hardly worthwhile.

6-21 a. (i) <u>Best Solution</u> is to use the binomial, with $n = 10$, $\pi = .50$:

$$Pr(S \geq 4) - Pr(S \geq 7) = .828 - .172 = .656$$

(ii) <u>Good Solution</u> is to use the normal approximation, with continuity correction:

$$\text{critical } P = \frac{6 + \frac{1}{2}}{10} = .65$$
$$\text{expected value} = \pi = .50$$

Thus $Z = \dfrac{P - \pi}{\sqrt{\dfrac{\pi(1-\pi)}{n}}} = \dfrac{.65 - .50}{\sqrt{\dfrac{.50(.50)}{10}}} = .95$

tail prob. $= .171$

central chunk $= 1 - 2(.171) = .658$

Note that this is a <u>very</u> good approximation to the correct value of .656 found above.

(iii) <u>Crude Solution</u> is to use the normal approximation without continuity correction. Thus critical $P = 6/10 = .60$, $Z = .63$, and answer $= .472$ -- a serious underestimate.

b.

with continuity correction	without continuity correction

$Z = \dfrac{60.5/100 - .50}{\sqrt{\dfrac{.50(.50)}{100}}} = 2.10$ $Z = \dfrac{60/100 - .50}{\sqrt{\dfrac{.50(.50)}{1000}}} = 2.00$

$Pr = 1 - 2(.018) = .964$ $Pr = 1 - 2(.023) = .954$

c. $Z = \dfrac{600.5/1000 - .50}{\sqrt{\dfrac{.50(.50)}{1000}}} = 6.36$ $Z = \dfrac{600/1000 - .50}{\sqrt{\dfrac{.50(.50)}{1000}}} = 6.32$

$Pr = 1 - 2(0.000...) \simeq 1$ $Pr = 1 - 2(0.000...) \simeq 1$

So probability grows from 66% to 96% to practically 100%. Note also that the continuity correction grows less and less important.

6-23
$E(S) = E(n\,P)$
by (4-29), $= n\,E(P)$
by (6-22), $= n\,\pi$

$SD(S) = SD(n\,P)$
by (4-29), $= n\,SD(P)$

by (6-23), $= n\sqrt{\dfrac{\pi(1 - \pi)}{n}} = \sqrt{n\pi(1 - \pi)}$ (4-13) proved

6-25 **a.** If $n/N = .10$, then

SE reduction factor $= \sqrt{1 - \dfrac{n}{N}} = \sqrt{1 - .10}$ (6-27)

$= .949 \simeq 1 - .05$

That is, the SE is reduced about 5%.

For $n/N = .05$ and .01, we find similar results:

n/N	SE reduction factor	SE reduction (%)
10% = .10	.9487 ≈ 1 - .05	5%
5% = .05	.9747 ≈ 1 - .025	2½%
1% = .01	.9950 ≈ 1 - .005	½%

To summarize: If the sampling percentage is small, then the SE is reduced half as much.

b.   Using the rule in (a), if we specify reduction = 1%, then

$$\text{sampling \%} = 2(1\%) = 2\%$$

$$\text{ie., } \frac{n}{N} = .02$$

$$N = \frac{n}{.02} = 50n$$

So N must be 50 times as large as n.

6-27 a.   The problem is easier to solve if we forget the irrelevant details (the colorful cards, suits, etc.) and imagine a bowlful of 52 chips marked with the appropriate number:

```
0  0  0  0  0  0  0  0  0  1  2  3  4
0  0  0  0  0  0  0  0  0  1  2  3  4
0  0  0  0  0  0  0  0  0  1  2  3  4
0  0  0  0  0  0  0  0  0  1  2  3  4
```

x	p(x)	xp(x)
0	36/52=9/13	0
1	4/52=1/13	1/13
2	1/13	2/13
3	1/13	or, by
4	1/13	calculator

$$\mu = 10/13 = .769$$

$$\sigma = 1.31$$

b.   13 cards totalling 13 points is equivalent to them averaging 13/13 = 1 point each.   To calculate $Pr(\bar{X} \geq 1)$, we first standardize:

$$Z = \frac{\bar{X} - \mu}{SE} = \frac{1 - .769}{\frac{1.31}{\sqrt{13}} \sqrt{\frac{52-13}{52-1}}} = .73$$

$$Pr(\bar{X} > 1) = Pr(Z > .73) = .233$$

For the continuity correction, we can express "at least 13 points" as "more than 12 points".   We therefore take 12½ as the compromise, which finally gives:

$$Pr(\bar{X} > .962) = Pr(Z > .61) = .271$$

6-29 b. From the dot graph given in Problem 6-28, we read the population moments as μ = 4.37 and σ = 4.50. According to the Normal Approximation Rule, therefore, the sampling distribution of $\bar{X}$ is approximately normal, with expected value 4.37 and SE = $\sigma/\sqrt{n}$ = 4.50/$\sqrt{5}$ = 2.01.

The left hand tail of the normal curve we graph as a dashed line, because here it is clearly just a crude approximation. (The true distribution should drop to zero immediately at the origin, since values of $\bar{X}$ below zero are impossible). We could get a better approximation by folding back the impossible tail over the region where $\bar{X}$ is possible:

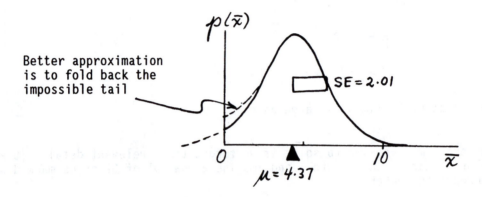

6-31 a. From Table II we draw a sample of five Z values. (Starting at line 3, for example, Z = 1.5, -.4, -.6, .7, .9). We convert these to X values using:

$$X = \mu + Z\sigma \qquad (6\text{-}28)$$

$$= 65 + 1.5(3) = 69.5$$

We continue this way for all n = 5 observations:

Z	X	
1.5	69.5	
- .4	63.8	
- .6	63.2	
.7	67.1	$<-\;\; \tilde{X} = 67.1$
.9	67.7	

$$\bar{X} = \frac{331.3}{5} = 66.3$$

b. The results indeed will be like Figure 6-11. In sampling from a <u>normal</u> population $\bar{X}$ is more accurate than $\tilde{X}$. (And so we see that the sample we happened to get in part (a) is typical: $\bar{X}$ = 66.3 is closer to μ = 65 than is $\tilde{X}$ = 67.1.)

6-33 Random sampling from a large population such as the U.S. voters is a form of very simple random sampling (VSRS), and so the relevant formula is

$$\text{Standard Error of } P = \sqrt{\frac{\pi(1-\pi)}{n}} \qquad (6\text{-}23)$$

That is, the standard error of the sample proportion depends on the <u>sample</u> size n, not the population size N. The U.S. sample should therefore be <u>equally</u> as large as the California sample.

6-35 **a.** Over the next 10 years, at 20 times a year and 1500 people per sample, they will interview about

$$10 \times 20 \times 1500 = 300,000 \text{ people}$$

Relative to the population of 160,000,000 this makes your chance of being interviewed:

$$\frac{300,000}{160,000,000} \approx .002$$

b. Yes the random sampling they do allows them to make a very legitimate claim. In fact, this claim can be quantified. Since this sampling is about equivalent to VSRS, the typical error of the binary (0-1) poll will be about:

$$SE = \sqrt{\frac{\pi(1-\pi)}{n}} = \sqrt{\frac{\pi(1-\pi)}{1500}}$$

Although π is unknown, we can find a bound: SE is biggest when π and $1-\pi$ are split .50-.50 (the maximum degree of uncertainty or variance in the population); thus

$$SE \approx \sqrt{\frac{(.50)(.50)}{1500}} \leq .013$$

6-37 **a.** The randomly-drawn height X fluctuates normally about a mean $\mu = 64$, with a standard deviation $\sigma = 3$. We use these to standardize the critical value X = 66,

$$Z = \frac{X - \mu}{\sigma} \qquad\qquad (4-23)$$

$$= \frac{66 - 64}{3} = .67$$

Thus,

$$Pr(X > 66) = Pr(Z > .67)$$

$$= .251 \approx 25\%$$

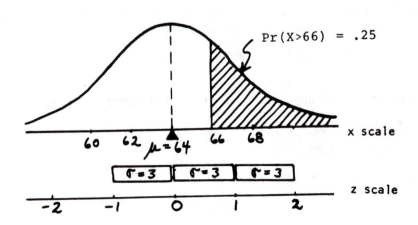

b. The sample average $\bar{X}$ fluctuates far less around $\mu = 64$, due to averaging out. In fact, its standard error is only $\sigma/\sqrt{n} = 3/\sqrt{25} = .60$. We use these to standardize the critical value $\bar{X} = 66$,

$$Z = \frac{\bar{X} - \mu}{SE} \qquad (4\text{-}8)$$

$$= \frac{66 - 64}{.60} = 3.3$$

Thus $Pr(\bar{X} > 66) = Pr(Z > 3.3)$

$$= .00048$$

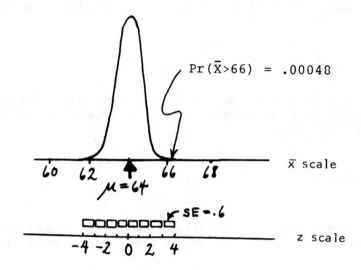

6-39 To use the normal approximation to the binomial, we have $n = 30$ and $\pi = .60$. The critical sample proportion P is $10/30 = .333$, and its standardized value is:

$$Z = \frac{P - \pi}{SE} = \frac{.333 - .60}{\sqrt{\dfrac{.60(.40)}{30}}} = -2.99$$

$$Pr(P < .333) = Pr(Z < -2.99) = .001$$

For the continuity correction, we could express "10 or fewer" equally well as "fewer than 11." Thus the compromise is $10.5/30$ and finally:

$$Pr(P < .35) = Pr(Z < -2.80) = .003$$

6-41 We will use the normal approximation rule for $\bar{X}$ given in (6-9) and (6-11):

$$Z = \frac{\bar{X} - \mu}{\sigma/\sqrt{n}} = \frac{12.00 - 12.30}{2.80/\sqrt{110}} = -1.12$$

$$Pr(\bar{X} > 12.00) = Pr(Z > -1.12)$$

$$= 1 - .131 = .869 \approx 87\%$$

6-43 a.

x = net win	p(x)	xp(x)
- 1	20/38	-20/38
+ 1	18/38	+18/38

$$\mu = -\,2/38$$
$$= \$-.0526$$

b.

x - μ	$(x-\mu)^2$	$(x-\mu)^2 p(x)$
-.95	.9025	.475
1.05	1.1025	.522

$$\sigma^2 = .997$$

b. On average, he loses \$.0526 (about a nickel) on each play.

(i) For a player to be a net loser in 5 plays, his total win, or equivalently, his average win, must be negative. His 5 plays may be regarded as a random sample of n = 5 from the population of all plays laid out in (a), and so we can use sampling theory. From day to day, $\overline{X}$ fluctuates normally, with:

$$\text{Expected value} = \mu = -\,.0526 \tag{6-5}$$

$$\text{Standard error} = \frac{\sigma}{\sqrt{n}} = \frac{\sqrt{.997}}{\sqrt{5}} = .447 \tag{6-7}$$

We require the probability that $\overline{X}$ is negative, i.e., below 0; To standardize this critical point,

$$Z = \frac{\overline{X} - \mu}{SE} \tag{6-11}$$

$$= \frac{0 - (-.0526)}{.447} = .12$$

Thus $\Pr(\overline{X} < 0) = \Pr(Z < .12)$

$$= 1 - .452 = .548 \simeq 55\%$$

(ii) Similarly, for n = 25, we obtain

$$Z = \frac{0 - (-.0526)}{\sqrt{.997}/\sqrt{25}} = .26$$

Hence $\Pr(\overline{X} < 0) = 1 - .397 = .603 \simeq 60\%$

(iii) And for n = 125, we obtain

$$Z = \frac{0 - (-.0526)}{\sqrt{.997}/\sqrt{125}} = .59$$

Hence $\Pr(\overline{X} < 0) = 1 - .278 = .722 \simeq 72\%$

Continuity Correction: When he plays an odd number of times, his total winning cannot come out exactly even at 0. The closest it can actually be is +1 or -1. Thus 0 as it stands is already a compromise between these two values, and no further compromise is required. That is, no continuity correction is necessary.
To confirm this, at least for part (i) when n = 5, we calculated the exact value using the binomial distribution, with n = 5, π = 20/38, and the probability of 0, 1 or 2 wins (i.e., total winning = -5, -3, or -1). This yields

$$\Pr(\text{net loss}) = p(0) + p(1) + p(2) = .549 \simeq 55\% \quad \text{again.}$$

7-1 **a.** True

b. Interchange μ and $\bar{X}$

c. If we <u>quadruple</u> the sample size ...

d. True

7-3 Let $\bar{X}_1$ denote the partial sample mean, with $n_1 = 320$, and let $\bar{X}_2$ denote the full sample mean, with $n_2 = 500$. Then

$$\text{efficiency of } \bar{X}_1, \text{ relative to } \bar{X}_2 = \frac{\text{var } \bar{X}_2}{\text{var } \bar{X}_1} \qquad \text{like (7-4)}$$

$$= \frac{\sigma^2/n_2}{\sigma^2/n_1} = \frac{n_1}{n_2} = \frac{320}{500} = .64 = 64\%$$

7-5 **a.** True.

b. Are you sure you have analyzed it efficiently -- not only using all the data, but analyzing it most effectively? If not, perhaps it would be wiser to spend $99,000 collecting data, and $1100 analyzing it.

7-7 We will use $\text{var } P = \frac{\pi(1-\pi)}{n} \simeq \frac{P(1-P)}{n}$ \qquad like (6-23)

a.
$$P^* = \tfrac{1}{2}(P_1 + P_2)$$

where $P_1 = \frac{60}{200} = .30$ and $P_2 = \frac{240}{1000} = .24$

Thus $\text{var } P^* = (\tfrac{1}{2})^2 [\text{var } P_1 + \text{var } P_2]$

$$\simeq \frac{1}{4} \left[\frac{.30(.70)}{200} + \frac{.24(.76)}{1000} \right] = .0003081$$

b. $\text{var } P_2 = \frac{.24(.76)}{1000} = .0001824$

$$\text{efficiency of } P_2 \text{ rel. to } P^* = \frac{\text{var } P^*}{\text{var } P_2} = \frac{.0003001}{.0001824} = 169\%$$

c. $P = \frac{300}{1200} = .25$

$$\text{var } P = \frac{.25(.75)}{1200} = .00015625$$

$$\text{efficiency of } P \text{ rel. to } P^* = \frac{\text{var } P^*}{\text{var } P} = \frac{.0003081}{.00015625} = 197\%$$

So P is the most efficient of all, which backs up our intuitive finding that it is best.

d. True. We saw how using the unreliable first source P_1 naively in part (a) (with the same weight as P_2) gave us a poorer estimate than P_2 alone.

7-9 $MSE = $ variance of estimator $+$ bias^2 (7-11)

$$= \frac{\sigma^2}{n} + bias^2$$

Presumably only one measurement is taken, so n=1 and the MSE reduces to:

$$MSE = \sigma^2 + bias^2$$

for A,	$= 10^2 + 0$		$=$	100
for B,	$= 0 + (-10)^2$	$=$		100
for C,	$= 5^2 + 5^2$		$=$	50
for D,	$= 8^2 + 2^2$		$=$	68

So gauge C has greatest accuracy.

Remarks Note that if there are 10 units of error to be split between bias and standard deviation, the greatest accuracy comes from the compromise 5/5 split.

7-11 Now we use the response rates to get the frequencies f for the subpopulation who would respond:

		given			
(1)	(2)	(3)	(4) = (2)×(3)	(5)	(6) = (1)×(5)
x	population f	response rate	subpopulation f	p(x) = f/N	xp(x)
0	20,000	60%	12,000	.541	0
1	12,000	40%	4,800	.216	.216
2	10,000	30%	3,000	.135	.270
3	10,000	30%	1,800	.081	.243
4	2,000	30%	600	.027	.108
	N = 50,000		N = 22,200		μ = .838

similarly, $\sigma^2 = 1.217$

The number of replies is approximately 22,200/50,000 × 100 = 44.4. Thus:

$$MSE = \text{var of } \bar{X} + bias^2$$

$$= \frac{1.217}{44.4} + (.838 - 1.160)^2$$

$$= .027 + .104 = .131$$

7-13 a. $MSE(P) = $ variance $+$ bias^2

from (6-22) and (6-23)

$$MSE(P) = \frac{\pi(1-\pi)}{n} + 0^2 = \frac{\pi(1-\pi)}{n}$$

Since MSE $\rightarrow$ 0 as n $\rightarrow \infty$, P is consistent according to (7-15).

b. $E(P^*) = E[(\frac{n}{n+2})P + (\frac{1}{n+2})]$

from (4-29) and (6-22),

$$E(P^*) = \left(\frac{n}{n+2}\right)\pi + \left(\frac{1}{n+2}\right)$$

$$\text{Bias} = E(P^*) - \pi$$

$$= \left(\frac{n}{n+2}\right)\pi + \left(\frac{1}{n+2}\right) - \pi = \frac{1 - 2\pi}{n+2}$$

$$\text{var}P^* = \text{var}\left[\left(\frac{n}{n+2}\right)P + \left(\frac{1}{n+2}\right)\right]$$

from (4-29) and (6-23),

$$\text{var}(P^*) = \left(\frac{n}{n+2}\right)^2 \frac{\pi(1-\pi)}{n} = \frac{n\pi(1-\pi)}{(n+2)^2}$$

$$\text{MSE}(P^*) = \text{variance} + \text{bias}^2$$

$$= \frac{n\pi(1-\pi)}{(n+2)^2} + \left(\frac{1-2\pi}{n+2}\right)^2$$

$$= \frac{1 + \pi(1-\pi)(n-4)}{(n+2)^2}$$

Since $(n+2)^2$ in the denominator swamps $(n-4)$ in the numerator, MSE $\to 0$ and so P^* is consistent too.

c. Consistency doesn't help, since both P and P^* are consistent. (This illustrates again what we meant by the last paragraph of section 7-4).

What _would_ help is MSE, or relative _efficiency_, which we will examine next in part (d).

d.

π	MSE(P^*) $= \dfrac{1 + 6\pi(1-\pi)}{144}$	MSE(P) $= \dfrac{\pi(1-\pi)}{10}$	ratio = efficiency of P^* relative to P
0, 1.0	.0069	.0000	0
.1, .9	.0107	.0090	84%
.2, .8	.0136	.0160	118%
.3, .7	.0157	.0210	134%
.4, .6	.0169	.0240	142%
.5	.0174	.0250	144%

e. P^* has greater efficiency when π is not very far from .50. In fact, with a little algebra we could show that P^* is more efficient **approximately** when

$$.50 - 1/\sqrt{8} < \pi < .50 + 1/\sqrt{8}$$

i.e., $.15 < \pi < .85$

This is illustrated for $n = 10$ in the table in part (d). There we see that between $\pi = .10$ and $\pi = .20$, the relative efficiency of P^* rises above 100% (from 84% to 118%)

7-15 a.

Scale	bias^2	variance of estimator $= \sigma^2/n$	MSE = sum
A	$0^2 = 0$	$.05^2/25 = .0001$	.000100
B	$(-.02)^2 = .0004$	$.02^2/25 = .000016$	.000416
C	$.08^2 = .0064$	$.01^2/25 = .000004$	.006404

Since it has the smallest MSE, scale A is most accurate for 25 weighings.

b. True, and very important to remember.

7-17 **a.** **(i)** $\dfrac{X_1^2 + X_2^2}{2} = \dfrac{5.9^2 + 6.1^2}{2} = 36.01$

(ii) $[\dfrac{X_1 + X_2}{2}]^2 = [\dfrac{5.9 + 6.1}{2}]^2 = 6.0^2 = 36.00$

They differ slightly, although they are practically the same.

b. We will extensively need the formula for the expected value of X^2:

$$E(X^2) = \mu^2 + \sigma^2 \tag{4-36}$$

For method (i), therefore,

$$E\,[\dfrac{X_1^2 + X_2^2}{2}] = \dfrac{E(X_1^2) + E(X_2^2)}{2} \qquad\qquad \text{like (5-17)}$$

$$= \dfrac{(\mu^2 + \sigma^2) + (\mu^2 + \sigma^2)}{2}$$

$$= \mu^2 + \sigma^2$$

Since the true area is μ^2, the bias is therefore σ^2.

For method (ii), we recognize $(X_1 + X_2)/2$ is just $\overline{X}$, whose moments are well known:

$$E(\overline{X}) = \mu \tag{6-5}$$

$$\text{var } \overline{X} = \sigma^2/n \tag{6-6}$$

Substitute these into (4-36):

$$E(\overline{X}^2) = \mu^2 + \dfrac{\sigma^2}{n}$$

That is, $E[\dfrac{X_1 + X_2}{2}]^2 = \mu^2 + \dfrac{\sigma^2}{2}$

Thus the bias is $\sigma^2/2$, and this is half the previous bias σ^2.

c. Since X_1 and X_2 are independent and hence uncorrelated, by Problem 5-38,

$$E(X_1 X_2) = E(X_1)\,E(X_2)$$

$$= (\mu)\,(\mu) = \mu^2$$

Thus, $X_1 X_2$ has no bias at all.

Remarks   It would be interesting to compare the three estimators in terms of their mean squared error (MSE). If the observations X_1 and X_2 are normally distributed then it may be shown by advanced techniques that the best estimator (with minimum MSE) is $\overline{X}^2$, and the next best is $X_1 X_2$. Here are the figures, starting with the best:

estimator	var	bias^2	MSE = sum
$\bar{X}^2 = (\dfrac{X_1 + X_2}{2})^2$	$2\mu^2\sigma^2 + .50\sigma^4$	$.25\sigma^4$	$2\mu^2\sigma^2 + .75\sigma^4$
$X_1 X_2$	$2\mu^2\sigma^2 + \sigma^4$	0	$2\mu^2\sigma^2 + \sigma^4$
$\dfrac{X_1^2 + X_2^2}{2}$	$2\mu^2\sigma^2 + \sigma^4$	σ^4	$2\mu^2\sigma^2 + 2\sigma^4$

7-19 a. $\sqrt{MSE}$ $= \sqrt{MSE}$

for P, $= \sqrt{.000242}$ $= .016$

or for P* $= \sqrt{.000328}$ $= .018$

This is a more understandable form. For example, P* has a typical deviation of 1.8% around the target of 3.4%.

b. Since total = NP

error in total = N x error in P

for P, $= 50,000,000 \times .016 \approx 800,000$

for P*, $= 50,000,000 \times .018 \approx 900,000$

70

8-1

    a. The sample mean [$\underline{\bar{X}}$, μ] is an unbiased estimate of the population mean [$\bar{X}$, $\underline{\mu}$]—assuming the sample is [$\underline{\text{random}}$, very large].

    b. $\bar{X}$ fluctuates from sample to sample with a standard deviation equal to [σ/n, $\underline{\sigma/\sqrt{n}}$], which is also called the [$\underline{\text{standard error SE}}$, population standard deviation].

    c. If we make an allowance of about [$\sqrt{n}$, $\underline{2}$] standard errors on either side of $\bar{X}$, we obtain an interval wide enough that it has a 95% chance of covering the target μ. This is called the 95% confidence interval for [$\bar{X}$, $\underline{\mu}$].

    d. A statistician who constructed a thousand of these 95% confidence intervals over his lifetime would miss the target [practically never, $\underline{\text{about 50 times}}$, about 950 times]. Of course, he [would, $\underline{\text{would not}}$] know just which times these were.

    e. For greater confidence such as 99%, the confidence interval must be made [narrower, $\underline{\text{wider}}$].

8-3

$$\mu = \bar{X} + 1.96 \frac{\sigma}{\sqrt{n}} = 3700 \pm 1.96 \frac{6000}{\sqrt{225}} \qquad (8\text{-}9)$$

$$= 3700 \pm 784$$

Total $= N\mu = 2700 \ (3700 \pm 784)$

$$= 9{,}990{,}000 \pm 2{,}116{,}800 \approx 10{,}000{,}000 \pm 2{,}000{,}000$$

We could get a slightly more accurate SE by using the correction factor for small populations:

$$SE = \frac{\sigma}{\sqrt{n}} \sqrt{\frac{N-n}{N-1}} = \frac{6000}{\sqrt{225}} \sqrt{\frac{2700-225}{2700-1}} = 383 \qquad (6\text{-}25)$$

Then we finally get:

Total $= 2700 \ (3700 \pm 1.96 \times 383)$
      $= \ \ 9{,}990{,}000 \pm 2{,}027{,}000$
      $\approx 10{,}000{,}000 \pm 2{,}000{,}000$ still

8-5   True.

8-7   a.   Our calculator gives $\bar{X}$ = 99.8 and s = 54.7. Since df = n-1 = 4, Table V gives $t_{.025}$ = 2.78. Then

$$\mu = \bar{X} \pm t_{.025} \frac{s}{\sqrt{n}}$$

$$= 99.8 \pm 2.78 \frac{54.7}{\sqrt{5}} \ = \ 99.8 \pm 67.9$$

    b.   Total $= N\mu = 50(99.8 \pm 67.9)$

$$= 4990 \pm 3397 \approx 5000 \pm 3400$$

    c.   Since the confidence interval runs from about 1600 to 8400, it nicely covers the true area of 3620.

8-9 To apply (8-11), we first find $\bar{X}$ and s. The easiest way of course is with a computer, or even a hand calculator that has a few statistical functions. Then we obtain $\bar{X} = 66.00$ and $s = 11.83$, so that:

$$\mu = \bar{X} \pm t_{.025}\ \frac{s}{\sqrt{n}} \tag{8-11}$$

$$= 66.0 \pm 2.02\ \frac{11.83}{\sqrt{40}}$$

$$= 66.0 \pm 3.8$$

Alternatively, without a calculator we could group into cells, of width 5 say, and centered at $X = 40, 45, \ldots$. This would yield $\bar{X} = 66.1$ and $s = 11.74$, which then gives practically the same confidence interval:

$$\mu = 66.1 \pm 3.8$$

8-11 a.

	WOMEN			MEN	
X_1	$X_1 - \bar{X}_1$	$(X_1 - \bar{X}_1)^2$	X_2	$X_2 - \bar{X}_2$	$(X_2 - \bar{X}_2)^2$
9	-2	4	16	0	0
12	+1	1	19	3	9
8	-3	9	12	-4	16
10	-1	1	11	-5	25
16	+5	25	22	6	36

$\bar{X}_1 = \dfrac{55}{5} \qquad\quad 0\ \checkmark \qquad 40 \qquad\qquad \bar{X}_2 = \dfrac{80}{5} \qquad\quad 0\ \checkmark \qquad 86$

$\phantom{\bar{X}_1} = 11 \qquad\qquad\qquad\qquad\qquad\qquad\qquad\ \ = 16$

$$s_p^2 = \frac{\Sigma(X_1 - \bar{X}_1)^2 + \Sigma(X_2 - \bar{X}_2)^2}{(n_1 - 1) + (n_2 - 1)} \tag{8-21}$$

$$= \frac{40 + 86}{4 + 4} = \frac{126}{8} = 15.75$$

Since d.f. = 8, $t_{.025} = 2.31$. Thus

$$(\mu_1 - \mu_2) = (\bar{X}_1 - \bar{X}_2) \pm t_{.025}\ s_p\ \sqrt{\frac{1}{n_1} + \frac{1}{n_2}} \tag{8-20}$$

$$= (11 - 16) \pm 2.31\ \sqrt{15.75}\ \sqrt{\frac{1}{5} + \frac{1}{5}}$$

$$\mu_W - \mu_M = -5 \pm 5.80 \approx -5 \pm 6$$

That is, women are estimated to earn 5 thousand dollars <u>less</u> (because of the minus sign).

We calculated the differences of women relative to men (in that order) merely because that was the given order. We could just as easily have used the other order, and found

$$\mu_M - \mu_W = (16 - 11) \pm \ldots$$

$$= +5 \pm 5.80 \approx +5 \pm 6$$

That is, men are estimated to earn 5 thousand dollars more than women. This statement has exactly the same meaning as our earlier statement that women earn 5 thousand dollars less than men.

b.　The simplest issue is that the estimate of 5 thousand dollars is obscured by a confidence allowance of + 6. That is, we cannot be sure that in the whole university, the men do earn more than the women; they might earn a little less.

But even if we did know that men earn more (from a very large sample, for example), we still wouldn't know whether it was _caused_ by discrimination, because this is an observational study. There are many other possible explanations besides discrimination. For example, men may be better qualified than women -- more experienced, perhaps, or better educated. What we really should do then, is compare men and women of the _same qualifications_. (This in fact will be done, to some extent, using multiple regression later in Chapter 14).

8-13　a.　Let μ_1 = the population mean IQ, for alcoholic mothers
Let μ_2 = the population mean IQ, for the control group

$$\mu_1 - \mu_2 = (\overline{X}_1 - \overline{X}_2) \pm t_{.025}\, s_p \sqrt{\frac{1}{n_1} + \frac{1}{n_2}} \qquad (8\text{-}20)$$

$$s_p^2 = \frac{\Sigma(X_1 - \overline{X}_1)^2}{(n_1 - 1)} + \frac{\Sigma(X_2 - \overline{X}_2)^2}{(n_2 - 1)} \qquad (8\text{-}21)$$

$$= \frac{1,805 + 11,520}{5 + 45} = \frac{13325}{50} = 266.5$$

Since d.f. = 50, $t_{.025} \approx 2.01$ (interpolating Table V). Thus

$$(\mu_1 - \mu_2) = (78 - 99) \pm 2.01 \sqrt{(266.5)} \sqrt{\frac{1}{6} + \frac{1}{46}}$$

$$= -21 \pm 2.01\,(7.086)$$

$$= -21 \pm 14.24 \approx -21 \pm 14$$

The negative sign means alcoholism causes a _drop_ of 21 IQ points; with 95% confidence, we estimate the drop to be between 7 and 35 IQ points.

b.　This is an observational study. To the extent they matched the control group on the whole with the alcoholic group (same average age, education, etc.), they have reduced bias. Yet the factors that were not matched remain as a possible source of bias, whose extent can only be guessed at.

8-15　a.

Treatment	Control	Difference D	$D - \overline{D}$	$(D - \overline{D})^2$
68	65	3	0	0
65	62	3	0	0
66	64	2	-1	1
66	65	1	-2	4
67	65	2	-1	1
66	64	2	-1	1
66	59	7	4	16
64	63	1	-2	4
69	65	4	1	1
63	58	5	2	4
		$\overline{D} = \dfrac{30}{10} = 3$	0 ✓	$s^2 = \dfrac{32}{9} = 3.56$

$$\Delta = \bar{D} \pm t_{.025} \frac{s_D}{\sqrt{n}} = 3 \pm 2.26 \sqrt{\frac{3.56}{10}} = 3.00 \pm 1.35$$

b.   It might be more meaningful to express this increase of 3 centigrams as a <u>percentage</u>. Since the mean control weight is about 60 centigrams,

$$\text{relative increase} \simeq \frac{3.00 \pm 1.35}{60} = 5\% \pm 2\%$$

In conclusion, there is good evidence that an interesting environment stimulates the growth of the cortex in rats more than an isolated environment does; it increases the weight by about 5% ± 2%. And we are 95% confident of this claim.

8-17 a.   In Figure 8-4, we find P = .10 on the x-axis. Hence

$$0 < \pi < .45$$

b. $$.01 < \pi < .30$$

c. $$.02 < \pi < .22$$

Or, since 5 observations are now "successes" (10% of n = 50), we can use the formula:

$$\pi = P \pm 1.96 \sqrt{\frac{P(1-P)}{n}} \tag{8-27}$$

$$= .10 \pm 1.96 \sqrt{\frac{.10(.90)}{50}} = .10 \pm .083$$

d. $$\pi = .10 \pm 1.96 \sqrt{\frac{.10(.90)}{200}} = .10 \pm .042$$

8-19 a.   For the U.S., $P_1 = .40$, $n_1 = 300$. For Japan, $P_2 = .33$, $n_2 = 300$. Thus

$$\pi_1 - \pi_2 = (.40 - .33) \pm 1.96 \sqrt{\frac{.40(.60)}{300} + \frac{.33(.67)}{300}} \tag{8-29}$$

$$= (.07) \pm 1.96 (.0392) = 7\% \pm 8\%$$

Thus the proportion of Americans (who say they are afraid to walk the neighboring streets at night) exceeds the proportion of Japanese -- by 7 percentage points (± 8, with 95% confidence).

b.   Now for Latin America, $P_3 = .57$ and $n_3 = 300$. Thus

$$\pi_1 - \pi_3 = (.40 - .57) \pm 1.96 \sqrt{\frac{.40(.60)}{300} + \frac{.57(.43)}{300}}$$

$$= (-.17) \pm 1.96 (.0402) = -17\% \pm 8\%$$

Thus the proportion of Americans is <u>less</u> than the proportion of Latin Americans -- by 17 percentage points (± 8, with 95% confidence).

8-21 a.

GROUP	NUMBER OF CHILDREN	NUMBER OF POLIO CASES	POLIO RATE (Cases per 100,000)
vaccinated	200,000	57	57/2 = 28.5
placebo (control)	200,000	142	142/2 = 71.0
refused to volunteer	340,000	157	157/3.4 = 46.2

b. To use the formulas, the proportions have to be expressed as decimals. Thus the proportion of vaccinated (or unvaccinated) children who contracted polio was $P_1 = .000285$ (or $P_2 = .000710$). Substituting into (8-29), we obtain the confidence interval for the difference in <u>population</u> proportions:

$$\pi_1 - \pi_2 = (.000285 - .000710) \pm 1.96 \sqrt{\frac{(.000285)(.999715)}{200,000} + \frac{(.000710)(.999290)}{200,000}}$$

$$= -.00425 \pm 1.96(.0000705) = -.000425 + .000138$$

$$\approx -.00043 \pm .00014$$

The minus sign indicates a reduction. Thus, with 95% confidence we can claim that the vaccine reduces the polio rate about 43 ($\pm$ 14) cases per 100,000.

c. **(i)** Such an observational study would confound the effect of the vaccine with the effect of volunteering.

And volunteering is indeed a substantial effect: To see how large, compare the volunteers who were not vaccinated (rate of 71 per 100,000) with the refusals, who also were not vaccinated of course (rate of only 46 per 100,000). Thus the children who volunteer have a higher polio rate, by about 25 cases per 100,000.

Incidentally, how do we explain this higher polio rate, in view of the fact that volunteers tend to come from better educated and more prosperous homes? Polio was a rather common childhood disease, and like other childhood diseases such as mumps and chicken pox, the earlier in childhood it was contracted, the less severe it was. Thus children who were born into a home with lots of dirt often contracted the disease so early that it did no damage, and was so mild that it was not even diagnosed as polio. This gave them subsequent immunity, so that they fared better than the children raised in cleaner homes.

(ii) The vaccinated children would have had a polio rate of about 28 per 100,000, while the unvaccinated would have had a rate of about 46 per 100,000. If these two groups were compared with a confidence interval as in part (b), we would have estimated that the vaccine reduces the polio rate by about:

$$(.00046 - .00028) \pm \ldots \approx 18 \pm \ldots \text{ per } 100,000$$

This would seriously underestimate the effect of the vaccine -- 18 is 25 lower than the unbiased estimate of 43 per 100,000 (the same 25 we mentioned in part i). And this underestimation would occur because the effect of the vaccine was "diluted" by being tried out on a much more susceptible group (the volunteers).

8-23 a.

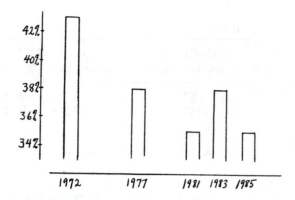

b.
$$\pi = P \pm 1.96 \sqrt{\frac{P(1-P)}{n}} \qquad (8\text{-}27)$$

For 1972, $\pi = .43 \pm 1.96 \sqrt{\dfrac{.43(.57)}{1500}} \quad \simeq .43 \pm .025 \quad \simeq 43\% \pm 3\%$

For 1985, $\pi = .35 \pm 1.96 \sqrt{\dfrac{.35(.65)}{1500}} \quad \simeq .35 \pm .024 \quad \simeq 35\% \pm 2\%$

c.
$$\pi_{85} - \pi_{72} = (.35 - .43) \pm 1.96 \sqrt{\frac{.35(.65)}{1500} + \frac{.43(.57)}{1500}} \qquad (8\text{-}29)$$

$$= -.08 \pm .0348 \quad \simeq \quad \text{drop } 8\% \pm 3\%$$

$$\pi_{83} - \pi_{81} = (.38 - .35) \pm 1.96 \sqrt{\frac{.38(.62)}{1500} + \frac{.35(.65)}{1500}} \qquad (8\text{-}29)$$

$$= .03 \pm .0344 \quad \simeq \quad \text{rise } 3\% \pm 3\%$$

d.
The change in the sample proportion *P* between 1981 and 1983 was relatively [large, <u>small</u>] and consequently [stood out, <u>did not stand out</u>] above the sampling allowance, that is, the ± figure.

By contrast, the change from 1972 to 1985 was [<u>large</u>, small] enough that it [<u>did</u>, did not] stand out above the sampling allowance. This illustrates the great [<u>value</u>, drawback] of confidence intervals: They [confuse, <u>distinguish between</u>] real and illusory changes. Looking back on the graphs in **a**, the fluctuations between 1972 and 1985 can now be interpreted as [fascinating detail, <u>mostly sampling "noise"</u>.]

8-25 a.   Our calculator gives $\bar{X}_1 = 61.0$, $\Sigma(X_1 - \bar{X}_1)^2 = 946$, and $\bar{X}_2 = 74.0$, $\Sigma(X_2 - \bar{X}_2)^2 = 770$.
To compare the regular (X_2) against the irregular (X_1), we take the difference $\bar{X}_2 - \bar{X}_1$, and the 95% confidence interval is:

$$(\mu_2 - \mu_1) = (\bar{X}_2 - \bar{X}_1) \pm t_{.025}\, s_p \sqrt{\frac{1}{n_2} + \frac{1}{n_1}} \qquad (8\text{-}20)$$

$$= (74.0 - 61.0) \pm 2.31 \sqrt{\frac{770 + 946}{4 + 4}} \sqrt{\frac{1}{5} + \frac{1}{5}}$$

$$= 13.0 \pm 2.31\,(9.26) \qquad = 13.0 \pm 21.4$$

76

b. This does not support the contention for two reasons:

(i) Since the confidence interval in part (a) includes both positive and negative values, we are not sure whether the "regulars" have a higher or a lower average grade.

(ii) Even if we were sure, we still would not know <u>why</u>. It might be the regular attendance, but it might be some confounding factor that was not controlled in this observational study -- for example, organizational skills, drive to do well, etc.

8-27   By far the most important issue is the possible bias in the data. As we stressed in Chapter 1, observational studies such as this cannot prove causation. For example, many of the right-to-work states are in the south, a poorer and more rural society that has traditionally had lower wages irrespective of the union laws. Maybe the cause-and-effect runs like this:

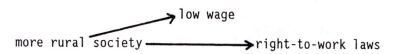

That is, low wages may be correlated with right-to-work laws, not because one causes the other, but because some third factor may cause them both. In fact, there are probably many other confounding "third factors", besides a more rural society: for example, a less skilled wage force, or attempts to reduce the unemployment rate.

How should we analyze the data? We should keep <u>all</u> the confounding factors constant, and see what relation (if any) remained between low wages and right-to-work laws. Ideally, this requires a randomized controlled experiment. But practically speaking, this just isn't feasible.

Instead, we have to live with an observational study. We take the data as it comes, and analyze it in a compensating way: As mentioned in (1-6), <u>multiple regression, insofar as possible</u>, gives the same answer as if the <u>measurable</u> third factors had been held constant. Not perfect, but the best we can do. In Chapter 13 we shall give the details.

Incidentally, should we meanwhile construct a 95% confidence interval on the meager data as it stands (without any confounding factors measured, and so multiple regression not possible)? It might do more harm than good, to give this sort of stamp of approval to such a biased figure. But if it were done, it should be done with the unmatched sample formula (8-20), and would give the 95% confidence interval

$$\mu_r - \mu_u = -.50 \pm .73$$
i.e., $-1.23 < \mu_r - \mu_u < .23$

This shows a nice point: <u>Even if</u> the data had been unbiased, the samples are too small to prove much anyhow; the right-to-work mean might be as much as $1.23/hr below the union shop mean, but then again it might be as much as $.23/hr <u>above</u>.

8-29   a.

x	f	xf	$(x - \overline{X})^2 f$
20	8	160	4685
40	16	640	282
60	12	720	2996
80	2	160	253
	38	$\overline{X} = \dfrac{1680}{38}$	$s^2 = \dfrac{10526}{37}$
		$= 44.21$	$= 284.5$

Or, our calculator gives $\bar{X} = 44.2$ and $s = 16.87$

$$\mu = \bar{X} \pm t_{.025} \frac{s}{\sqrt{n}} \tag{8-11}$$

$$= 44.21 \pm 2.02 \frac{(16.87)}{\sqrt{38}}$$

$$= 44.2 \pm 5.5$$

We could get a slightly better answer by applying the small-population correction factor to the SE, and hence the confidence allowance:

$$\sqrt{\frac{N-n}{N-1}} = \sqrt{\frac{380-38}{380-1}} = .950 \tag{6-24}$$

Thus $\mu = 44.2 \pm 5.53(.950) = 44.2 \pm 5.3$

b. Total $= N\mu$

$$= 380 (44.2 \pm 5.5)$$

$$= 16,800 \pm 2,100$$

8-31 a.

$$\pi = P \pm 1.96 \sqrt{\frac{P(1-P)}{n}} \tag{8-27}$$

Using this formula, we obtain the following CI:

groups	n	P	95% CI
all marriages	3864	3492/3864 = .904	90.4% ± 0.9%
weekly or more	1113	1071/1113 = .962	96.2% ± 1.1%
sometimes	1467	1339/1467 = .913	91.3% ± 1.4%
rarely or never	1284	1082/1284 = .843	84.3% ± 2.0%

b. Substitute $P_1 = .962$ and $P_2 = .843$ into (8-29):

$$(\pi_1 - \pi_2) = (.962 - .843) \pm 1.96 \sqrt{\frac{.962(.038)}{1113} + \frac{.843(.157)}{1284}}$$

$$= .119 \pm .023 \simeq 12\% \pm 2\%$$

c. In this observational study, there are many confounding variables changing at the same time -- for example, age at marriage, city size, and so on. And their effect is included in the 12% difference found in (b). How much, if any, is due to church attendance alone is anybody's guess.

<u>Remarks</u> To reduce this bias, the authors of this study used a "hazards" model -- a refinement of the multiple regression model that is especially suited to survival analysis over time (survival of marriage, survival after surgery, survival of certain machinery, etc.).

Like multiple regression, the "hazards" analysis controls for the confounding variables that can be measured. In this study, the authors controlled for several variables, including the following:

(1)   age at marriage (teenage marriages are risky)
(2)   year of marriage (marriages before 1965 were much more enduring)
(3)   city size (large cities are risky)

All these factors were important, as important as church attendance itself. So controlling for them gave a substantial improvement to the 12% difference found in part (b) -- the improved estimate being a 7% difference between weekly and rare church attendance.

Of course, there remain important factors too subtle to be measured that make this 7% figure still biased -- for example, personality traits such as conventionality, spiritual experiences outside of church, etc. So there remains lots of work to be done.

9-1

Problem	95% CI	Is it discernible, i.e., Does estimate stand out above "fog"?
8-24	$\Delta = -4.0 \pm 5.8$	no
8-25a	$\mu_2 - \mu_1 = 13 \pm 21$	no
8-26b	$\pi_2 - \pi_1 = -45\% \pm 9\%$	yes!

9-3

A	B	Selling Price S	A's error A^*	B's error B^*	difference $D = A^* - B^*$
94	81	86	8	$|-5| = 5$	3
60	55	50	10	5	5
39	32	30	9	2	7
116	106	119	$|-3| = 3$	$|-13| = 13$	-10
136	121	126	10	$|-5| = 5$	5

Our calculator gives, from the last column, $\bar{D} = 2.0$ and $s_D = 6.86$. Thus the 95% CI is

$$\Delta = \bar{D} \pm t_{.025}\, s_D/\sqrt{n} \qquad (8\text{-}24)$$

$$= 2.0 \pm 2.78\,(6.86)/\sqrt{5} = 2.0 \pm 8.5$$

The following parts are then equivalent manifestations of statistical indiscernability (much like Example 9-2):

b. The estimate 2.0 is overwhelmed by the fog (± 8.5)

c. By Example 9-2(d), it follows from (b) that the difference (between A and B's errors) is statistically indiscernible.

d. No. Specifically, the CI covers negative as well as positive values: $-6.5 < \Delta < 10.5$.

e. $H_0: \Delta = 0$ cannot be rejected (is acceptable), since it is within the CI in (d).

9-5

Problem	95% CI, i.e. estimate $\pm t_{.025}$SE	t=estimate/SE	df	last critical t surpassed	p-value
8-24	$-4.0 \pm 2.78(2.07)$	$-4.0/2.07 = -1.93$	4	$t_{.10} = 1.53$	$< .10$
8-25a	$13.0 \pm 2.31(9.26)$	$13.0/9.26 = 1.40$	8	$t_{.10} = 1.40$	$= .10$
8-26b	$-.45 \pm 1.96(.044)$	$-.45/.044 = -10.2$	large n,	last z = 5.9	$\ll 10^{-8}$

9-7

a. If H_0 is true, a "false alarm" could occur, called a type _I_ error, with probability denoted by _α_.

b. If H_A is true, a "missed alarm" could occur, called a type _II_ error, with probability denoted by _β_.

c. By making the equipment more sensitive and reliable, it is possible to reduce both _α_ and _β_.

9-9 **a.** H_0: the proportion of defective gloves is the old value of 10%, i.e., $\pi = .10$
H_A: the proportion of defective gloves is greater than 10%, i.e., $\pi > .10$

b. We need to find the critical proportion P_c such that:

$$\text{Critical } Z = \frac{P_c - \pi_0}{\sqrt{\dfrac{\pi_0(1-\pi_0)}{n}}} = z_{.09} = 1.34 \qquad \text{like (9-24)}$$

$$\frac{P_c - .10}{\sqrt{\dfrac{.10(.90)}{100}}} = 1.34$$

$$\frac{P_c - .10}{.030} = 1.34$$

$$P_c = .10 + 1.34(.030) = .140$$

Thus, reject H_0 if the proportion of defective exceeds 14%.

c. Reject shipments with 25%, 16%, 24%, and 21% defective -- that is, all but the first and third shipments.

9-11 We need a confidence interval that has 5 times the precision, that is:

$$\pm z \frac{\sigma}{\sqrt{n}} \text{ is to be reduced by a factor of 5.}$$

To achieve this we must increase n by a factor of 25. Hence, a sample of n = 2500 is needed.

9-13 **a.** Accept H_0, since $\overline{X} = 1245$ is less than the critical value 1249.

b. Follow common sense, and reject H_0 in favour of H_A. Your engineering knowledge should have some influence over your decision. Classical testing unfortunately excludes this and many other common sense aspects, because it considers only the data of this particular sample. And it arbitrarily sets α at 5%.

c. Substituting into (9-25)

$$\frac{\overline{X}_c - \mu_0}{\sigma/\sqrt{n}} = 1.64$$

$$\frac{\overline{X}_c - 1200}{300/\sqrt{200}} = 1.64$$

$$\overline{X}_c = 1235$$

Since $\overline{X} = 1245$ exceeds the critical value $\overline{X}_c = 1235$, H_0 is now rejected at the level $\alpha = .05$. The problem may indeed have been inadequate sample size.

d.   Substituting into (9-25),

$$\frac{\bar{X}_c - \pi_0}{\sigma/\sqrt{n}} = 1.64$$

$$\frac{\bar{X}_c - 1200}{300/\sqrt{1,000,000}} = 1.64$$

$$\bar{X}_c = 1200.5$$

Since $\bar{X} = 1201$ exceeds $\bar{X}_c = 1200.5$, H_0 is now rejected at the level $\alpha = .05$, and the improvement is statistically discernible. So the final statement in (d) is true, and shows that classical tests are not very satisfactory for very large samples, either.

9-15   Jurors would probably be more reluctant to risk condemning an innocent man. That is, they would reduce α. Consequently, ß, would increase.

<u>Remarks:</u>   It would be possible to keep ß from increasing, by simply giving the jury the choice among <u>three</u> verdicts: not guilty, guilty of second degree murder (with imprisonment), and guilty of first degree murder (with capital punishment). Then juries would no longer be in a bind: If they were reasonably sure the defendant was guilty, but not absolutely sure enough to irretrievably impose capital punishment, they could then choose the middle verdict. This solution has been proposed as a way to maximize the possible deterrent effect of capital punishment, while minimizing one of its terrible drawbacks (executing an innocent man).
   Like courts, statisticians have to also be urged to look for creative third alternatives, alternatives to "accept" or "reject" H_0. For example, when $\bar{X}$ follows close to the critical cutoff, "collect more data" is often a wise intermediate choice (a choice not available to the courts, unfortunately). This means taking a second, and possibly more, samples, and is known as "sequential sampling."

9-17 a. H_A: $\pi = .30$

b.   From the lower left corner of Table 9-1,

ß = Pr(accepting H_0 when it is false)

The test is based on the number of defective gloves S in a sample of n = 10 gloves. In Problem 9-10, we were given that the rejection region was $S \geq 2$. Thus, from the binomial table (using n = 10 and $\pi = .30$),

$$\begin{aligned}Pr(\text{rejecting } H_0 \text{ when it is false}) &= Pr(S \geq 2) \\ &= .851\end{aligned}$$

ß is the probability of <u>accepting</u> H_0 when it is false, that is, the complement:

$$ß = 1 - .851 = .149 \approx 15\%$$

9-19 a.   Test H_0: $\mu = 8.5$ vs. H_A: $\mu > 8.5$ ("better" plants).

critical $Z = \dfrac{\bar{X}_c - \mu_0}{\sigma/\sqrt{n}} = 1.64$ (9-24)

$$\text{critical } Z = \frac{\overline{X}_c - 8.5}{1/\sqrt{100}} = 1.64$$

$$\overline{X}_c = 8.664$$

b. Since $\overline{X} = 8.8$ exceeds $\overline{X}_c = 8.664$, reject H_0

c. A typical calculation, for $\mu_1 = 8.6$, goes as follows: The type II error occurs when H_1 is true, and H_0 is wrongly accepted (which occurs when $\overline{X} < 8.664$). Let us assume that σ remains 1, even if μ changes. Then

$$Z = \frac{\overline{X}_c - \mu_A}{\sigma/\sqrt{n}} = \frac{8.664 - 8.6}{1/\sqrt{100}} = .64$$

$$\beta = Pr(\overline{X} < 8.664) = Pr(Z < .64)$$

$$= 1 - .261 = .74$$

Similarly, we could calculate a few other values of β, obtaining

μ_A	β
(8.5)	(.95)
8.6	.74
8.66	.500
8.8	.09
9.0	.00

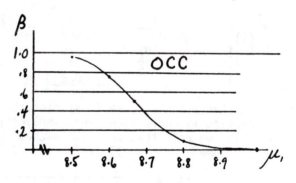

d. From the graph in (c), we read off the value of β to be approximately .10. Calculation would confirm this ($\beta = .009$).

9-21 a. The critical value is $P_c = 25/100 = .025$. To calculate α, we assume the null hypothesis is true, i.e. $\pi_0 = .020$ -- including the calculation of the standard error in the denominator:

$$Z = \frac{P_c - \pi_0}{\sqrt{\dfrac{\pi_0(1-\pi_0)}{n}}}$$

$$= \frac{.025 - .020}{\sqrt{\dfrac{.020(.980)}{1000}}} = 1.13$$

Thus $\alpha = Pr(P > P_c)$

$$= Pr(Z > 1.13) = .129 \approx 13\%$$

For the continuity correction, we read carefully, "If more than 25 in a sample of 1000, ...", which can be expressed as 26 or more, i.e., .026. Splitting the difference between .025 and .026, we get $P_c = .0255$. Then $Z = 1.24$ and finally $\alpha = .107 \approx 11\%$. The continuity correction for later parts of course uses the same critical value, $P_c = .0255$.

b. **(i)** We go through the same calculations as in part (a), except that now we calculate the complementary probability, and use the alternative hypothesis $\pi_A = .025$ everywhere in place of π_0 (see Figure 9-6 for example):

$$Z = \frac{P_c - \pi_A}{\sqrt{\dfrac{\pi_A(1-\pi_A)}{n}}}$$

$$= \frac{.025 - .025}{\sqrt{\dfrac{.025(.975)}{1000}}} = 0$$

Thus $\beta = Pr(P < P_c)$
$= Pr(Z < 0) = .50$

Similarly we could calculate the other values:

	Z	β	Z(wcc)	β(wcc)
(i)	0	.500	.10	.540
(ii)	-.93	.176	-.83	.203
(iii)	-1.72	.043	-1.63	.052
(iv)	-2.42	.008	-2.34	.010

c. To sketch the OCC, we first plot the 4 points found in part (b) (with no continuity correction, for simplicity). To help fill in the detail on the left, we note that as π approaches $\pi_0 = 2\%$, the type II error approaches the complement of $\alpha = .13$, which is .87

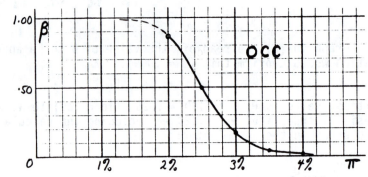

d. If we plot the values $1-\beta$ we will find this power curve is the same shape as the occ, just flipped upside down:

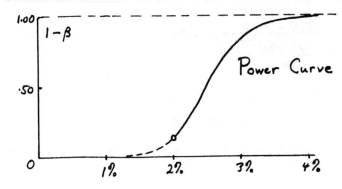

84

e. Reading from the power curve, power $\approx$ .82. Or more exactly from part b(ii), power = 1 - .176 = .824. Then the expected number detected is:

$$E = n\pi = .82 \times 50 = 41$$

Or more informally, 82% of 50 = 41

9-23 a. We are interested in the change in the population proportion who were afraid to walk alone at night. In symbols, we want $\pi_2 - \pi_1$ where

π_1 = the population proportion who were afraid in 1972
π_2 = the population proportion who were afraid in 1975

$$(\pi_2 - \pi_1) = (.45 - .42) \pm 1.96 \sqrt{\frac{(.45)(.55)}{1,500} + \frac{(.42)(.58)}{1,500}} \qquad (8\text{-}29)$$

$$= .03 \pm 1.96(.0181)$$
$$= .03 \pm .0355 \approx .030 \pm .036$$

b. From the second last line in part (a), we find the estimate is .03 and the SE is .0181. Thus

$$t = \frac{\text{estimate}}{\text{SE}} = \frac{.03}{.0181} = 1.66 \qquad (9\text{-}17)$$

We can use the Z table [since we used $z_{.025}$ = 1.96 in part (a) because n was large] and we find:

$$Pr(Z > 1.66) = .048$$

Thus the two-sided p-value = 2(.048) = .096

c. We cannot reject H_0 at level α = 5% (difference is indiscernible), for either of two reasons:

(i) $(\pi_2 - \pi_1) = 0$ is included in the 95% confidence interval in (a).

(ii) In (b), the p-value is .096, and this measure of credibility exceeds α = 5%.

9-25 a. $\mu > \bar{X} - 3.05\ \sigma/\sqrt{n}$ \qquad (9-31)

$\mu > 14,740 - 1.64\ (2000)/\sqrt{25}$

$\mu > 14,740 - 1.64(400)$

$\mu > 14,084$

b. From the second last line in part (a), we find the estimate in 14,740 and its standard error is 400. Thus

$$Z = \frac{\text{estimate} - \mu_0}{\text{exact SE}} \qquad (9\text{-}14)$$

$$= \frac{14,740 - 14,000}{400} = 1.85$$

p-value = $Pr(Z > 1.85) = .032$

c. We can reject H_0 at level $\alpha = 5\%$ (improvement is discernible), for either of two reasons:

(i) $\mu_0 = 14{,}000$ is excluded from the 95% confidence interval in a.

(ii) The p-value in (b) is .032 and this measure of credibility falls below $\alpha = 5\%$.

9-27 The null hypothesis is that no train is coming. Thus the type I error is to unnecessarily leap of the tracks.

This leaves the alternative hypothesis that a train is indeed coming. Thus the type II error is to keep walking and get killed -- obviously much more serious. So of course we would leap off the tracks immediately.

9-29 a. The null hypothesis is that the judge is fair, that is, he is drawing a random sample from a population whose proportion of women is 29%. In symbols,

$$H_0: \quad \pi = .29$$

b.
$$t = \frac{\text{estimate - null hypothesis}}{SE} = \frac{P = \pi_0}{\sqrt{\dfrac{\pi(1-\pi)}{n}}} \qquad (9\text{-}16)$$

For the SE, it would be best to consistently use the same π_0 as in the numerator. Then we have the exact SE, and hence a z-value:

$$z = \frac{P - \pi_0}{\sqrt{\dfrac{\pi_0(1-\pi_0)}{n}}} = \frac{.15 - .29}{\sqrt{\dfrac{.29(.71)}{700}}} = -8.16$$

p-value = $\Pr(Z < -8.16) \simeq 0$

That is the judge's fairness (H_0) had almost no credibility -- unless there is some <u>alternative</u> explanation such as a larger non-response from women, for example. (The appeal court did not rule on these complex statistical issues, but dismissed Dr. Spock on constitutional grounds).

<u>Remarks</u>: We would get almost as good an answer by estimating π with P:

$$t = \frac{P - \pi_0}{\sqrt{\dfrac{P_0(1-P_0)}{n}}} = \frac{.15 - .29}{\sqrt{\dfrac{.29(.85)}{700}}} = -10.4$$

Again, p-value $\simeq 0$.

c. H_0 can certainly be rejected, because

$$\text{p-value} \le \alpha \quad (0 \le 5\%) \qquad (9\text{-}27)$$

10-1

	B	A	C	
	74	75	60	
	78	70	64	
	72	66	65	
	68	69	55	
$\overline{X}$	73	70	61	$\overline{\overline{X}} = 68$
$X - \overline{\overline{X}}$	5	2	-7	0
$(X - \overline{\overline{X}})^2$	25	4	49	78
$\Sigma(X - \overline{X})^2$ within sample	52	42	62	156

Source	SS	df	MS	F	p-value
between fert.	4(78) = 312	2	156	9.0	p < .01 ($F_{.010} = 8.02$)
within fert.	156	9	17.3		
total	468	11			

Optional check on arithmetic:

Total SS among the 12 observations, disregarding their classification into columns, is 468 (which agrees with 312 + 156). Also, df = 11 (which agrees with 2 + 9).

10-3

given $\overline{X}$	given $\Sigma(X - \overline{X})^2$
148	8,510
61	3,480
73	2,910
118	11,410
	$SS_E = 26,310$

From the given column of $\overline{X}$, our calculator finds its average is $\overline{\overline{X}} = 100.0$ and $\Sigma(\overline{X}-\overline{\overline{X}})^2 = 6504$. Hence $SS_A = 5(6504) = 32,520$. We substitute SS_A and SS_E into the ANOVA Table:

Source	SS	df	MS	F	P
cities	24,390	3	8,130	4.94	< .05
residual	26,310	16	1,644		($F_{.05} = 3.24$)
total	50,700	19			

10-5 a. The arithmetic is so easy, we shall show it in detail

given X 33   29   40 $\bar{\bar{X}} = 102/3 = 34$

$X-\bar{\bar{X}}$ -1   -5   6   0

$(X-\bar{\bar{X}})^2$ 1   25   36   62, Hence $SS_A = 10 \times 62 = 620$

given $\Sigma(X-\bar{X})^2$ 240   363   315 $SS_E = 918$

Source	SS	df	MS	F	p-value
oils	620	2	310	9.1	<.001
residual	918	27	34.0		$(F_{.001} \simeq 8.77)$
total	1538	29			

10-7 a. When $n_1 = n_2 = \ldots = n$, then we have the following reductions of the formulas in Table 10-5:

$$\bar{\bar{X}} = \frac{n_1 \bar{X}_1 + n_2 \bar{X}_2 + \ldots}{n_1 + n_2 + \ldots}$$

$$= \frac{n\bar{X}_1 + n\bar{X}_2 + \ldots}{n + n + \ldots}$$

$$= \frac{n[\bar{X}_1 + \bar{X}_2 + \ldots]}{na}$$

$$= \frac{\bar{X}_1 + \bar{X}_2 + \ldots}{a} = \bar{\bar{X}} \text{ in Table 10-4a}$$

$$SS_A = n_1(\bar{X}_1 - \bar{\bar{X}})^2 + n_2(\bar{X}_2 - \bar{\bar{X}})^2 + \ldots$$

$$= n(\bar{X}_1 - \bar{\bar{X}})^2 + n(\bar{X}_2 - \bar{\bar{X}})^2 + \ldots$$

$$= n[(\bar{X}_1 - \bar{\bar{X}})^2 + (\bar{X}_2 - \bar{\bar{X}})^2 + \ldots]$$

$$= n \Sigma(\bar{X} - \bar{\bar{X}})^2 = SS_A \text{ in Table 10-4a}$$

residual d.f. $= (n_1 - 1) + (n_2 - 1) + \ldots$

$$= (n - 1) + (n - 1) + \ldots$$

$$= a(n - 1) = \text{residual d.f. in Table 10-4a}$$

total d.f. $= n_1 + n_2 + \ldots -1$

$$= n + n + \ldots -1$$

$$= na - 1 = \text{total d.f. in Table 10-4a}$$

10-9

	X_{ij}			$X_{.j}$	$(X_{.j}-\bar{X})$	$(X_{.j}-\bar{X})^2$
	24	19	20	21	1	1
	23	17	1	18	-2	4
	25	21	17	21	1	1
$\bar{X}_{i.}$	24	19	17	20	0 √	6
$(\bar{X}_{i.}-\bar{X})$	4	-1	-3	0 √		
$(\bar{X}_{i.}-\bar{X})^2$	16	1	9	26 √		

To find the residual sum of squares, we first tabulate the fitted values:

25	20	18
22	17	15
25	20	18

for example, as in (10-16), 20 + (-2) + 4 = 22

residuals				squared residuals			
-1	-1	2		1	1	4	
1	0	-1		1	0	1	sum = 10
0	1	-1		0	1	1	

ANOVA Table

Source	SS	df	MS	F	p-value
between hours	3(6) = 18	2	9	3.6	since $F_{.25} = 2.00$, $p < .25$
between men	3(26) = 78	2	39	15.6	since $F_{.05} = 6.94$, $p < .05$
residual	10	4	2.5		
total	106 √	8 √			

Optional check on arithmetic:

Total SS among the 9 observations, disregarding their classification into rows and columns, is 106 (which agrees with 18 + 78 + 10). Also d.f. = 8 (which agrees with 4 + 2 + 2).

10-11 We find the residual SS by the requirement that all four SS add up to the total. Then the ANOVA table proceeds as usual:

Source	SS	df	MS	F	p
fertilizers	608	2	304	51.7	< .001
seeds	183	1	183	31.1	< .001
blocks	261	3	87	14.8	< .001
residual	100	17	5.88		
total	1152	23			

10-13 a. Considering a move from Rochester (city 3) to San Diego (city 4), the change in mean house prices is $\mu_4 - \mu_3$ (new-old). Therefore

$$\mu_4 - \mu_3 = (\bar{X}_4 - \bar{X}_3) \pm t_{.025} \, s_p \sqrt{\frac{1}{n_4} + \frac{1}{n_3}} \qquad \text{like (10-21)}$$

$$= (118 - 73) \pm 2.12\sqrt{1644} \sqrt{1/5 + 1/5}$$

$$= 45 \pm 54$$

Here we used $s_p = \sqrt{MSE}$ in the ANOVA table in Problem 10-3, whose df = $a(n-1)$ = $4(5-1) = 16$, so that $t_{.025} = 2.12$.

<u>Remarks:</u> This formula, like all of ANOVA, assumes the variance within all cities is the same. But that clearly is wrong: cities with a high mean level likely have a high variance level too. So we could get a better answer by leaving out the first two cities, and just sticking to the relevant formula from Chapter 8:

$$\mu_4 - \mu_3 = (\bar{X}_4 - \bar{X}_3) \pm 1.96 \sqrt{\frac{\sigma_4^2}{n_4} + \frac{\sigma_3^2}{n_3}} \qquad \text{(like (8-18)}$$

$$\approx (\bar{X}_4 - \bar{X}_3) \pm t_{.025} \sqrt{\frac{s_4^2}{n_4} + \frac{s_3^2}{n_3}}$$

where $s_4^2 = \dfrac{\Sigma(X_4 - \bar{X}_4)^2}{n_4 - 1} = \dfrac{11,410}{4} = 2852$

Similarly $s_3^2 = \dfrac{2,910}{4} = 728$

We will use df = 4 + 4 = 8 as a rough approximation, so that $t_{.025} = 2.31$. Thus

$$(\mu_4 - \mu_3) = (118 - 73) \pm 2.31 \sqrt{\frac{2852}{5} + \frac{728}{5}}$$

$$= 45 \pm 62$$

b. We replace $t_{.025}$ in part (a) with

$$\sqrt{(k-1)F_{.025}} = \sqrt{(4-1)3.24} = 3.12 \qquad (10\text{-}24)$$

This gives an appropriately wider CI:

$$\mu_4 - \mu_3 = 45 \pm 3.12 \sqrt{1644} \sqrt{\frac{1}{5} + \frac{1}{5}}$$

$$= 45 \pm 80$$

10-15 a. When run through MINITAB, the data gives the following 2-way ANOVA table:

ANALYSIS OF VARIANCE ON C1

SOURCE	DF	SS	MS
SOILS	2	186.00	93.00
SEEDS	2	54.00	27.00
ERROR	4	24.00	6.00
TOTAL	8	264.00	

b. The 3 variety means are $\bar{X}_1 = 20$, $\bar{X}_2 = 23$, and $\bar{X}_3 = 17$. The ANOVA table gives the residual $s^2 = 6.0$ with d.f. = 4. Thus

$$(\mu_1 - \mu_2) = (\bar{X}_1 - \bar{X}_2) \pm \sqrt{(k-1)F}_{.05} \; s \sqrt{\frac{1}{n_1} + \frac{1}{n_2}} \qquad (10\text{-}25)$$

$$= (20 - 23) \pm \sqrt{2(6.94)} \; \sqrt{6.0} \sqrt{\frac{1}{3} + \frac{1}{3}}$$

$$\mu_1 - \mu_2 = -3.00 \pm 7.45$$

Similarly $\quad \mu_1 - \mu_3 = +3.00 \pm 7.45$

$$\mu_2 - \mu_3 = +6.00 \pm 7.45$$

c. He seems to have succeeded -- B's yield in loam (31) is much higher than any other yield in the table. This means the additivity assumption is suspect, and so therefore is the analysis in parts a and b above.

10-17 Suppose that a 95% confidence interval for a population mean was calculated to be $\mu = 170 \pm 20$. Answer True or False; if False, correct it:

a. F: Any hypothesis in the interval $150 < \mu < 190$ is called an <u>acceptable</u> hypothesis, while any hypothesis outside this interval is called a <u>rejected</u> hypothesis.

b. F: The <u>sample</u> mean is a random variable with expectation μ and approximate standard deviation <u>10</u>.

c. F: If this sampling experiment were repeated many times, and if each time a confidence interval were similarly constructed, 95% of these confidence intervals would cover <u>the true but unknown</u> μ.

10-19 Let P_1 (or P_2) denote the proportion of men (or women) applicants who are admitted.

a. (i) For Arts,

$P_1 = 700/2300 = .304$, while $P_2 = 900/3200 = .281$

$$(\pi_1 - \pi_2) = (P_1 - P_2 \pm 1.96 \sqrt{\frac{P_1(1-P_1)}{n_1} + \frac{P_2(1-P_2)}{n_2}} \qquad (8\text{-}29)$$

$$= (.304 - .281) \pm 1.96 \sqrt{\frac{.304(.696)}{2300} + \frac{.281(.719)}{3200}}$$

$$= .023 \pm .024$$

(ii) $P_1 = 3000/6000 = .500$ while $P_2 = 600/1100 = .545$

Thus, $(\pi_1 - \pi_2) = (.500 - .545) \pm 1.96 \sqrt{\dfrac{.500(.500)}{6000} + \dfrac{.545(.455)}{1100}}$

$$= -.045 \pm .032$$

(iii) $P_1 = 3700/8300 = .446$ while $P_2 = 1500/4300 = .349$

$(\pi_1 - \pi_2) = (.446 - .349) \pm 1.96 \sqrt{\dfrac{.446(.544)}{8300} + \dfrac{.349(.651)}{4300}}$

$$= .097 \pm .018$$

b.   In this problem there was no sampling actually carried out. Yet to make sense of a confidence interval, there has to be an underlying population whose parameter $(\pi_1 - \pi_2)$ is being estimated. So we can imagine a hypothetical population of all those students with the same sorts of qualifications who might have applied.

Many statisticians, with good reason, feel uneasy about such a vague concept (an excellent critique is given in Friedman, Purvis, and Pisani, 1978). They would prefer to make no inference at all in a case like this. Or, if a confidence interval is calculated at all, it should be interpreted as a formal measure of variability rather than literally.

c.   The only faculty with discernibly different rates is Science, where women have a <u>higher</u> admission rate. The reason women have a discernibly lower admission rate in the whole school is that they tend to apply to the tougher faculty. (It is not sex discrimination.) For more detail, see Problem 1-18 on p. 23 of the text.

10-21 a.   Let P_H (or P_L) denote the proportion of infants on high (or low) concentration of oxygen who survived. The $P_H = 36/45 = .80$, while $P_L = 28/40 = .70$, and consequently the 95% confidence interval is:

$(\pi_1 - \pi_2) = (.80 - .70) \pm 1.96 \sqrt{\dfrac{.80(.20)}{45} + \dfrac{.70(.30)}{40}}$

$$= .10 \pm 1.96 \ (.094)$$

$$= .10 \pm .184$$

b.   From (a) the estimate .10 and its standard error (.094) can be substituted into (9-17):

$$t = .10/.094 = 1.06$$

Use the normal table as an easy approximation, since d.f. is large but too complex to bother with. Thus

$$\text{p-value} \simeq .145$$

c.   In words: With 95% confidence we estimate the 3-month survival rate is better for high concentration of oxygen than for low -- better by 10 ± 18 percentage points. That is, the survival rate may be 28 percentage points higher, or 8 lower. (Since we are unsure which is better, we call the result statistically indiscernible).

Part b: If the true effect is zero, there is a 15% chance that a sampling fluke would produce survival rates as different as those actually observed.

10-23 First, we rephrase the question: For the <u>total</u> weight of 100 persons to be more than 18,000 lbs., is equivalent to the <u>average</u> to be more than $18,000/100 = 180$ lbs. And $\bar{X}$ has an approximately normal distribution with expected value $\mu = 175$ and standard error $= \sigma/\sqrt{n} = 30/\sqrt{100} = 3.0$. We can then standardize the critical value $\bar{X} = 180$ pounds,

$$Z = \frac{180 - 175}{3.0} = 1.67$$

Thus

$$Pr(\bar{X} > 180) = Pr(Z > 1.67) = .047 \approx 5\%$$

$$\mu = \bar{X} \pm t_{.025} \; s/\sqrt{n} \tag{8-11}$$

$$= 186 \pm 2.20 \; (84)/\sqrt{12} = 186 \pm 53.3$$

10-25 a.   type I error, $Pr = \alpha$

b.   type II error, $Pr = \beta$

10-27 a.   From part (a) of Problem 10-26 we found the confidence interval for the mean difference in income was:

$$(\mu_1 - \mu_2) = (\bar{X}_1 - \bar{X}_2) \pm t_{.025} s_p \sqrt{\frac{1}{n_1} + \frac{1}{n_2}}$$

$$= (16.0 - 10.0) \pm 2.78 \sqrt{\frac{8 + 38}{2 + 2}} \; \sqrt{\frac{1}{3} + \frac{1}{3}}$$

$$= 6.0 \pm 2.78 \; (2.769)$$

To convert this to a p-value, we just take the ratio:

$$t = \frac{estimate}{SE} = \frac{6.0}{2.769} = 2.17 \tag{9-17}$$

From Table V, with d.f. $= 4$, we find the observed t of 2.17 lies beyond $t_{.05} = 2.13$. Thus

$$p\text{-value} < .05$$

$$two\text{-sided } p\text{-value} < .10$$

b.   From part (b) of Problem 10-26 we also found:

$$(\mu_1 - \mu_2) = (\bar{X}_1 - \bar{X}_2) \pm \sqrt{(k-1)F_{.05}} \; s \sqrt{\frac{1}{n_1} + \frac{1}{n_2}} \tag{10-25}$$

$$= (16.0 - 10.0) \pm \sqrt{(2.1)7.71} \; \sqrt{11.5} \sqrt{\frac{1}{3} + \frac{1}{3}}$$

$$= 6.0 \pm 2.78 \; (2.769)$$

which agrees with part (a). And it gave us the denominator s^2 of the F ratio. For the numerator, we find the explained variation:

$$SS = n\Sigma(\bar{X}_i - \bar{X})^2 = 3\ [(16 - 13)^2 + 10 - 13)^2] = 54$$

$$df = 2-1 = 1$$

$$MS = SS/df = 54/1 = 54$$

Thus $F = 54/11.5 = 4.70$

From Table VI, with d.f. = 1, 4, we find $F_{.10} = 4.54$ and so:

$$\text{p-value} < .10$$

c. The answers to (a) and (b) agree. Note also that $F = t^2$ (that is, 4.70 = 2.17^2. And this is equally true of the critical value: $F_{.10} = t_{.05}^2$, that is, 4.54 = 2.13^2). Thus what we have seen here in this example will be <u>generally</u> true.

   [Because of the squaring, the two-tailed t test corresponds to the one-tailed F test: Whether t is very positive or very negative (two tails), F = t^2 will be very positive (one tail).]
   We made exactly the same assumptions in the t test and F test:

   1) Our foremost assumption was that the random samples were independent.

   2) We assumed the two underlying populations were normally distributed, with equal variances. (As stated in footnote 1 at the beginning of Chapter 10, however, these two assumptions are not critical).

   3) As always, in calculating a p-value we assumed H_0 was true, i.e., the two populations were identical.

10-29 a. True

   b. True

10-31 Since this is just an observational study, there are <u>many</u> possible reasons why the last group has an average income that is more than double the first group. It might be their education, but then again, it might be their ambition, or their native intelligence, or their middle class upbringing, or . . . ..

11-1 a.

X	Y	$x = X - \bar{X}$	$y = Y - \bar{Y}$	xy	xy
1	70	-2	-10	20	4
2	70	-1	-10	10	1
4	80	+1	0	0	1
5	100	+2	+20	40	4
$\bar{X} = 12/4$ $= 3$	$\bar{Y} = 320/4$ $= 80$	0 ✓	0 ✓	70	10

$$b = \frac{\Sigma xy}{\Sigma x^2} = \frac{70}{10} = 7.0 \tag{11-5}$$

$$a = \bar{Y} - b\bar{X} = 80 - 7.0(3) = 59 \tag{11-6}$$

Thus, $\hat{Y} = 59 + 7.0X$

b.

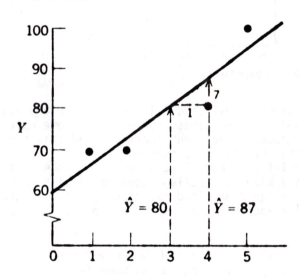

c. **(i)** $X = 3, \hat{Y} = 59 + 7(3) = 80$

(ii) $X = 4, \hat{Y} = 59 + 7(4) = 87$

(iii) We can go through the argument from first principles. In parts (i) and (ii) above, we saw that as X increased 1 pound (from 3 to 4), then Y increased 7 bushels (from 80 to 87). And as the graph shows, because the slope is constant, this same increase in Y will occur whenever X increases by 1 pound -- whether from 3 to 4, or 1.4 to 2.4, or whatever.
   Alternatively we can appeal to the text, where this same argument has been used to develop (11-8), which tells us that:

slope b = 7 is the change in Y that accompanies
a unit increase in X

11-3 a.

$$b = \frac{\Sigma xy}{\Sigma x^2} = \frac{876}{97.0} = 9.0 \tag{11-5}$$

$$a = \bar{Y} - b\bar{X} = 160 - 9.0(4.6) = 119 \tag{11-6}$$

Hence $\hat{Y} = 119 + 9.0X$

b.   if X = 5, $\hat{Y}$ = 119 + 9(5) = 164
if X = 0, $\hat{Y}$ = 119 + 9(0) = 119

c.

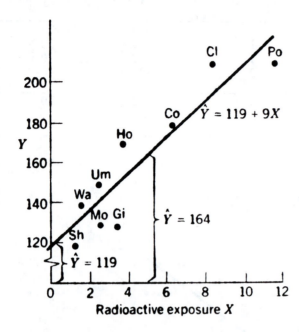

d.   Since this is an observational study, it does not in any way provide proof. As radioactive exposure X increases, for example, some extraneous variable such as degree of urbanization might increase, and this might be the cause, or partial cause of the increase in cancer mortality Y.

There does exist elsewhere lots of good evidence that radioactivity causes cancer --randomized controlled experiments with animals, for example. And for humans, although randomized experiments are unthinkable, nevertheless victims of Hiroshima and industrial accidents provided strong evidence.

11-5

    a. OLS may be regarded as the extension of a familiar technique— fitting [the median, <u>mean</u>] to a sample as in Chapter 2—and so shares many of its virtues.

    b. For example, OLS is efficient if the underlying population is [<u>normal</u>, extremely long-tailed].

    c. The OLS formulas for the slope b and intercept a are relatively [<u>easy</u>, difficult] to compute.

    d. Weighted least squares or WLS is a very flexible modification of [<u>OLS</u>, MAD]. For example [BLUE, <u>LOWESS</u>] uses WLS to fit many bits of line locally, which are then strung together to form a [<u>curve</u>, the optimal straight line].

11-7 a.

P	R		p = P - $\bar{P}$	r = R - $\bar{R}$		pr	r^2
50	0		0	0		0	0
60	40		10	0		0	0
40	30		-10	-10		100	100
50	50		0	+10		0	100
$\bar{P}$ = 50	$\bar{R}$ = 40		0 ✓	0 ✓		+100	200

$$b = \frac{\Sigma p \cdot r}{\Sigma r^2} = \frac{100}{200} = .50$$

$$a = \bar{P} - b\bar{R} = 50 - .5(40) = 30$$

Thus, $\hat{R} = 30 + .50R$

b.

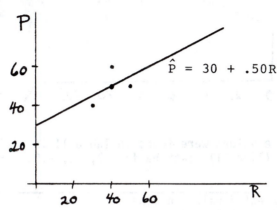

c. This line fails to "show how research generates profits" on two accounts:

1) It is based on a very small sample of firms, and no allowance for the sampling fluctuation has been made. This will be discussed in Chapter 12.

2) Even if the whole population of firms were graphed and fitted with a line (so that no sampling fluctuation occurred), there would only be a line showing a relation. Nothing could necessarily be said about <u>causation</u>. (Does R cause P, or does P cause R, or does good management cause both etc.).

12-1 a.

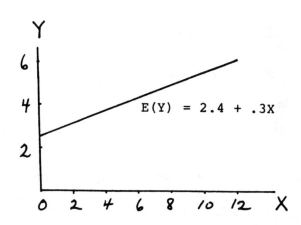

E(Y) = 2.4 + .3X

The following e values were found in Table II, starting at a place blindly with a pencil (line 31), last half: .7, .1, -.9, -.6, .6. Thus

| | expected value on line | | simulated Y |
X	E(Y) = 2.4 + .30X	e	sum
2	3.0	.7	3.7
4	3.6	.1	3.7
6	4.2	-.9	3.3
8	4.8	-.6	4.2
10	5.4	.6	6.0

b.

X	Y	x = X - X̄	y = Y - Ȳ	xy	x²
2	3.7	-4	-.48	1.92	16
4	3.7	-2	-.48	.96	4
6	3.3	0	-.88	0	0
8	4.2	+2	+.02	.04	4
10	6.0	+4	+1.82	7.28	16
X̄ = 30/5 = 6	Ȳ = 20.9/5 = 4.18	0 ✓	0 ✓	10.20	40

$$b = \frac{\Sigma xy}{\Sigma x^2} = \frac{10.2}{40} = .255 \tag{11-5}$$

$$a = \bar{Y} - b\bar{X} = 4.18 - .255(6) = 2.65 \tag{11-6}$$

Hence, $\hat{Y} = 2.65 + .255$

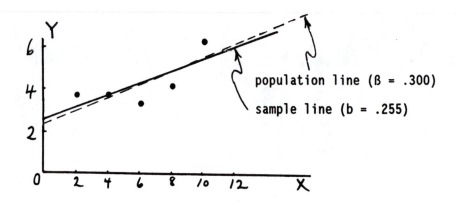

population line (ß = .300)

sample line (b = .255)

c. If your class is very very large, the distribution of b will be normal, with an expected value of .30 and standard error of .16. The smaller your class, the rougher this distribution will be approximated.

d. The "Monte Carlo" distribution in part (c) is only approximate, of course, because it is found from just a few possible samples. We could improve it by going to a computer to get thousands of possible samples. Or perhaps we could work out the distribution of b theoretically, as we did for X in Chapter 6 (in fact, we will do this in Section 12-2).

12-3 a. true slope = rise/run

If the right-hand point is off by .01 inches then estimate slope

$$= \frac{rise \pm .01}{run} = \frac{rise}{run} \pm \frac{.01}{run}$$

So the error involved is $\pm$ .01/run.

For points 1 inch apart, run $\simeq$ 1, so error $\simeq \pm$ .01
For points 4 inches apart, run $\simeq$ 4, so error $\simeq \pm$ .01/4

So the estimate from points 4 inches apart is 4 times more accurate.

b. We can measure the accuracy of the slope estimate b using SE $= \sigma/\sqrt{\Sigma x^2}$

The only difference in the two situations is in $\sqrt{\Sigma x^2}$.

When the points are 4 times as far apart, this makes the deviation (x) 4 times as large. Since the square root cancels the effect of the squaring, the change in $\sqrt{\Sigma x^2}$ would also be 4 times, and so the SE would be only 1/4 as large.

Alternatively, here is the calculation in detail:

For two points 1 inch apart,

$\Sigma x^2 = (\tfrac{1}{2})^2 + (-\tfrac{1}{2})^2 = \tfrac{1}{2}$

SE $= s/\sqrt{\tfrac{1}{2}} = \sqrt{2}s$

For two points 4 inches apart,

$\Sigma x^2 = (-2)^2 + (2)^2 = 8$

SE $= s/\sqrt{8} = \sqrt{2}s/\sqrt{16} = \sqrt{2}s/4$

That is, the second SE is only 1/4 as large.

12-5 a.

X	S	x = X - $\bar{X}$	s = S - $\bar{S}$	xs	x^2
22	2.0	+1	-.2	-.2	1
18	2.0	-3	-.2	+.6	9
17	1.6	-4	-.6	+2.4	16
27	3.2	+6	+1.0	+6.0	36
$\bar{X}$ = 84/4	$\bar{S}$ = 8.8/4	0 $\checkmark$	0 $\checkmark$	8.8	62
= 21	= 2.2				

99

$$b = \frac{\Sigma X S}{\Sigma X^2} = \frac{8.8}{62} = .142$$

$$a = \bar{S} - b\bar{X} = 2.2 - (.142)21 = -.782$$

Thus, $\hat{S} = -.782 + .142 \ X$

b.

X	S	$\hat{S} = -.782 + .142X$	$S - \hat{S}$	$(S - \hat{S})^2$
22	2.2	2.34	-.34	.1156
18	2.0	1.77	+.23	.0529
17	1.6	1.63	-.03	.0009
27	3.2	3.05	+.15	.0225
				.1919

$$s^2 = \frac{1}{n-2} \Sigma(S-\hat{S})^2$$

$$= \frac{1}{2}(.1919) = .0960$$

df = n - 2 = 2, from Table V, $t_{.025} = 4.30$. Thus

$$\beta = .142 \pm t_{.025} \ s/\sqrt{\Sigma X^2}$$

$$= .142 \pm 4.30 \ \sqrt{.0960}/\sqrt{62}$$

$$= .142 \pm 4.30(.0393)$$

$$= .142 \pm .169$$

$$\approx .14 \pm .17$$

Thus, the 95% confidence interval for β is $-.03 < \beta < .31$.

c.

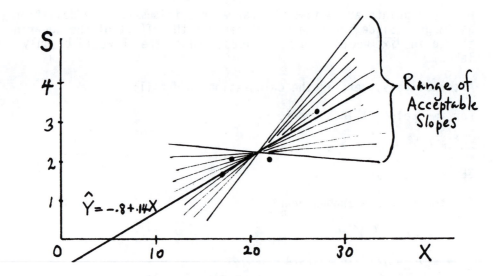

d. From part b, the 95% confidence interval for β is

$$-.03 < \beta < .31$$

According to (9-5), since the first three values of β ($\beta = 0, .05, .10$) are inside this confidence interval, they are acceptable. The fourth value $\beta = .50$ is rejected.

12-7 a. The summary statistics are $\bar{X} = 40$, $\bar{S} = 3$

$$\Sigma xs = 180, \ \Sigma x^2 = 1600$$

so $b = \dfrac{\Sigma xs}{\Sigma x^2} = \dfrac{130}{1600} = 0.081$

$$
\begin{aligned}
a &= \bar{S} - b\bar{X} \\
&= 3 - (.081)(40) = -0.24
\end{aligned}
$$

So $\hat{S} = -.24 + .081X$

b. From this, we can calculate $\Sigma(S-\hat{S})^2 = 3.4376$

So $s^2 = \dfrac{\Sigma(S - \hat{S})^2}{n - 2} = \dfrac{3.4376}{5 - 2} = 1.146$

For d.f. = 5-2=3, $t_{.025} = 3.18$. Therefore with 95% confidence

$$\beta = b \pm t_{.025} \ s/\sqrt{\Sigma x^2} = .081 \pm 3.18 \ \sqrt{1.146}/\sqrt{1600}$$

$$= .081 \pm 3.18(.0268) = .081 \pm .085$$

i.e. $-.004 < \beta < .166$

c.

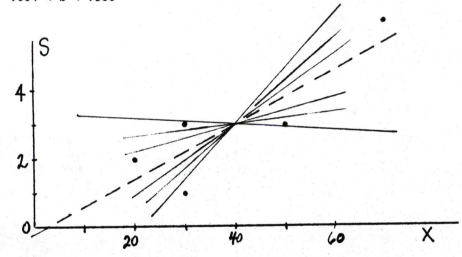

d. All the hypotheses are now acceptable except H_0: $\beta = .50$ (since .50 is not contained in the 95% CI.)

<u>Now for the answers for the last half (Problem 12-6):</u>

a. H_0: $\beta = 0$
H_A: $\beta > 0$

b. $t = b/SE = .081/.0268 = 3.02$ (12-16)

where b and SE were copied down from the confidence interval above. With d.f. = 5-2=3, we find this observed t exceeds $t_{.05} = 2.35$ Thus p-value < .05

c. $\beta > b - t_{.05} \ SE$
$\beta > .081 - 2.35(.0268) = .081 - .063$
$\beta > .018$

d. Reject H_0 because

(i) p-value < 5% or

(ii) $\beta = 0$ is excluded from the confidence interval

12-9 b.

$$\mu = (a + bX_0) \pm t_{.025} \; s \sqrt{\frac{1}{n} + \frac{(X_0 - \bar{X})^2}{\Sigma x^2}} \tag{12-19}$$

Since d.f. = n - 2 = 48 - 2 = 46, we will use the conservative value d.f. = 40. (Although we could interpolate between d.f. = 40 and d.f. = 60 and use $t_{.025}$ = 2.01, it would give the same rounded answer.)

(i)

$$\mu = 3.0 + 2.0(6) \pm 2.02(6) \sqrt{\frac{1}{48} + \frac{(6-30)^2}{6900}}$$
$$= 15.0 \pm 3.9$$

(ii)

$$\mu = 3.0 + 2.0(18) \pm 2.02(6) \sqrt{\frac{1}{48} + \frac{(18-30)^2}{6900}}$$

$$= 39.0 \pm 2.5$$

(iii)

$$\mu = 3.0 + 2.0(30) \pm 2.02(6) \sqrt{\frac{1}{48} + \frac{(30-30)^2}{6900}}$$

$$= 63.0 \pm 1.7$$

(iv) We saw in part (iii) that when $X_0 = \bar{X} = 30$, we get the narrowest interval. And now that $X_0 = 42$, it is the same distance (12 units) from $\bar{X}$ as in part (ii), and so we get the same confidence allowance:

$$\mu = 3.0 + 2.0(42) \pm 2.5 = 87.0 \pm 2.5$$

c.

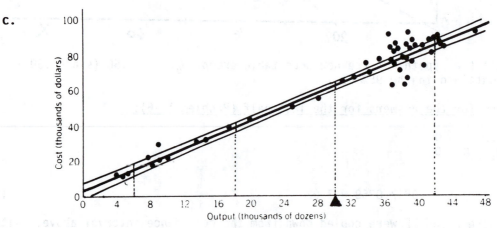

As the figure shows, the band is narrowest at the centre, at $\bar{X}$ = 30. It contains far fewer than 95% of the data points, of course. (Since it has a 95% chance of capturing the <u>mean</u> height at any given level of X, it has a much smaller chance of capturing an individual point that wanders from the mean.)

12-11 a. Since d.f. = n - 2 = 48, in table V we go about halfway between d.f. = 40 and d.f. = 60, to get $t_{.025}$ = 2.01. Thus

$$\beta = b \pm t_{.025} s/\sqrt{\Sigma x^2} \tag{12-10}$$

$$= 800 \pm 2.01(7300)/\sqrt{900}$$

$$= 800 \pm 489 \approx 800 \pm 490$$

b. Since the estimate (800) stands out above the sampling allowance (± 490), the slope is indeed statistically discernible.

c.

$$\hat{Y} = (a + bX_0) \pm t_{.025} \, s \sqrt{\frac{1}{n} + \frac{(X_0 - \bar{X})^2}{\Sigma x^2} + 1} \tag{12-20}$$

$$= 1200 + 800(10) \pm 2.01(7300) \sqrt{\frac{1}{50} + \frac{(10 - 11)^2}{900} + 1}$$

$$= \$9,200 \pm \$14,800$$

Since the population of incomes is skewed rather than normal, this interval turns out to include some impossible (negative) values of income. This serves as a warning that it has only an <u>approximate</u> 95% chance of bracketing the actual income.

d. Not fair, because this observational study is likely biased.

12-13 a. The sampling allowance (± .27) equals ± $t_{.025}$ SE, given in (12-9).

That is,
$$.27 = t_{.025} \, SE$$

Since d.f. is much larger than 120, we use the last entry in Table V, $t_{.025}$ = 1.96. Thus

$$.27 = 1.96 \, SE$$

$$SE = .27/1.96 = .138$$

Having found SE, we can use it to get the p-value:

$$t = b/SE = .38/.138 = 2.76 \tag{12-16}$$

Continuing to use the z table (since d.f. are very large), we find from Table IV:
$$p\text{-value} = .003$$

12-15 a.

$$b = \frac{\Sigma xy}{\Sigma x^2} = \frac{46,100}{36,400} = 1.266$$

$$a = \bar{Y} - b\bar{X} = 140 - 1.266(110) = 0.7$$

Thus $\hat{Y} = 0.7 + 1.266X$

b.

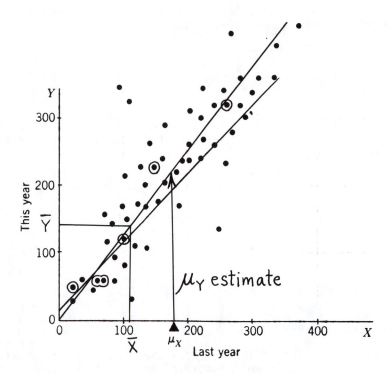

c. μ_Y will correspond to μ_X as shown on the graph above. To use (12-19), we will therefore set $X_0 = \mu_X$. And to get the residual s, we will need the following table:

X	Y	$\hat{Y} = 0.7 + 1.266X$	$(Y - \hat{Y})$	$(Y - \hat{Y})^2$
70	60	89.3	-29.3	860
260	320	329.9	- 9.9	100
150	230	190.6	+39.4	1550
100	120	127.3	- 7.3	50
20	50	26.0	24.0	580
60	60	76.7	-16.7	280
				3420

$$s^2 = \frac{1}{n-2} \Sigma(Y-\hat{Y})^2 = 3420/4 = 855$$

Thus

$$\mu_o = (a + bX) \pm t_{.025}s \sqrt{\frac{1}{n} + \frac{(X_0 - \bar{X})^2}{\Sigma x^2}} \qquad (12\text{-}19)$$

$$= 0.7 + 1.266(180) \pm 2.78 \sqrt{855} \sqrt{\frac{1}{6} + \frac{(180 - 110)^2}{36400}}$$

$$= 229 \pm 45$$

d. If only the 6 given Y values were available, we would use the standard confidence interval for a mean:

$$\mu_Y = \bar{Y} \pm t_{.025} \; s/\sqrt{n} \qquad\qquad\qquad \text{like (8-11)}$$

$$= 140 \pm 2.57 \sqrt{\frac{61,800/5}{6}}$$

$$= 140 \pm 117$$

e. The regression CI in part (c) is more accurate because it exploits the linear relation between the (unknown) Y values and the (known) X values. It is centred better, as well as being narrower.

For the CI in part (c) to work, however, an important assumption is that the population scatter is <u>linear</u>. If it is <u>curved</u>, then the simple CI in part (d) would be more reliable.

12-17 a. The population mean at any level X_0 is denoted by μ_0, and it has the 95% confidence interval:

$$\mu_0 = (a + bX_0) \pm t_{.025} \; s \sqrt{\frac{1}{n} + \frac{(X_0 - \bar{X})^2}{\Sigma x^2}} \qquad\qquad (12\text{-}19)$$

We want a CI for the Y-intercept α, where X = 0. We therefore substitute $X_0 = 0$:

$$= (a + b.0) \pm t_{.025} \; s \sqrt{\frac{1}{n} + \frac{(0 - \bar{X})^2}{\Sigma x^2}}$$

$$= a + t_{.025} \; s \sqrt{\frac{1}{n} + \frac{\bar{X}^2}{\Sigma x^2}}$$

Since $a = \bar{Y} - b\bar{X}$ according to (11-6),

$$\alpha = (\bar{Y} - b\bar{X}) \pm t_{.025} \; s \sqrt{\frac{1}{n} + \frac{\bar{X}^2}{\Sigma x^2}} \qquad\qquad (12\text{-}12) \text{ proved}$$

b. Into (12-12) above we substitute the values given in Problem 12-15 (including $s^2 = 855$ found in Problem 12-15 c):

$$\alpha = 140 - 1.266(110) \pm 2.78 \sqrt{855} \sqrt{\frac{1}{6} + \frac{(110)^2}{36,400}}$$

$$= 0.7 \pm 57.4$$

13-1   a.

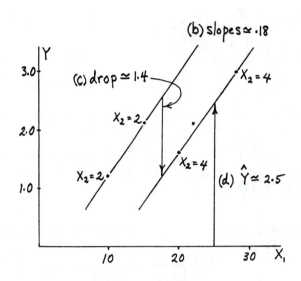

b.   When X_2 is constant, at $X_2 = 2$ for example, we have the top line in the graph. There the slope is about .18 (to be exact, slope $= \Delta Y/\Delta X_1 = (2.1 - 1.2)/(15-10) = .9/5 = .18$). The slope on the line where $X_2 = 4$ is about the same.

As we saw in (11-8), the change in Y that accompanies a unit increase in X_1 is just this slope, .18.

13-3   a.   If fertilizer is held constant at $X_1 = 400$ and rainfall changed from 10 to 30 inches, yield would increase by about 15 bushels/acre (distance between lines at $X_1 = 400$). This is an increase of about

$15/20 = 0.75$ bushels/acre per inch of rainfall.

b.   From the top line of the graph ($X_2 = 30$) we predict the yield to be about 66 bushels/acre when $X_1 = 300$.

13-5   a.   When $X_2 = 100$, the given multiple regression yields:

$$\hat{Y} = 10.9 - .13X_1 - .034\,(100)$$
$$= 7.5 - .13X_1$$

This is graphed as the lowest line in the figure. When $X_2 = 50$, 0 and -50 we similarly get the next three lines.

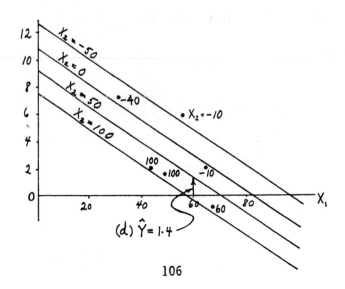

b. When X_2 is constant, the lines have a slope of $-.13$. As we saw in (11-8), the change in Y that accompanies a unit change in X_1 is just this slope, $-.13$. This is the coefficient of X_1, of course.

c. As the graph shows, while we keep X_1 constant, at $X_1 = 0$ say, Y drops by 3.4 when X_2 changes by 100. That is, Y drops .034 per unit change in X_2. And this is the coefficient of X_2, of course.

d. We substitute $X_1 = 60\%$ aand $X_2 = \$50$ into the given regression equation:

$$\hat{Y} = 10.9 - .13 (60) - .034 (50) = 1.4$$

This is confirmed on the graph.

e. The easiest solution by far is to use a computer. MINITAB gave us:

```
    READ C1,C2,C3
--  7.3   32   -40
--  2.0   43   100
--  2.3   65   -10
--  5.9   56   -10
-- -.8    67    60
--  1.7   48   100
--

    REGRESSC1 ON 2,C2,C3

THE REGRESSION EQUATION IS
Y =     10.9 - 0.129 X1 -0.0337 X2
```

	COLUMN	COEFFICIENT	ST. DEV. OF COEF.	T-RATIO = COEF/S.D.
	--	10.898	2.453	4.44
X1	C2	-0.1294	0.0460	-2.81
X2	C3	-0.0337	0.0101	-3.33

13-7 If $b_2 = 0$, (13-5) becomes

$$\Sigma x_1 y = b \Sigma x_1^2 + 0$$

Solve for b:

$$b = \frac{\Sigma x_1 y}{\Sigma x_1^2}$$

This agrees with the equation (11-5) for b in the simple regression case -- as it should.

13-9 a. We have d.f. $= n - k - 1 = 6 - 2 - 1 = 3$. Thus, for the coefficient of X_1,

$$\beta_1 = b_1 \pm t_{.025}\ SE \qquad (13\text{-}13)$$

$$= -.13 \pm 3.18(.046)$$

$$= -.13 \pm .15$$

$$t = b/SE = -.13/.046 = -2.8 \qquad (13\text{-}5)$$

from Table V, p-value $< .05$

Along with similar computations for the coefficient of X_2, we obtain the equation form:

$$\hat{Y} = 10.9 - .13X_1 - .034X_2$$

SE	0.46	.010
95% CI	±.15	±.032
t ratio	-2.8	-3.4
p-value	<.05	<.025

b. Confidence intervals and p-values are for underlying <u>population</u> parameters. We are therefore assuming that the 6 years represents a random sample from a large hypothetical population. But just exactly what this population may be, it is hard to say, since U.S. elections are unique historical events.

So it might be more honest to regard the confidence intervals as just familiar ways of expressing how much the data is scattered away from the fitted model. (The residual standard deviation s might be a better way, since it is just as familiar, and makes no pretence about an underlying population.)

c. The regressor X_2 (change in real income) has the smallest p-value (< .025), and consequently is most discernible.

d. We would keep it, for two reasons:

(i) <u>A priori</u>, we expect the President's popularity X_1 to have <u>some</u> effect on his party's election prospects (as X_1 goes up, the vote loss Y should go down).

(ii) The statistical evidence confirms this prior expectation: X_1 has a substantial negative coefficient (which is discernible at the one-sided 5% level.)

13-11 a. Other things being equal, the price per front foot for a lot that was 3 acres bigger (3=5-2) was greater by

$$(-1.1)3 = \$-3.30 \tag{13-29}$$

That is, $3.30 per front foot <u>less</u>. This makes sense: although a bigger lot sells for more, it sells for less <u>per front foot</u>.

b. Other things being equal, for a lot 1/2 mile less distant, the price per front foot was greater by

$$(-1.34)(-1/2) = + \$.67$$

c. <u>For the same kind of lot</u>, the price trend was up -- by $1.50 per front foot, per year.

However, the kinds of lots being sold probably changed over time. So the actual prices for these <u>changing lots</u> would have a different trend.

13-13 a. By (13-29), we use the multiple regression coefficient:

increase = 3.38(3) = 10.14

b. Again, by (13-29) we use the multiple regression coefficient

increase = .0364(10) = .364

c. We sum the individual changes, according to (13-32):

total increase = 10.14 + .364 = 10.504

d. As mentioned in example 13-4, it is the <u>simple</u> regression that measures the change in response while the extraneous factors are varying. So we use $\hat{Y} = 12.2 + 3.22R$, and find:

$$\text{increase} = 3.22(3) = 9.66$$

e. By (13-32),

$$\text{increase} = 3.38(3) + .0364(-13) = 9.67$$

Incidentally, this answer is the same as (d), and so we can deduce what happened in (d): When rainfall increased 3, apparently temperature decreased 13 on average.

f. As in part (d), it is the <u>simple</u> regression that measures the change in response while the extraneous factors are varying. So we use $\hat{Y} = 40.4 - .208T$, and find:

$$\text{increase} = (-.208)(10) = -2.08$$

That is, a decrease of 2.08, on average.

13-15 a. False: . . . the second equation would correctly predict that a year with <u>above</u>-average rainfall would <u>tend to</u> produce above average yield.

b. Could be improved: In view of the positive multiple regression coefficient, it would improve the crop to irrigate, <u>assuming</u>:

  (i)   irrigation water acts like rain water
  (ii) the level of water is not near the saturation point, where further water would cause the average yield to start to fall nonlinearly.
  (iii) there are not other extraneous variables (besides temperature) whose effects are so strong that including them in the multiple regression might change the sign of R.

13-17 a. The direct relation is the multiple regression coefficient, 3.38

b. total relation $= b_1 + bb_2$ (13-41)
                     $= 3.38 - 4.33 (.0364)$
                     $= 3.22$

c. We want the direct relation, i.e., the multiple regression coefficient where other factors are held constant (after all, when we irrigate we don't change the temperature). Thus the answer is 3.38.
    Of course, this assumes that irrigation water acts like rainwater, and so on (just as in Problem 13-15b above).

d. The simple regression coefficient is just the total effect, as we remarked just before (13-41). Thus, to repeat part (b),

      total effect of rainfall $= b_1 + bb_2$
                          $= 3.38 - 4.33 (.0364)$
                          $= 3.22$

      total effect of temperature $= .0364 - .0725(3.38)$
                               $= -.208$

Note that these two simple regression coefficients agree with those given in Problem 13-13 -- as they should, of course.

13-19 a. From the multiple regression equation in the top figure, we obtain the two direct coefficients leading into Y. And from the simple regression equation in the lower figure, we obtain the coefficient leading from X_1 to X_2:

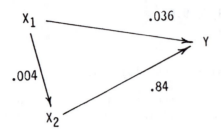

b. total relation = $b_1 + bb_2$
$$= .036 + .004(.84) = .039$$

c.

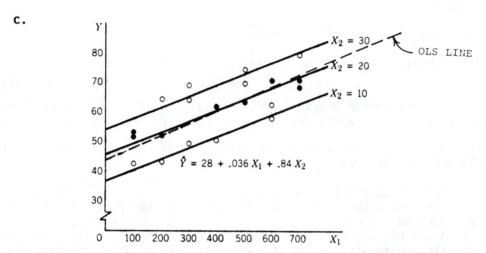

Since it is the least-squares line, this line fits the dots as well as any single line possibly can. (Of course, the 3 parallel lines of multiple regression fit better.)

d. Consider the split that occurs by chance in the small sample in the lower figure: The 3 levels of X_2 on average were slightly higher when $X_1 = 700$ than when $X_1 = 100$. And it was this sort of fluke that gave the line its slight tilt.

But randomization is blind. Thus in the long run, such flukes would average out, so that the average level of X_2 would be the same for all levels of X_1. That is, the regression coefficient b (of X_2 against X_1) would be zero, and hence:

$$\text{bias = indirect effect}$$
$$= bb_2 = 0b_2 = 0$$

This of course is the great virtue of randomization: It removes the bias of every extraneous effect, even those we couldn't measure or even think of.

13-21 a. Since we are holding X_1 and X_2 constant, we want the <u>multiple</u> regression coefficient of Y against X_3. This is just the arrow from X_3 to Y, the direct effect - .26

b. Again we want the multiple regression coefficient, the arrow from X_2 to Y, the direct effect - .07

Or to rephrase it: The intermediate variable X_3 was specified as

110

constant, so we do <u>not</u> want to include its indirect effect (defined as the change in Y induced via changes in X_3).

c. Now X_3 <u>is</u> changing, so we do want to include its indirect effect, and take the total effect from X_2 to Y. This was found in Problem 13-20 to be

$$b_2 + bb_3 = -.07 + .33(-.26) = -.16$$

d. Again we want the total effect, since all the intermediate variables may be changing. This was found in Problem 13-20 to be .069

13-23 a.

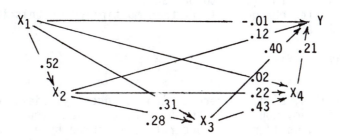

b.   (i)   <u>total effect of X_3</u>

direct	= .40
indirect via X_4	(.43)(.21) = .0903
	total effect = .4903

(ii)   <u>total effect of X_2</u>

direct	= .12
indirect via X_4	(.22)(.21) = .0462
via X_3: via X_3 alone	(.28)(.40) = .1120
via X_3 and X_4	(.28)(.43)(.21) = .0253
	total effect = .3035

Note that the last two lines -- the indirect effect via X_3 -- could have been condensed into one line instead, by looking at it this way: Fro X_2 to X_3, the coefficient is .28. Then from X_3 to Y there are two paths, which we <u>already found totalled</u> .4903 in part (i). So we simply condense the last two lines as (.28)(.4903) = .1373.

Then the total effect of X_2 can be written more briefly as:

direct	= .12
indirect via X_4	(.22)(.21) = .0462
via X_3	(.28)(.4903) = .1373
	total effect = .3035

(iii) We shall use the same condensation as in part (ii), a couple of times now:

<u>total effect of X_1</u>	
direct	= -.01
indirect via X_4	(.02)(.21) = .0042
via X_3	(.31)(.4903) = .1520
via X_2	(.52)(.3035) = .1578
	total effect = .3040

c.   (i)   If all the other variables are held constant, we want the multiple regression coefficient. This is just the arrow from X_1 to Y, the direct effect .01.

Or to rephrase it: The intermediate variables were specified as constant, so we do not want to include their indirect effects (defined as the changes in Y induced via changes in them).

In any case, the 3 units change in X_1 is multiplied by -.01 to give the change in Y:

$$(-.01)(3) = -.03$$

(ii) Now the intermediate variables are changing, so we do want to include their indirect effects, and take the total effect from X_1 to Y. This was found in part (b)(iii) to be .304.

The 3 units change in X_1 is then multiplied by this factor to give the change in Y:

$$(.304)3 = .912$$

13-25 Because extraneous variables, such as exercise habits, obesity, diet, or alcohol intake were not included, they would make the 5 years a biased figure.

The effect of smoking would be more accurately measured by a multiple regression that included these extraneous variables. Since it is impossible to include all the extraneous variables, however, this could never be completely unbiased. This, incidentally, is the same issue raised in Problem 13-24e.

An unbiased estimate might be obtained by a randomized controlled experiment -- that took strong measures to keep the control group from smoking, while it let the treatment group smoke as much, or as little, as they wished. This is hardly feasible, however, so we ultimately have to make an intelligent guess what the unbiased figure would be. Let us take a figure of about 3 years, rather than 5, as our "guesstimate" for smoking a pack a day.

The major defect in the given statement is not a formal statistical problem, however. It is a question of accurate reporting: Smoking doesn't take years off the end of your life, when you are old and ready to die anyhow. Instead, smoking takes out the best years of your life -- the years of vigorous living. This is because a pack-a-day smoker by the age of 30, say, has the lungs and heart and stamina of a nonsmoker who is about 33. For evidence about lungs, see Problem 13-24 (d). That is the smoker "loses" the 3 years of young adulthood from 30 to 33.

So smoking a pack a day doesn't cut out 3 years of arthritis and senility; it cut out 3 years of skiing and sex.

13-27 a. We substitute the given levels of the regressors into the regression equation:

$$\hat{M} = 19.6 + .041(170) + .71(6.0) + .001(790) + .41(6.8) + 6.87(9.5)$$
$$= 99.673 \approx 100 \text{ (deaths per 10,000 annually).}$$

This prediction is quite close to the actual figure of 103 for Pittsburg.

b. Likewise substitute in the average values:

$$\bar{M} = 19.6 + .041(120) + .71(4.7) + .001(760) + .41(12.5) + 6.87(8.4) = 91.45$$
$$\approx 91 \text{ (deaths per 10,000 annually)}$$

Incidentally, for a rigorous justification of this, in the case of 2 regressors at least, we could appeal to (13-7):

$$a = \bar{Y} - b_1\bar{X}_1 - b_2\bar{X}_2$$

that is, $\bar{Y} = a + b_1\bar{X}_1 + b_2\bar{X}_2$

c.　(i)　$\Delta E = 4.2 - 8.4 = -4.2$

　　　　　Thus $\Delta M = b\Delta E$　　　　　　　　　　　　　　like (13-28)

　　　　　　　$= 6.87(-4.2) = -28.85$

　　　That is, mortality decreases by 29 (deaths per 10,000 annually).

　　(ii)　　$\Delta D = 380 - 760 = -360$

　　　Thus $\Delta M = b\,\Delta D = .001(-360) = -.36$

　　(iii)　　$\Delta P = 60 - 120 = -60$

　　　　　$\Delta SP = 2.35 - 4.7 = -2.35$

　　　Thus $\Delta M = b_1\,\Delta P + b_2\,\Delta SP$　　　　　　like (13-32)

　　　　　　$= .041(-60) + .71(-2.35) = -4.13$

　　　To summarize, the effects of age are very strong, the effect of pollution is intermediate, and the effect of density is very weak (in fact, hardly discernible, if you look at its t ratio of 1.7).

d.　(i)　$\beta = b \pm t_{.025}\ SE$　　　　　　　　　　　　(13-13)

　　　　$= .041 \pm 1.98(.016)$

　　　　$= .041 \pm .032$

　　(ii)　$t = b/SE = .041/.016 = 2.56$

　　Since $n = 117$, and $k = 5$ regressors, therefore
　　　d.f. $= 117 - 5 - 1 = 111$

　　　From Table V, we use d.f. $= 120$ as the closest approximation, and find this observed t of 2.56 lies beyond $t_{.01} = 2.36$. Thus p-value $< .01$.

　(iii) We can reject H_0 either because:

　　　1)　　it lies outside the CI
　　　2)　　its p-value is small enough ($< 5\%$)

　　That is, pollution is statistically discernible.

13-29 old $Y = a + b_1X_1 + b_2X_2 + b_3X_3$
　　new $X_1 = (X_1 + \Delta X_1)$, new $X_2 = (X_2 + \Delta X_2)$, new $X_3 =$ old $X_3 = X_3$
　　So new $Y = a + b_1(X_1 + \Delta X_1) + b_2(X_2 + \Delta X_2) + b_3X_3$
　　　　　$= a + b_1X_1 + b_2X_2 + b_3X_3 + b_1\Delta X_2 + b_2\Delta X_2$
　　　　　$=$ old $Y + b_1\Delta X_1 + b_2\Delta X_2$
　　So ΔY　　$=$ new Y-old $Y = b_1\Delta X_1 + b_2\,\Delta X_2$

14-1 a. (i) SAL = 43.4 + 1.24(7) + 3.60(6) + .74(1)
$$= 74.42 \text{ (thousand \$)}$$

(ii) 126 − 74.42 = 51.58 and s = 16.4. So his salary is 51.58/16.4 = 3.15 standard deviations higher than the fitted value. This shows that Fred's salary is indeed exceptional (almost all of the observations should be within 3 standard deviations of the fitted values).

(iii) We should add <u>at least</u> 2 years to EDUC (perhaps even more since a prestigious Rhodes Scholarship is more of a learning experience than 2 ordinary years of university). So:

$$\begin{aligned} SAL &= 43.4 + 1.24(7) + 3.60(8) + .74(1) \\ &= 81.62 \end{aligned}$$

$$126 − 81.62 = 44.38$$

So his salary is only 44.38/16.4 = 2.7 standard deviations higher than the fitted value. This is still quite exceptional, but what do you expect from a Rhodes Scholar? (He is probably exceptional in other factors that were not measured as well.)

b. (i) To test for evidence of sex discrimination, we look at the coefficient of MALE.

$$H_0: \beta = 0 \quad \text{(No discrimination)}$$
$$H_a: \beta > 0 \quad \text{(Males earn more than females)}$$

$$t = \frac{b}{SE} = \frac{.74}{1.10} = .67$$

$$\text{p-value} = Pr(t > .67)$$

But df = 270 − 4 = 266, so we use the z-distribution instead.

$$Pr(Z > .67) = .251 = \text{p-value} \quad \text{(large)}$$

We fail to reject H_0, and conclude that there is practically no evidence of sex discrimination here.

<u>Note</u>: The above procedure is of limited use for reasons discussed in (ii) below.

(ii) Our coefficient for EDUC is b = 3.60, which seems to indicate that each extra year of post-secondary education increases income of executives by $3600 a year, on average.

But this value is based on a sample of 270, and therefore is just an estimate. With 95% confidence the true value is between 3.60 ± 1.96(1.20) = 3.60 ± 2.35 i.e., between $1250 and $5950.

Furthermore, this is an observational study and therefore we must temper our conclusions somewhat. We have controlled some of the important confounding factors (experience and sex), but there are surely others (intelligence, interpersonal skills, etc.) that were not controlled by inclusion in the regression equation.

So it would be better to say that each extra year of education is <u>related</u> to an increase of about $3600 in extra salary.

For the same reasons, even if our test in (i) above had shown a discernible coefficient of MALE, it would not necessarily be proof of sex discrimination. The apparent discrimination might actually be explained by other factors not included in the study.

114

14-3 a. $$\beta = b \pm t_{.025}SE \qquad\qquad (13\text{-}13)$$

Thus, for the coefficient of AGE, for example,

$$\beta = -39 \pm 1.96\,(1.8) = -39 \pm 3.5$$

Similarly, all the other confidence allowances are found, and turn out to be ± 4.3, ± 90, ± 104, ± 106.

b. How would the prediction for a chemical worker differ from the prediction for a doctor with other things equal? Only by changing the dummy CHEMW from 0 to 1. According to (13-31), therefore, the coefficient of CHEMW (-350) gives this change; that is, gives the air capacity of the chemical worker relative to the physician. Thus, the blanks are:

<u>age and cigarette smoking, 350 ml lower</u>

c. The chemical worker has an air capacity that is 350 less than the physician, and the farm worker similarly has an air capacity that is 380 less than the physician:

physician (reference group)

-350   - 380

chemical workers

farm workers

Thus, the chemical worker has an air capacity of $-350 - (-380) = +30$ relative to the farm worker, and so the blanks are:

<u>30 ml higher</u>

d. Again using (13-31), if we increase AGE by 1 year, the coefficient (-39) gives the accompanying change in the response AIRCAP. Thus, the blanks are:

<u>39 ml lower</u>

e. For 20 cigarettes, the effect is 20 times the effect of one cigarette, so that we multiply the relevant coefficient by 20, obtaining $20 \times (-9.0) = -180$. Thus the blanks are:

<u>180 ml. lower</u>

f. Let x be the unknown number of years. Then let us set the effect of aging equal to the effect of smoking:

$$x(-39) = 20(-9)$$

$$x = \frac{180}{39} = 4.6$$

Thus, the blanks are:

<u>4.6 years</u>. But this estimate may be biased because of <u>important variables being omitted from the regression</u>.

14-5 a. We check off ($\checkmark$) the first two patients. Then we graph the regression equation as follows: Since the weight-axis does not go back to 0, we take as our reference weight = 200, say, where BP is then:

```
for D = 0:   BP = 54.0 + 10.6(0) + .139(200) = 81.8
for D = 1:   BP = 54.0 + 10.6(1) + .139(200) = 92.4
```

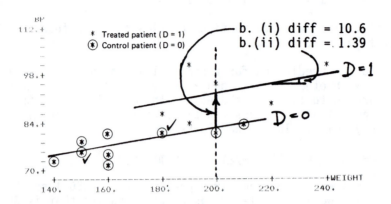

b.   Since "other things are constant", we use the multiple regression
coefficients:

(i) $\Delta Y = b_1 \Delta X_1 = 10.6(1) = 10.6$ (13.28)

(ii) $\Delta Y = b_2 \Delta X_2 = .139(10) = 1.39$

d.   Since simple regression looks at just the 2 variables (BP and weight) shown on
the graph above, it would fit a steeper line to the given points. The added
steepness would be the bias for omitting D.

14-7   We want to see how admission rate Y depends on sex S, holding faculty F constant.
We therefore run a multiple regression of Y against S and F, using the following
dummy variables defined for each student:

      Let Y = 1 if admitted, 0 otherwise

         F = 1 if faculty of Science, 0 otherwise

         S = 1 if female, 0 otherwise

Note that in the given table in Problem 18-1, the second entry, for example, records
700 males admitted to Arts, that is,

      Y = 1, F = 0, and S = 0 occurs 700 times.

This is accordingly typed into the computer in the third row of data below. As
another example, the first entry of the given table shows altogether 2300 males
applying to Arts. Since 700 were admitted, the remaining 1600 were not, that is,

      Y = 0, S = 0 and F = 0 occurs 1600 times

This is typed into the computer, in the first row of data below.

116

```
MTB > PRINT C1-C4

ROW     Y     F     S     FREQ

  1     0     0     0     1600
  2     0     1     0     3000
  3     1     0     0      700
  4     1     1     0     3000
  5     0     0     1     2300
  6     0     1     1      500
  7     1     0     1      900
  8     1     1     1      600

MTB > REGRESS 'Y' ON 2 REGRESSORS, 'F' AND 'S';
SUBC> WEIGHT BY 'FREQ'.

THE REGRESSION EQUATION IS
Y = 0.288 + 0.218 F + 0.005 S
```

The weighted regression subcommand gave us a regression equation that is easy to interpret:

Compared to males in the <u>same faculty</u>, females have practically the same admission rate (higher by .005, or ½ percentage point, on average).

Compared to Arts students of the <u>same sex</u>, Science students have a much higher admission rate (higher by .218, or 22 percentage points, on average).

Note how these answers provide a simple and routine alternative to the answers given in Problem 1-18.

14-9 a. **(i)** Set $D_A = D_B = 0$ in the regression equation:

$$\hat{Y} = 61 + 9(0) + 12(0) = 61$$

(ii) Now set $D_A = 1$, $D_B = 0$:

$$\hat{Y} = 61 + 9(1) + 12(0) = 70$$

(iii) Finally set $D_B = 1$, $D_A = 0$:

$$\hat{Y} = 61 + 9(0) + 12(1) = 73$$

b.

60	75	74
64	70	78
65	66	72
55	69	68

$$\bar{X} = \frac{244}{4} \qquad \frac{280}{4} \qquad \frac{292}{4}$$

$$= 61 \qquad\qquad = 70 \qquad\qquad = 73$$

These averages are the same as in part (a)--as they ought to be.

c. This is one-factor ANOVA, with the response being the yield, and the factor being fertilizer types.

d.

```
ROW      Y     DA    DB
  1     60     0     0
  2     64     0     0
  3     65     0     0
  4     55     0     0
  5     75     1     0
  6     70     1     0
  7     66     1     0
  8     69     1     0
  9     74     0     1
 10     78     0     1
 11     72     0     1
 12     68     0     1
```

MTB > REGRESS 'Y' ON 2 REGRESSORS, 'DA' AND 'DB'

THE REGRESSION EQUATION IS
Y = 61.0 + 9.00 DA + 12.0 DB

14-11 a.   Let us see, for example, how the NE cell would be fitted (males on drug A).
Then $D_A = 1$, $D_B = 0$, while $M = 1$. Thus the fitted values are:

additive $\hat{Y} = 65 + 5(1) - 10(0) + 10(1) = 80$

interactive $\hat{Y} = 68 + 6(1) - 15(0) + 5(1) - 2(1)(1) + 9(0)(1) = 77$

Continuing in this way, we obtain the following tables:

additive		interactive	
70	80	74	77
55	65	53	67
65	75	68	73

b.   In the additive model, ...   the same for both sexes.

14-13 a.   Eventually more water will cease to help, and in fact hinder. So the expected
yield cannot be perfectly linear; instead, it might be something like
quadratic, with a downward bend (negative term in I^2).

b. $t = \dfrac{b}{SE} = -\dfrac{1.5}{.4} = -3.75$

With df = 24 - 1 - 2 = 21, we find the observed t of -3.75 exceeds in
magnitude $t_{.001} = 3.53$, so that

p-value < .001

Thus the data shows H_0 has very little credibility, which confirms part (a).

c.   We can calculate $\hat{Y}$ at various levels of I, and so plot the curve. For
example,

at I = 0, $\hat{Y} = 42 + 12(0) - 1.5(0^2) = 42$
at I = 2, $\hat{Y} = 42 + 12(2) - 1.5(2^2) = 60$
at I = 3, $\hat{Y} = 42 + 12(3) - 1.5(3^2) = 64.5$

118

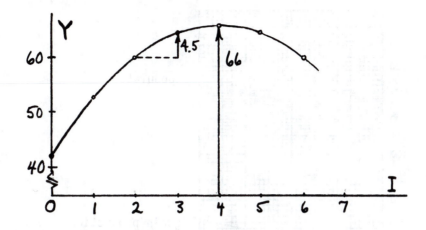

At I = 4 the maximum yield $\hat{Y}$ = 66 occurs. This is the appropriate level to irrigate only if irrigation is free. To the extent it is costly, irrigation should be less.

d.   In part (c), we already found Y at I = 2 and I = 3, and so the increase is, as shown on the graph:

$$\Delta Y = 64.5 - 60.0 = 4.5$$

This is not the coefficient of X, of course, because this is not a linear fit.

14-15 a.   Grain production seems to have risen more slowly than population.

   b.   **(i)**   From the graph, we find grain production increased from about 210 to 260 -- an increase of 50. The relative change was therefore

$$\frac{50}{210} = .24 = 24\%$$

   (ii)   Similarly, we find population increased from about 520 to 625 -- an increase of 125. The relative change was therefore

$$\frac{105}{520} = .20 = 20\%$$

So grain increased a little more.

c.

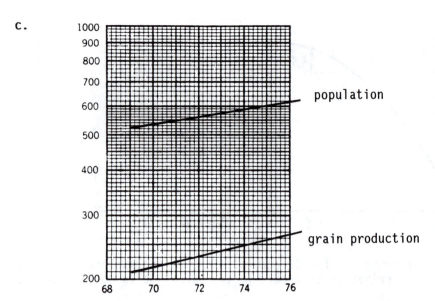

This graph does indeed make clear that grain production is increasing more.

<u>Remarks</u> Problem 2-28 confirms this analysis with the actual numbers. And as the solution there shows, this upward trend in per capita grain production has continued for many years.

14-17 Yes, it makes good sense to take logs in ANOVA whenever the model is multiplicative -- just as in regression. Not only will it linearize the model and make the error term additive, but it also may make the error term more normally distributed. This is shown in the figure below: if the distribution of u is skewed to the right, the distribution of log u usually is more symmetric, hence closer to normal. This provides certain advantages, such as more valid t tests.

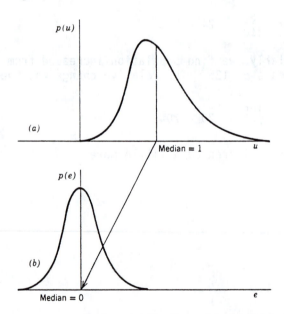

FIGURE The error term in the multiplicative model. (a) Original skewed error. (b) The more symmetric error after the log transformation.

14-19 $Q = \beta_0 K^\beta L^\beta$

Take logs:

$$\log Q = \log \beta_0 + \beta_1 \log K + \beta_2 \log L$$

This is of the standard form:

$$y = \alpha + \beta_1 X_1 + \beta_2 X_2$$

where, of course, $Y \equiv \log Q$, $\alpha \equiv \log \beta_0$, $X_1 = \log K$, and $X_2 = \log L$

Thus, ordinary multiple regression can be used to estimate the coefficients.

14-21 In each case we would use regression as follows:

a. $$Y = \beta_0 + \beta_1 X + \beta_2 X^2 + \beta_3 X^3$$

Regress Y against X, X^2, X^3

b. $$Y = \beta_0 + \beta_1 T + \beta_2 \sin \frac{2\pi T}{12}$$

Regress Y against T, $\sin \frac{2\pi T}{12}$

c. $$Y = \beta_0 (1 + \beta_1)^T$$

Take logs: $\log Y = \log \beta_0 + T \log (1 + \beta_1)$

So regress log Y against T

d. $$Y = \beta_0 \beta_1^T \beta_2^X$$

Take logs: $\log Y = \log \beta_0 + T \log \beta_1 + X \log \beta_2$

So regress Y against T, X

e. $$Y = \beta_0 + \beta_1 X + \beta_2 T + \beta_3 X^2 + \beta_4 T^2 + \beta_5 XT$$

Regress Y against X, T, X^2, T^2, XT

f. $$Y = \beta_0 + \beta_1 e^{\beta x}$$

No transformation will work here so we have to find the least squares estimates by computing methods.

14-23 a.

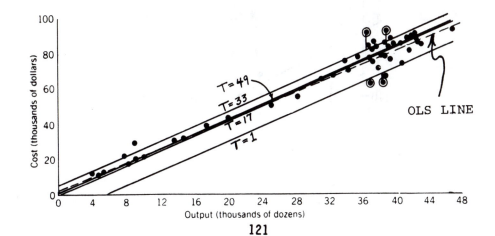

121

b.   We substitute $T = 1$ into the multiple regression:

$$\hat{Y} = -13.6 + 2.07X + 1.3(1) - .022(1^2) = -12.32 + 2.07X$$

Similarly we substitute $T = 17$, and so on, obtaining:

(i) $\hat{Y} = -12.32 + 2.07\ X$

(ii) $\hat{Y} = 2.14 + 2.07\ X$

(iii) $\hat{Y} = 5.34 + 2.07\ X$

(iv) $\hat{Y} = -2.72 + 2.07\ X$

When we plot these, we obtain the 4 lines shown in the Figure. They do indeed produce smaller residuals.

We also note as T increases, the lines rise and then fall, reflecting the parabolic dependence of Y on T.

14-25 a.   It can handle categorical factors such as [income, <u>race</u>], by using [non-negative variables, <u>dummy variables</u>].

b.   It can handle ANOVA, which deals with [<u>just categorical factors</u>, just numerical factors]. In fact, it is particularly [<u>suitable</u>, unsuitable] to handle ANOVA when the number of observations in each cell varies.

c.   It can handle polynomials, by using [dummy variables, <u>X and X^2 and X^3 ... as the regressors</u>].

d.   It [<u>can</u>, cannot] help to remove the bias of extraneous factors in observational studies, because each extraneous factor that can be [<u>measured</u>, conceived of] can be entered into the regression equation.

Then the coefficient of interest is interpreted as the change in Y that accompanies a [<u>unit</u>, significant] change in a regressor, if these confounding factors were [insignificant, <u>constant</u>].

e.   In observational studies, multiple regression [can, <u>cannot</u>] tell us exactly how X causes Y, because [<u>some omitted confounding factors may be causing X and Y to move together</u>, the sign and size of the coefficient of X tells us the direction and size of the change that X produces in Y].

14-27 a.

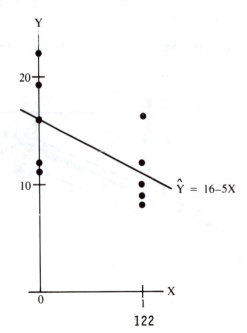

$\hat{Y} = 16 - 5X$

b. The regression line should pass through the center of the men's distribution (Y = 16, when X = 0) and the center of the women's distribution (Y = 11 when X = 1). This means the line must have a Y-intercept of 16 and a slope of:

$$\frac{\Delta Y}{\Delta X} = \frac{(11-16)}{1-0} = -5$$

Thus its equation is:

$$\hat{Y} = 16 - 5X$$

c. A computer solution is easiest. If we do it by hand, however, we will very clearly see the close analogy with Problem 8-11:

X	Y	$x=X-\bar{X}$	$y=Y-\bar{Y}$	xy	x^2	$\hat{Y}=a+bX$	$(Y-\hat{Y})$	$(Y-\hat{Y})^2$
0	12	-.5	-1.5	0.75	.25	16	-4	16
0	11	-.5	-2.5	1.25	.25	16	-5	26
0	19	-.5	5.5	- 2.75	.25	16	3	9
0	16	-.5	2.5	- 1.25	.25	16	0	0
0	22	-.5	8.5	- 4.25	.25	16	6	36
1	9	.5	-4.5	- 2.25	.25	11	-2	4
1	12	.5	-1.5	- 0.75	.25	11	1	1
1	8	.5	-5.5	- 2.75	.25	11	-3	9
1	10	.5	-3.5	- 1.75	.25	11	-1	1
1	16	.5	2.5	1.25	.25	11	5	25
		0 ✓	0 ✓	-12.50	2.50			126

$$\bar{X} = \frac{5}{10} \qquad \bar{Y} = \frac{135}{10}$$

$$= .5 \qquad = 13.5$$

$$b = \frac{\Sigma xy}{\Sigma x^2} = \frac{-12.5}{2.5} = -5.0 \tag{11-5}$$

$$a = \bar{Y} - b\bar{X} \tag{11-6}$$

$$= 13.5 - (-5.0)(.5) = 16.0$$

Thus $\hat{Y} = 16.0 - 5.0X$

This agrees with the graphical solution in b.

d.
$$\beta = b \pm t_{.025} \frac{s}{\sqrt{\Sigma x^2}} \tag{12-10}$$

$$= 5.0 \pm 2.31 \sqrt{\frac{126/8}{2.5}} = -5.0 \pm 5.8$$

To interpret β, let us quote (13-26): If X is increased one unit (from 0 for males to 1 for females) the accompanying increase in Y is -5(±5.8). That is, as we pass from males to females, there is an average decrease in Y of 5(±5.8).
　　Or, to state it as simply as possible: Women earn on average $5,000 (±$5,800) less than men.

e. This is the same confidence interval as in Problem 8-11. And we note it corresponds component by component too: Regression gives Y = 16 and 11 for the men and women--exactly the same sample means as in Problem 8-11. Consequently the residual s^2 is exactly the same.

f.   Although we estimate that there is a difference of $5,000 in men's and women's salaries, this may be due to things other than discrimination--for example, due to different qualifications such as publications, age, etc. It would be interesting to do a study that held these qualification variables constant, or at least analyzed the data as if they were constant. That is what Problem 14-28 will do.

14-29 Since the regression did not include all possible confounding factors, the given conclusion is not perfectly free of bias. While we agree that sex discrimination likely explains most of the $2400 difference between men and women with the same measured qualifications, there may be other explanations.

For example, suppose in starting their careers, married couples tend to accept offers from universities where the husband's offer is higher, and reject offers (equally frequent, perhaps) from universities where the wife's offer is higher (in order to maximize lifetime family income, including those years when the wife is more likely to quit in order to stay home). Then published salaries would show men earning more than women, even if the universities as a whole were absolutely evenhanded.

14-31 Severe rounding makes the coefficient easy to state and interpret. However, rounding loses some information, and hence the t-ratio is likely weakened.

Furthermore, in some ways severe rounding makes the coefficient _too_ easy to state. In just comparing the top and bottom half of the faculty, it transforms shades of gray into black and white. If original student evaluation score had been used as a regressor, its coefficient would have reflected the value of increasing it by various shades--which is the goal of most professors.

15-1

X	Y	$x=X-\bar{X}$	$y=Y-\bar{Y}$	xy	x^2	y^2
3400	24	+800	+3	+2400	640,000	9
2600	20	0	-1	0	0	1
2200	17	-400	-4	+1600	160,000	16
2400	19	-200	-2	+ 400	40,000	4
2900	26	+300	+5	+1500	90,000	25
2100	20	-500	-1	+ 500	250,000	1
$\bar{X}=2600$	$\bar{Y}=21$	0 $\checkmark$	0 $\checkmark$	+6400	1,180,000	56

$$r = \frac{\Sigma xy}{\sqrt{\Sigma x^2}\,\sqrt{\Sigma y^2}} = \frac{6400}{\sqrt{1,180,000}\,\sqrt{56}} \qquad (15\text{-}2)$$

$$= .787 \approx 79\%$$

b. Interpolating Figure 15-4, the 95% confidence interval for ρ is approximately

$$-.05 < \rho < .97$$

c. Since $\rho = 0$ is included in the 95% confidence interval, the null hypothesis (cigarette consumption and lung cancer are uncorrelated) is acceptable at the $\alpha = .05$ level. That is, there is no discernible correlation.

   If there had been more data (15 states, say), we likely would have found that there <u>was</u> a discernible relation. Nevertheless, it would not have proved <u>causation</u>, because it is merely an observational study.

15-3 Although we could calculate these like Problem 15-1, it is more instructive to compute them on MINITAB:

a.
```
ROW     C1      C2

 1     0.22    0.26
 2     0.26    0.31
 3     0.25    0.24
 4     0.31    0.29
 5     0.26    0.25
```

MTB > CORR C1 C2

Correlation of C1 and C2 = 0.450

b. Using n = 5 and r = .45 in Figure 15-4, we find $-.61 < \rho < .92$. We are assuming that the batting average from these 2 years have a bivariate normal distribution. This assumption is not exactly true, but it may be approximately true.

c.
MTB > REGRESS C2 ON 1 C1

The regression equation is
C2 = 0.165 + 0.405 C1

Predictor	Coef	Stdev	t-ratio	p
Constant	0.1648	0.1214	1.36	0.268
C1	0.4048	0.4639	0.87	0.447

So a 95% CI for the slope ß is given by ß = b ± t$_{.025}$SE   (12-9)

i.e.,   ß = .4048 ± 3.18(.4639) = .4048 ± 1.4752

d. MTB > PLOT C2 VS C1

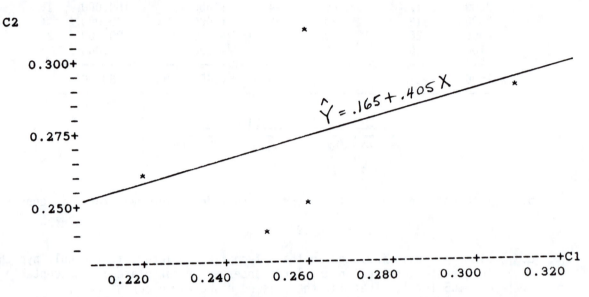

e.   **(i)** Since the confidence interval in (c) contains ß = 0, we cannot reject it.

      (ii) Likewise, since the confidence interval in (b) contains ρ = 0, we cannot reject it.

15-5 a.

$$b = r\frac{s_y}{s_x} = .693 \frac{.493}{14.7} = .0232$$

$$a = \bar{Y} - b\bar{X} = 2.1 - .0232(41) = 1.15$$

$$\hat{Y} = 1.15 + .0232X$$

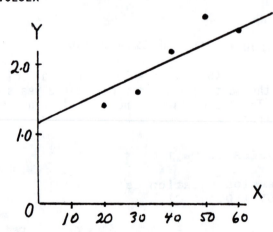

b. $b^2 \Sigma x^2 = .02324^2(10,600) = 5.73$

We subtract this explained variation from the total variation of Y to get the residual variation:

126

Source	SS	df	MS	F	p
regression	5.73	1	5.73	44.6	<<.001
residual	6.17	48	.1285		
total	11.9	49			

Reject H_0 at the 5% level, since its p-value is less than 5%.

c.
$$\beta = b \pm t_{.025} \frac{s}{\sqrt{\Sigma x^2}}$$

$$= .0232 \pm 2.01 \sqrt{\frac{.1285}{10,600}}$$

$$= .0232 \pm .0070$$

Since $\beta = 0$ is well outside the 95% confidence interval, reject it at the 5% level.

d. From Table 15-4, using $n = 50$ and $r = .693 \approx .69$, we find approximately:

$$.50 < \rho < .81$$

Since $\rho = 0$ is well outside the 95% confidence interval, reject it at the 5% level.

e. Parts (b), (c), and (e), are all consistent: H_0 can be rejected at the 5% level.

f. From the ANOVA Table, the SS column gives:

$$\text{proportion explained} = \frac{5.73}{11.9} = .48$$

This agrees with $r^2 = .693^2 = .48$

It logically follows that the complements must agree too. Just to check our arithmetic:

$$\text{proportion unexplained} = \frac{6.17}{11.9} = .52$$

This agrees with $1 - r^2 = 1 - .693^2 = .52$

15-7 a. This scatter is similar to Figure 15-2(a), so we would guess r is about .6. To actually calculate it,

$$r = \frac{\Sigma xy}{\sqrt{\Sigma x^2}\sqrt{\Sigma y^2}} = \frac{11,000}{\sqrt{18,000}\sqrt{21,000}} = .566$$

b.
$$\hat{X}_2 = a + bX_1$$

where $b = \frac{\Sigma x_1 x_2}{\Sigma x_1^2} = \frac{11,000}{18,000} = .611$

and $a = \bar{X}_2 - b\bar{X}_1 = 62 - .611(62) = 24$

Thus $\hat{X}_2 = 24 + .611X_1$

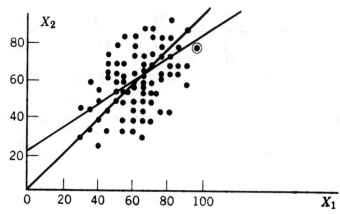

c. $\hat{X}_2 = 24 + .611(90) = 79$

$\hat{X}_2 = 24 + .611(40) = 48.4$

d. For the 3 pilots whose X_1 score was 90, the X_2 scores were 90, 70, 60. The average is 73, which agrees (within sampling variability) with the X_2 prediction of 79 in part (c).

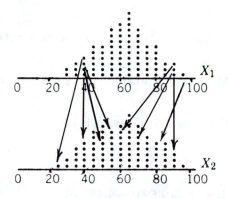

e. For the 4 pilots whose X_1 score was 40, the X_2 scores were 25, 40, 50, 55. The average is 42.5, which agrees (within sampling variability) with the X_2 prediction of 48 in part (c).

f. True, with a minor qualification: The pilots who scored very well or very badly on the first test X_1 <u>tended</u> to be closer to the average on the second test X_2.

15-9 a. In this observational study, the effect of criticism (or praise) cannot be distinguished from (is confounded with) the natural regression toward the mean discussed in Problem 15-7(f). The effect of criticism might be positive, but then again it might be negative--this data can't tell.

b. It is possible to design an experiment that <u>would</u> measure the effect of praise and criticism: Assign students <u>at random</u> to be praised or criticized. Then the comparison of praise and criticism would be valid since randomization makes "all other things equal" on average.

15-11 a.

Y	$\hat{Y}$	$y=Y-\bar{Y}$	$\hat{y}=\hat{Y}-\hat{\bar{Y}}$	y^2	$\hat{y}^2$	$y\,\hat{y}$
40	42.3	-20	-17.7	400	313	354
50	48.2	-10	-11.8	100	139	118
50	54.1	-10	- 5.9	100	35	59
70	60.0	10	0	100	0	0
65	65.9	5	5.9	25	35	30
65	71.8	5	11.8	25	139	59
80	77.7	20	17.7	400	313	354
$\bar{Y}=60$	$\hat{\bar{Y}}=60$			1150	974	974

$$R = \frac{\Sigma y\hat{y}}{\sqrt{\Sigma y^2}\,\sqrt{\Sigma \hat{y}^2}} = \frac{974}{\sqrt{1150}\,\sqrt{974}} = .920$$

b. From part (a) we have $\Sigma y^2 = 1150$. From Table 11-2, $\Sigma x^2 = 28{,}000$ and $\Sigma xy = 16{,}500$. Thus we get an answer that agrees with (a):

$$r = \frac{\Sigma xy}{\sqrt{\Sigma x^2}\,\sqrt{\Sigma y^2}} = \frac{16{,}500}{\sqrt{280{,}000}\,\sqrt{1150}} = .920$$

15-13 Statements (a) and (e) are equivalent. Statements (b), (c), and (d) are equivalent.

15-15 In the table below, we will find $\bar{X}_1 = 0$ and $\bar{X}_2 = 0$, so that they are already in deviation form. This is one of the many convenient features of orthogonal polynomials.

a.

X	$X_1 =$ $X-3$	$X_2 =$ X^2-6X+7	$x_1^2 =$ X_1^2	$x_2^2 =$ X_2^2	$X_1X_2 =$ X_1X_2
1	-2	2	4	4	-4
2	-1	-1	1	1	+1
3	0	-2	0	4	0
4	1	-1	1	1	-1
5	2	2	4	4	+4
	$\bar{X}_1 = 0$	$\bar{X}_2 = 0$	10	14	0

b. Since r = 0, there is absolutely no problem of multicollinearity.

$$SE_1 = \frac{s}{\sqrt{\Sigma x_1^2(1-R_1^2)}} \qquad (15\text{-}33)$$

$$= \frac{\sqrt{15.7}}{\sqrt{10\,(1-0)}} = 1.25$$

$$SE_2 = \frac{\sqrt{15.7}}{\sqrt{14\,(1-0)}} = 1.06$$

d. To predict Y from X_1 above, we should use the best possible prediction equation of the form
$$Y = a + bX_1$$

The best equation is the least-square line--the simple regression. Is its coefficient just the same as the multiple regression coefficient (what we get if we just "drop off" the X_2 term)? Equation (13-41) showed us that when the regressors are uncorrelated, the simple regression coefficient does indeed exactly coincide with the multiple regression coefficient.

Therefore in this special case of orthogonal polynomials, we can just "drop off" an insignificant regressor. We do not need to calculate the regression equation afresh using just the regressor X_1 (the simple regression). This is one more advantage of orthogonal polynomials.

15-17 The correlation would be exactly 1, as there would be a perfect positive linear relationship between husband's height (X) and wife's height (Y): When graphed, all couples would be exactly on the line Y = X - 4.

15-19 a. True. By symmetry, $\sigma_X = \sigma_Y$ (Or, you can see that the spread of X and Y are equal by looking at the ranges: X and Y both range from about 40 to 120.) Thus

$$\beta = \rho \frac{\sigma_Y}{\sigma_X} = .50(1) = .50 \qquad\qquad \text{like (15-21)}$$

also $\alpha = \mu_Y - \beta\mu_X = 80 - .50(80) = 40$

Thus the regression line is

$$\hat{Y} = 40 + .50X$$

and this is the line shown in the graph. Thus (a) is true -- although it would be better notation to use E(Y) instead of Y.

b. False. As already stated in part (a), $\sigma_X = \sigma_Y$. So we should write, "The variance of Y equals the variance of X".

Or we could correct it another way: The explained variation of Y is what is given by the values on the line (as in Figure 15-6). Since the slope is only 1/2, we conclude:

"the explained variation of Y compared to the variation of X is only $(1/2)^2 = 1/4$".

c. True. This is what we showed in part (b). Or equivalently, we could show it using the given value $\rho = .50$:

ρ^2 = proportion of variation of Y explained by X   like (15-16)
   = $(.50)^2 = 1/4$

d. True.
        proportion unexplained = $1 - \rho^2 = 1 - 1/4 = 3/4$

e. False. The best predicted X score would be obtained from the regression of X on Y:

$$\beta_* = \rho \frac{\sigma_X}{\sigma_Y} = .50(1) = .50 \qquad\qquad \text{like (15-24)}$$

also $\alpha_* = \mu_X - \beta_*\mu_Y = 80 - .50(80) = 40$

Thus the regression line is

$$\hat{X} = 40 + .50Y$$

When Y = 70, $\hat{X} = 40 + .50(70) = 75$

15-21 a. Clue: It can be shown that b is a weighted sum, with weights proportional to x (the distance from the center X̄). For the 2 circled points, x = 0, so they are irrelevant to the fitted slope. Thus the fitted line can go exactly through the remaining two points:

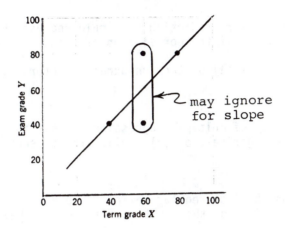

b. Clue: to minimize the horizontal deviations, we run the line midway between each indicated pair.

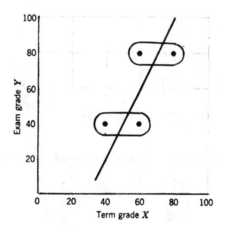

c. From Problem 15-20c, $r = \sqrt{bb_*} = \sqrt{(1)(.50)} = .71$

d. Using graph (a), we predict $\hat{Y} = 70$

e. Using graph (b), we predict $\hat{X} = 65$

15-23 a. True. This is another example of the "regression toward the mean" already seen in Problem 15-9, for example.

b. False. Profits in 1985 and 1984 are <u>equally</u> extreme, and so it is silly to look for reasons why they are "less extreme".

To see why they are equally extreme, we could compare this figure with Problems 15-19 or 15-9. They too were symmetrical, yet had a regression slope less than 1.

Or, we could give another reason: While the extreme firms tended to become more middling, what happened to the middling firms? They changed too, of course, with nowhere to go but more extreme. And when it all averaged out, the variation in 1985 remained the same as in 1984.

c. True, and similar to statement (a).

d. False: ...the best single prediction of its 1985 profit would be 9.5% (on the regression line)--which illustrates part (c).

15-25 a. True.

b. False: Nevertheless, for predicting Y, simple regression can be very effective -- especially if the correlation of X and Y is near <u>one</u>.

c. False: ... <u>many</u> but not <u>all</u> of the confounding factors ...

d. True.

e. False: One <u>advantage</u> of multiple regression is that it <u>can</u> include (1) factors that are categorical, or (2) nonlinearities such as polynomials and exponentials.

15-27 a. Since this exceeds the last regular row of Table V, we shall use the very last row where $t_{.025} = 1.96$. For the first coefficient, we have therefore:

$$\beta = b \pm t_{.025}\ SE = .09 \pm 1.96(.01) = .09 \pm .02$$

$$t = \frac{b}{SE} = \frac{.09}{.01} = 9.0$$

p-value $\ll .0005$

$$\text{partial } r = \frac{t}{\sqrt{t^2 + (n-k-1)}} \qquad\qquad \text{like (15-31)}$$

$$= \frac{9}{\sqrt{9^2 + (200-3-1)}} = .54$$

Similarly we can work out the other two coefficients, obtaining finally:

95% CI	.09 ± .02	-.24 ± .10	2.61 ± 1.61
t	9.0	-4.8	3.18
p	< .0005	< .0005	< .0010
partial r	.54	-.32	.22

b. **(i)** If nothing else is known, we have to use the average, which was given in the opening paragraph: $\bar{Y} = 32$

(ii) Now we can substitute into the regression equation:

```
DRLATE = 10 + 30 + 0 + 60 = 100
PALATE = 15
SHORT  = 0
```

Then $\hat{Y} = 22 + .09\ (100) - .24(15) + 2.61(0)$
$= 27.4$ minutes

c. The prediction errors were:

(i) $32-22 = 10$

(ii) $27.4 - 22 = 5.4$

Thus, the regression prediction had about half as much error.

d. In part (c), the squared prediction errors, with and without regression, were in the ratio

$$\left(\frac{5.4}{10.0}\right)^2 = .29$$

For all 200 patients, we likewise would obtain

$$\frac{\Sigma(Y-\hat{Y})^2}{\Sigma(Y-\bar{Y})^2} = 1 - R^2 = 1 - .72 = .28$$

So the one patient in part (c) was indeed typical of all 200 patients.

16-1 a. From the given graph, we see there are S = 5 observations above ν = 90°, out of a total of n = 6 observations. From Table IIIc, therefore,

$$\text{p-value} = \text{Pr } (S \geq 5) = .109 \approx 11\%$$

b. Now there are S = 4 observations below ν = 92°, so that

$$\text{p-value} = \text{Pr } (S \geq 4) = .344 \approx 34\%$$

16-3

		a.	**b.**	**c.**
B	S	B $\overset{?}{\gtrless}$ 66	S $\overset{?}{\gtrless}$ 63	B-S $\overset{?}{\gtrless}$ 0
65	63		tie,omit	√
67	62	√		√
69	64	√	√	√
70	65	√	√	√
71	68	√	√	√
73	66	√	√	√
76	71	√	√	√
77	69	√	√	√
		S=7	S=6	S=8
		(n=8)	(n=7)	(n=8)

From Table IIIc, with π = .50:

a. n = 8, Pr $(S \geq 7)$ = .035
b. n = 7 (because of tie), Pr$(S \geq 6)$ = .062
c. n = 8, Pr$(S \geq 8)$ = .004

16-5 This confidence interval goes from the very smallest to the very largest measurement. Using an argument like Figure 16-3c, we see that it will miss its target if all 6 observations are above ν. The chance of this is found from Table IIIc, with n = 6 and π = .50:

$$\text{Pr } (S \geq 6) = .016$$

There is an equal chance of missing the target when all 6 observations are below ν, and the chance of being right is the complement:

$$1.00 - 2 \,(.016) = .968 \approx 97\%$$

16-7 a.

(i)			(ii)	(iii)
B	S	B-S	ordered S	ordered B-S
65	63	2	62	2
67	62	5	63	3
69	64	5	64	5
70	65	5	65	5
71	68	3	66	5
73	66	7	68	5
76	71	5	69	7
77	69	8	71	8

From the ordered data above,

(i)   67 < ν < 76   **(ii)**   63 < ν < 69   **(iii)**   3 < ν < 7

134

b. Using an argument like Figure 16-3c, we see that the confidence interval will miss its target if 7 (or more) of the 8 observations are above ν. The chance of this is found from Table IIIc, with n = 8 and π = .50:

$$Pr\ (S \geq 7) = .035$$

There is an equal chance of missing the target when 7 (or more) observations are below it, and the chance of being right is the complement:

$$1.00 - 2(.035) = .930 = 93\%$$

16-9 a. Men's height, like many other biological measurements, is approximately normally distributed.

b. When the distribution is normal, the classical CI based on t is shortest, on average. We therefore would expect the nonparametric CI to be wider.

c. For men's height, our calculator gives $\overline{X}$ = 71.0 and s = 4.17. The 93% CI (leaving 3 1/2% error in each tail) is therefore:

$$\mu = \overline{X} \pm t_{.035}\ \frac{s}{\sqrt{n}} \qquad\qquad \text{like (8-11)}$$

$$= 71.0 \pm 2.14\ \frac{(4.17)}{\sqrt{8}}\ = 71.0 \pm 3.2$$

That is, $\qquad\qquad 67.8 < \mu < 74.2$

The nonparametric CI for ν in Problem 16-7(a) was $67 \leq \nu \leq 76$, which was indeed wider.

16-11 a. We estimate the population median ν with the sample median $\overset{\shortmid}{X}$ = 15.

b. The interval is $X_{(6)} \leq \nu \leq X_{(20)}$, and we follow the same logic as Figure 16-3c. We see that the confidence interval will miss its target if 20 (or more) of the 25 observations are above ν. The chance of this is found from the binomial, with n = 25 and π = .50. Since this exceeds Table IIIc, we use the normal approximation (6-12):

$$Z = \frac{P - \pi}{\sqrt{\dfrac{\pi(1-\pi)}{n}}} \qquad\qquad \text{like (6-13)}$$

$$= \frac{20/25 - .50}{\sqrt{\dfrac{.50(.50)}{25}}} = 3.00$$

$$Pr(Z \geq 3.00) = .001$$

There is an equal chance of missing the target when 20 or more observations are <u>below</u> ν, and the chance of being right is the complement:

$$1.00 - 2(.001) = .998 = 99.8\%$$
(wcc, critical P = 19.5/25, Z = 2.80, Pr = .003, and confidence = .994)

c. As the hint suggests, we will work our way backwards, starting out with the specification:

confidence level = 1.00 -2 (one tailed error) = .95
one-tailed error = .025
From Table IV, Z = 1.96
That is,

$$\frac{P-\pi}{\sqrt{\frac{\pi(1-\pi)}{n}}} = 1.96$$

$$\frac{P-.50}{\sqrt{\frac{.50(.50)}{25}}} = 1.96$$

$$P = .696$$

A proportion P = .696 corresponds to how many observations out of n = 25?

$$.696 \times 25 = 17.4 \approx 17$$

So the confidence interval should be

$$X_{(9)} \le \nu \le X_{(17)}$$
$$12 \le \nu \le 19$$

For the continuity correction, we note in part (b) that P = 19.5/25 corresponds to using $X_{(20)}$. From 19.5 to 20 we moved up .5. Similarly then, P = 17.4/25 corresponds to using $X_{(17.9)}$, which is a lot closer to $X_{(18)}$ than $X_{(17)}$. So the 95% confidence interval (wcc) is closer to

$$X_{(8)} \le \nu \le X_{(18)}$$
$$10 \le \nu \le 23$$

16-13 According to (16-9), we are to look for the smaller sample (the men, with $n_1 = 4$) and start ranking at the end where they are concentrated (the bottom of the table):

| Combined Ordered Incomes | | Combined Ranks | |
men	women	men	women
	14		10
	18		9
	25		8
	36		7
38		6	
	45		5
46		4	
	48		3
52			
77		2	
		1	
$n_1 = 4$	$n_2 = 6$	W = 13	

From Table VIII, we look up W = 13 where $n_1 = 4$, $n_2 = 6$, and find:

$$\text{p-value} = .033$$

16-15 According to (16-9), we are to look for the smaller sample (the make A, with $n_1 = 5$) and start ranking at the end where they are concentrated (the bottom of the table):

Combined Ordered Mileages		Combined Ranks	
A	B	A	B
	22		13
	26		12
30	30	$10\frac{1}{2}$	$10\frac{1}{2}$
	32		9
	36		8
	39		7
41	41,41	5	5,5
48		3	
49		2	
61		1	
$n_1 = 5$	$n_2 = 8$	$W = 21.5$	

In Table VIII, we look up W = 21 and 22, and find the p-value = .023 and .033. Splitting the difference gives

$$\text{p-value} \approx .028$$

16-17 Our calculator gives $\overline{X}_1 = 4.5$, $\Sigma(X_1 - \overline{X}_1)^2 = 41.0$, and $\overline{X}_2 = 6.17$, $\Sigma(X_2 - \overline{X}_2)^2 = 34.8$.

$$t = \frac{\text{estimate}}{SE} = \frac{\overline{X}_1 - \overline{X}_2}{SE} \qquad (9\text{-}17)$$

$$= \frac{\overline{X}_1 - \overline{X}_2}{s_p \sqrt{\frac{1}{n_1} + \frac{1}{n_2}}} \qquad \text{like } (8\text{-}20)$$

$$= \frac{4.5 - 6.17}{\sqrt{\frac{41.0 + 34.8}{3 + 5}} \sqrt{\frac{1}{4} + \frac{1}{6}}} = \frac{-1.67}{1.99} = -.84$$

We scan Table V along the row where d.f. = 8, and find that the observed t-value of magnitude .84 lies beyond the first tabulated value $t_{.25} = .71$. Thus
$$\text{p-value} < .25$$

This p-value agrees pretty well with the earlier p-value of .24 found in (16-8).

16-19 b. Our calculator gives $\overline{D} = 3.62$ and $s_D = 3.75$. Thus

$$t = \frac{\text{estimate}}{SE} = \frac{\overline{D}}{SE} \qquad (9\text{-}19)$$

$$= \frac{\overline{D}}{s_D/\sqrt{n}} = \frac{3.62}{3.75/\sqrt{8}} = 2.73 \qquad \text{like } (8\text{-}24)$$

We scan Table I, along the row where d.f. = 7, and find the observed t of 2.73 lies beyond $t_{.025} = 2.36$. Thus
$$\text{p-value} < .025$$

c. This p-value is considerably sharper (smaller) than the earlier p-value of .145 found in the sign test (16-4). No surprise, since the rank test used more information than the earlier sign test. (This excellent performance is fairly typical of rank tests.)

16-21

	two samples	k samples
independent	Wilcoxon test for two independent samples	Kruskal-Wallis one-factor ANOVA
matched	Wilcoxon test for two paired samples	Friedman two-factor ANOVA

16-23 The ranks are treated just like X and Y values, for calculating the correlation coefficient r:

ranks		deviations		products		
X	Y	$x = X - \bar{X}$	$y = Y - \bar{Y}$	x^2	y^2	xy
6	5	2.5	1.5	6.25	2.25	3.75
4	3.5	.5	0	.25	0	0
2	1	-1.5	-2.5	2.25	6.25	3.75
3	2	-.5	-1.5	.25	2.25	.75
5	6	1.5	2.5	2.25	6.25	3.75
1	3.5	-2.5	0	6.25	0	0
3.5	3.5	0 ✓	0 ✓	17.5	17.0	12.00

$$r = \frac{\Sigma xy}{\sqrt{\Sigma x^2} \sqrt{\Sigma y^2}} = \frac{12.0}{\sqrt{17.5}\sqrt{17.0}} = .70 \qquad (15\text{-}2)$$

From Figure 15-4, the 95% confidence interval is formed by interpolating the bands for n = 5 and n = 7:

$$-.24 < \rho < +.95$$

Since this includes $\rho = 0$, it is not discernibly different from 0.

16-25 First of all, we must find the sample median: A simple tabulation gives $\overset{\downarrow}{X}$ = 51. Thus we can mark the observations as High or Low:

H	H	H	H	H		H	H /	L /	H	H /		L	L	L	L	L
67	63	58	79	62		55	56	50	57	55		43	47	23	31	38

L	L	L	L	L		*/	H	H /	L /	H
49	33	43	34	42		51	66	54	46	55

Thus R = 7, and to standardize it, we calculate its moments (remembering that after the median observation is deleted, "n" = 24):

$$E(R) \simeq \frac{n}{2} + 1 = \frac{24}{2} + 1 = 13 \qquad (16\text{-}12)$$

$$SE = \frac{\sqrt{n-1}}{2} = \frac{\sqrt{24-1}}{2} = 2.40$$

Thus $Z = \frac{R-\mu}{SE} = \frac{7-13}{2.40} = -2.50$

$$p\text{-value} = \Pr(Z \leq -2.50) = .006$$

For the continuity correction, use R = 7.5. Then Z = -2.29, and p-value = .011

16-27 a. For a normal population, according to Section 7-2, the most efficient estimator is $\bar{X} = 8.1$.

b. Because of possible outliers, the best estimate is $\bar{X}_{.25} = 7.9\%$, or perhaps $\overset{\shortmid}{X} = 8.0\%$.

c. Because of possible outliers, the best estimate is $\bar{X}_{.25} = 15.18$.

16-29 a.

$$\left.\begin{array}{l} 91 \\ 104 \\ 104 \leftarrow \overset{\shortmid}{X} = 104 \\ 108 \\ 140 \end{array}\right\} \quad \bar{X}_{.25} = \tfrac{1}{3}(104 + 104 + 108) \left.\begin{array}{l} \\ \\ \\ \\ \end{array}\right\} \bar{X} = \tfrac{1}{5}(547)$$

$$= 105.3 \qquad\qquad = 109.4$$

b.

c. $\overset{\shortmid}{X}$ happens to be closest to the target of 100.

16-31 $IQR = 108 - 104 = 4$

Thus $Z = \dfrac{X - \overset{\shortmid}{X}}{3(IQR)} = \dfrac{X - 104}{12}$ \hfill (16-15)

X	Z	$w(X)=(1-Z^2)^2$	$Xw(X)$
91	-1.08	0 ($\|Z\| > 1$)	0
104	0	1.00	104
104	0	1.00	104
108	.333	.79	85.32
104	3.0	0 ($\|Z\| > 1$)	
	$\Sigma w(X) = 2.79$		293.32

$$\bar{X}_b = \frac{\Sigma Xw(X)}{\Sigma w(X)} = \frac{293.32}{2.79} = 105.13 \qquad (16\text{-}16)$$

16-33
a. [NPS, <u>CS</u>] are based on averages, and therefore [<u>appropriate</u>, inappropriate] whenever a total is required.

b. [<u>NPS</u>, CS] are often based on medians or ranks.

c. [<u>NPS</u>, CS] are often easier to calculate, and sometimes called quick-and-dirty.

d. If you have prior knowledge that the distribution is normal, or nearly normal, you gain by exploiting this by using [NPS, <u>CS</u>].

e. [<u>NPS</u>, CS] are particularly useful for data that is ordered, for example from best to worst, without any actual numerical values.

f. [<u>NPS</u>, CS] are particularly appropriate when it is important for the actual level of confidence to equal the specified level of 95%, even when populations are very non-normal.

16-35 a. The simplest test is the sign test. Since S = 6 out of the 8 observations are above $\nu = 0$, we find from Table III c,

$$\text{Pr}(S \geq 6) = .145$$

Alternatively, we could get a more powerful test using the Wilcoxon matched-sample test (like Problem 16-19). The improvement in sales performance is shown on the graph, running from -8 up to +18. We temporarily ignore the signs, and rank them from smallest to largest. Then we put back the + and - signs, obtaining:

values ordered by size	signed ranks D
+2	+1
+3	+2.5
-3	-2.5
-8	-4
+9	+5
+10	+6
+12	+7
+18	+8

For the sample in the last column, our calculator gives $\bar{D}$ and $s_D = 4.43$. Then

$$t = \frac{\text{estimate}}{\text{SE}} = \frac{\bar{D}}{\text{SE}} \qquad (9\text{-}17)$$

$$= \frac{2.88}{4.43/\sqrt{8}} = 1.84 \qquad \text{like } (8\text{-}24)$$

We scan Table V, along the row where d.f. = 7, and find the observed t of 1.84 lies beyond $t_{.10} = 1.41$. Thus

$$p\text{-value} < .10$$

Incidentally, to be perfectly valid, this test requires the population to be symmetric about ν (the price paid for the sharper p-value).

b. Using the same logic as part (a), the sign test gives

$$\text{Pr}(S \geq 7) = .035$$

and the Wilcoxon test gives

values ordered by size	signed ranks D
+1	+1
-2	-2
+6	+3
+8	+4
+14	+5
+17	+6
+19	+7
+27	+8

$$t = \frac{\bar{D}}{s_D/\sqrt{n}} = \frac{4.0}{3.30/\sqrt{8}} = 3.43$$

140

Since $t_{.010} = 3.00$,

$$p\text{-value} < .01$$

c. For the Wilcoxon test, we can work graphically and informally:

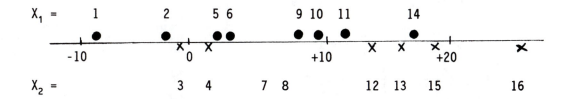

● = Program A

X = Program B

Proceeding as in Problem 16-17, we just use the two-sample t test (8-20) on the ranks. Our calculator gives $\bar{X}_1 = 7.25$, $\Sigma(X_1-\bar{X}_1)^2 = 143.5$, and $\bar{X}_2 = 9.75$, $\Sigma(X_2-\bar{X}_2)^2 = 171.5$. Thus

$$t = \frac{\text{estimate}}{SE} = \frac{\bar{X}_1 - \bar{X}_2}{s_P\sqrt{\frac{1}{n_1} + \frac{1}{n_2}}} \tag{9-17}$$

$$= \frac{7.25 - 9.75}{\sqrt{\frac{143.5 + 171.5}{7 + 7}}\sqrt{\frac{1}{8} + \frac{1}{8}}} = -1.05$$

From Table V, with df = 14, $t_{.25} = .68$. Thus

$$p\text{-value} < .25$$

16-37

RANK OF CHILD	①	2	③	④	⑤	6	⑦	⑧	9	⑩	11	12	13	14
Art Program	B	A	B	B	B	A	B	B	A	B	A	A	A	A

The null hypothesis is that education programs A and B are equally effective (in terms of the best painting they can bring out in a child.)

To calculate the p-value for H_0, we proceed as in Problem 16-17, using the two-sample t test on the ranks. For the first sample ($X_1 = 1,3,4,5,7,8$, and 10, the ranks circled above) our calculator gives $\bar{X}_1 = 5.43$, $\Sigma(X_1-\bar{X}_1)^2 = 57.7$. And for the second sample ($X_2 = 2,6, \ldots$, the remaining ranks above), $\bar{X}_2 = 9.57$, $\Sigma(X_2-\bar{X}_2)^2 = 109.7$. Thus

$$t = \frac{\text{estimate}}{SE} = \frac{\bar{X}_1 - \bar{X}_2}{s_P\sqrt{\frac{1}{n_1} + \frac{1}{n_2}}} \tag{9-17}$$

$$= \frac{5.43 - 9.57}{\sqrt{\frac{57.7 + 109.7}{6 + 6}}\sqrt{\frac{1}{7} + \frac{1}{7}}} = -2.07$$

From Table V, with df = 12, $t_{.05} = 1.78$. Thus

$$p\text{-value} < .05$$

141

16-39 a. To apply the runs test we first need the sample median: A simple tabulation gives $\tilde{X}$ = 29. Thus we can mark the observations as High or Low:

$$
\begin{array}{llll}
\text{H / L L L} & \text{L / H/ L L} & \text{L */ H H H} & \text{H H / L H} \\
33,26,28,24 & 28,34,28,23 & 27,29,31,32,35 & 30,32,26,31
\end{array}
$$

To standardize R = 7, we need the moments remembering that after the median observation is deleted, "n" = 16):

$$E(R) = \frac{n}{2} + 1 = \frac{16}{2} + 1 = 9 \qquad\qquad (16\text{-}12)$$

$$SE \simeq \frac{\sqrt{n-1}}{2} = \frac{\sqrt{16-1}}{2} = 1.94$$

Thus $Z = \frac{R-\mu}{SE} = \frac{7-9}{1.94} = -1.03$

$$p\text{-value} = Pr(Z \le -1.03) = .152$$

For the continuity correction, we use R = 7.5. Then Z = -.77 and p-value = .221

b. Even before a formal test is made, there is no reason to expect a time series like this to be a random sample. And the formal test in part (a) does nothing to allay our fears that we have dependence. (The p-value for independence is only 16%, in a small sample). We therefore find it of questionable validity to proceed with a test for the median being ν = 33.

17-1 a.

period	0	π	$E = n\pi$	$0 - E$	$(0 - E)^2/E$
8-10	31	.25	40	- 9	2.02
10-12	30	.25	40	-10	2.50
1-3	41	.25	40	1	.03
3-5	58	.25	40	18	8.10

$$n = 160 \qquad\qquad 0 \checkmark \quad \chi^2 = 12.65$$

Referring to Table VII, with d.f. = 3, we find the observed χ^2 of 12.65 exceeds $\chi^2_{.01} = 11.3$.   Thus

$$\text{p-value} < .01$$

b.   Since p-value < .05, by (9-27) we reject H_0.

c.   95% CI:

$$\pi = P \pm 1.96\sqrt{\frac{P(1-P)}{n}} \qquad\qquad (8-27)$$

for first period, P = 31/160 = .194

and $\pi = .194 \pm 1.96\sqrt{\dfrac{.194\,(.806)}{160}} = .194 \pm .061$

Compare this with the null π = .25 if H_0 were true:

$$\frac{\text{true } \pi}{\text{null } \pi} = \frac{.194 \pm .061}{.25} = .78 \pm .24$$

For the other periods, we calculate similar confidence intervals, for the ratio of (actual accidents)/(expected accidents if H_0 true):

period	P	95% CI for ratio
8-10	.194	.78 ± .24
10-12	.188	.75 ± .24
1-3	.256	1.03 ± .27
3-5	.362	1.45 ± .30

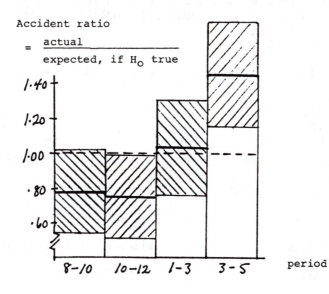

17-3 We shall show one typical simulation. And to make our work easy to follow, we shall start at the beginning of the random number Table I, rather than picking a random start. When we discard the digits 0, 7, 8 and 9, the tally is as follows.

Simulation			(a) Test			
face	tally	0	π	$E = n\pi$	0 - E	$(0 - E)^2/E$
1		4	1/6	5	-1	.2
2		4	1/6	5	-1	.2
3		3	1/6	5	-2	.8
4		5	1/6	5	0	0
5		5	1/6	5	0	0
6		9	1/6	5	4	3.2
		30 $\checkmark$		30 $\checkmark$	0 $\checkmark$	χ^2 = 4.4

Since the observed χ^2 = 4.4 falls short of the critical $\chi^2_{.25}$ = 6.63 (d.f. = 5),

$$\text{p-value} > .25$$

b. Since the p-value (credibility level) exceeds the 5% level, we do not reject H_0. (In this case, where H_0 is indeed true, this experiment happened to lead to the correct conclusion.)

c. In testing a fair die (or simulating it), the correct decision is to accept its fairness (H_0), and the erroneous decision is to reject H_0. This test was conducted at the 5% error level, i.e., the testing procedure will lead to an erroneous decision to reject H_0 5% of the time in the long-run--or about 5% of the time in a large classroom.

Or, to put it another way, suppose we made a frequency distribution of all the calculated values of χ^2 from the classroom--our own value (χ^2 = 4.4) plus several hundred more. What would this χ^2 distribution look like? Like the figure in Table VII. And by definition, the value $\chi^2_{.05}$ = 11.1 is exceeded 5% of the time. These are precisely the times when H_0 is rejected.

17-5 a. Since only the aces are in question, we shall "concentrate our fire" by counting the <u>proportion of aces</u> as the test statistic.

If we use the same random digits as in Problem 17-4 (line 10 of the random digits in Table I), the observed proportion of aces is

$$P = 9/30 = .30$$

To carry out the test calculations, we standardize this:

$$Z = \frac{P - \pi}{\sqrt{\frac{\pi(1 - \pi)}{n}}}$$

like (6-12) or
(9-16)

In testing H_0, we use the H_0 value $\pi = 1/6 \approx .17$, of course, and so

$$Z = \frac{.30 - .17}{\sqrt{\frac{.17(.83)}{30}}} = 1.90$$

To find the p-value, we look up the tail area in the normal distribution, Table IV:

$$\text{p-value} = .029 \approx 3\%$$

b. Since the p-value (credibility level) is less than the 5% level, we reject H_0. (In this case, where H_0 is in fact false, this experiment happened to lead to the correct decision).

c. This probability can be estimated by the relative frequency among the students who carried out the experiment in your class.

You will find that this proportion is considerably larger than in Problem 17-4, where the χ^2 test was used. That is, the Z test more often correctly detects when the null hypothesis is false. And this is the value of "concentrating our fire." The Z test is technically called a <u>more powerful</u> test than χ^2.

17-7 a. The null hypothesis is that education and occupation are independent, or equivalently, that all occupations have the same distribution of education.

b.

Observed frequencies O				Totals		P_j
194	146	27	10	377		.754
18	79	18	8	123		.246
totals						
212	225	45	18	500		
P_i						
.424	.450	.090	.036			1.00

Assuming independence, estimated joint probabilities,
$$P_{ij} = P_i P_j$$

.320	.339	.068	.027
.104	.111	.022	.009

Expected frequencies $E = n\, P_{ij}$

160	170	34	14
52	55	11	4

O-E

34	-24	-7	-4
-34	24	7	4

$(O-E)^2/E$

7.2	3.4	1.4	1.1
22.2	10.5	4.5	4.0

total, $\chi^2 = 54.3$

With less rounding, we would find $\chi^2 = 52.64 \simeq 53$. Since this observed χ^2 far exceeds the critical $\chi^2_{.001} = 16.3$ (with d.f. = 3),

p-value $\ll$ .001

Of course, the computer can do χ^2 calculations very easily with a standard program. Here is the MINITAB version for this Problem, for example:

```
EXPECTED COUNTS ARE PRINTED BELOW OBSERVED COUNTS

           C1       C2       C3       C4     TOTAL
    1     194      146       27       10       377
        159.85   169.65    33.93    13.57

    2      18       79       18        8
         52.15    55.35    11.07     4.43

TOTAL    212      225       45       18       500

CHISQ =  7.297 +  3.297 +  1.415 +  0.940 +
        22.365 + 10.105 +  4.338 +  2.881 = 52.639
DF = 3
1 CELLS WITH EXPECTED COUNTS LESS THAN 5.0
```

c.   95% CI:

$$\pi = P \pm 1.96 \sqrt{\frac{P(1-P)}{n}}$$

For white collar workers, the proportion of better educated workers is P = 194/212 = .915. Thus

$$\pi = .915 \pm 1.96 \sqrt{\frac{.915(.085)}{212}} = .915 \pm .038$$

Similarly we obtain confidence intervals for the other occupations, obtaining:

Occupation	95% CI for proportion who are better educated
white collar	.915 ± .038
blue collar	.649 ± .062
services	.600 ± .143
farm work	.556 ± .230

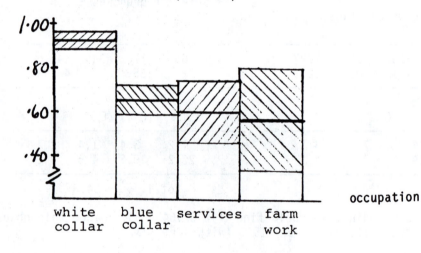

proportion who are
better educated (95% CI)

17-9 a.

	farm	small urban	urban
survival rate =	$\frac{287}{305}$ = .941	$\frac{1124}{1213}$ = .927	$\frac{2081}{2346}$ = .887

146

b. H_0: Survival rate is independent of residence. To test this, here is the MINITAB output:

```
EXPECTED COUNTS ARE PRINTED BELOW OBSERVED COUNTS

              C1       C2       C3    TOTAL
     1       287     1124     2081     3492
          275.64  1096.22  2120.14

     2        18       89      265      372
           29.36   116.78   225.86

  TOTAL      305     1213     2346     3864

CHISQ =    0.468 +   0.704 +   0.723 +
           4.398 +   6.608 +   6.784 = 19.685
  DF = 2
```

Referring to Table VII, with d.f. = 2, we find the observed x^2 of 19.7 exceeds $x^2_{.001}$ = 13.8. Thus

$$p\text{-value} < .001$$

c. Since p-value < 5% we reject H_0, according to (9-27).

17-11 a. The null hypothesis to be tested is that newspaper and social class are independent; or equivalently, that all newspapers have the same class of reader.

b.

	Observed O			Totals	P_j
	31	11	12	54	.18
	49	59	51	159	.53
	18	26	31	75	.25
	2	4	6	12	.04
totals	100	100	100	300 ✓	1.00
P_i	.333	.333	.333	1.00 ✓	

If independent, $P_{ij} = P_i P_j$			Expected $E = n\, P_{ij}$		
.060	.060	.060	18	18	18
.177	.177	.177	53	53	53
.083	.083	.083	25	25	25
.013	.013	.013	4	4	4

(O-E)			$(O-E)^2/E$		
13	-7	-6	9.4	2.7	2.0
-4	6	-2	.3	.7	.1
-7	1	6	2.0	.0	1.4
-2	0	2	1.0	0	1.0

$$x^2 = 20.6$$

Since the observed x^2 of 20.6 exceeds $x^2_{.005}$ = 18.5 (with d.f. = 2 x 3 = 6),

$$p\text{-value} < .005$$

Since p > .001, we cannot reject H_0 at the .001 level according to (9-27). We conclude that the newspapers are not discernibly different (at this very stringent level of .001).

17-13 a. The null hypothesis to be tested is that type of degree and sex are independent, or equivalently, the proportion of women is the same for all degrees.

b. Here is the MINITAB output that finds $\chi^2 = 3.25$:

```
        EXPECTED COUNTS ARE PRINTED BELOW OBSERVED COUNTS

                  C1        C2        C3      TOTAL
          1       534       144        22       700
                537.16    145.94     16.90

          2       515       141        11       667
                511.84    139.06     16.10

     TOTAL       1049       285        33      1367

     CHISQ =   0.019 +   0.026 +   1.540 +
               0.020 +   0.027 +   1.616 = 3.248
     DF = 2
```

Since d.f = 2, we scan the second row of Table VII. Since the observed χ^2 of 3.25 approximately exceeds $\chi^2_{.25} = 2.77$,

p-value < .25

c. The sample proportion of the Bachelor degrees granted to women is

$$P = \frac{515}{1049} = .491$$

Thus, the population proportion π has the 95% confidence interval:

$$\pi = P \pm 1.96 \sqrt{\frac{P(1-P)}{n}} \qquad\qquad (8\text{-}27)$$

$$= .491 \pm 1.96 \sqrt{\frac{(.491)(.508)}{910}} = .491 \pm .030$$

That is, the proportion who are women

among BA's	= 49% ± 3%	
Similarly, among MA's	= 49% ± 6%	
among PhD's	= 33% ± 16%	

A graph of these three CI shows more clearly than χ^2 just how degree depends upon sex: the PhD degree has relatively few women.

17-15 Here is the MINITAB output that finds $\chi^2 = 14.0$:

EXPECTED COUNTS ARE PRINTED BELOW OBSERVED COUNTS

	C1	C2	C3	C4	TOTAL
1	112	105	154	113	484
	121.00	121.00	121.00	121.00	
2	888	895	846	887	3516
	879.00	879.00	879.00	879.00	
TOTAL	1000	1000	1000	1000	4000

CHISQ = 0.669 + 2.116 + 9.000 + 0.529 +
           0.092 + 0.291 + 1.239 + 0.073 = 14.009

DF = 3

Since the observed χ^2 of 14.0 exceeds $\chi^2_{.005} = 12.8$ (with d.f. = 3),

$$p\text{-value} < .005$$

18-1 a.

$$L(\pi) = \binom{n}{s} \pi^s (1-\pi)^{n-s} = \binom{8}{2}\pi^2(1-\pi)^6 \tag{18-2}$$

Rather than calculating $L(\pi)$, it is easier to read it from Table IIIb, with n = 8 and s = 2. Reading across, we obtain (to 2 decimals):

π	.1	.2	.3	.4	.5	.6	.7	.8	.9
$L(\pi)$	.15	.29	.30	.21	.11	.04	.01	.00	.00

When $\pi = 0$ or 1, substituting into (18-2) easily shows that $L(\pi) = 0$. Thus, the graph is:

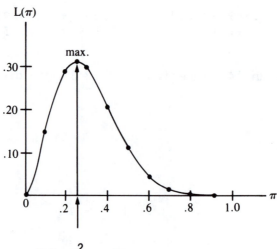

$$\text{MLE} = \frac{2}{8} = .25$$

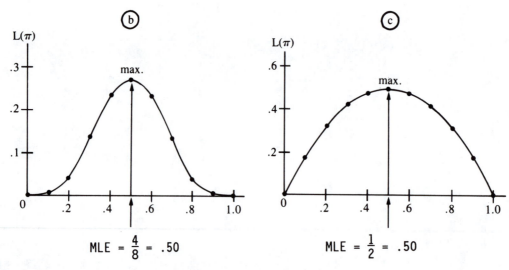

$$\text{MLE} = \frac{4}{8} = .50 \qquad \qquad \text{MLE} = \frac{1}{2} = .50$$

d.

$$L(\pi) = \binom{n}{s}\pi^s(1-\pi)^{n-s} = \binom{2}{0}\pi^0(1-\pi)^2 = (1-\pi)^2$$

In this case, when $\pi = 0$, we have $L(\pi) = 1$. When $\pi = 1$, we have $L(\pi) = 0$, as usual. The rest of the values are read across Table IIIb, of course, and so the graph is:

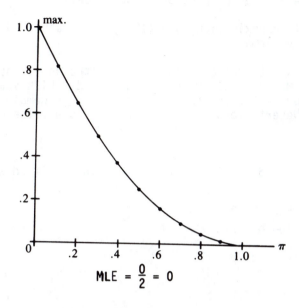

$$\text{MLE} = \frac{0}{2} = 0$$

18-3 In all cases, the MLE and MME are the same -- the familiar estimate already studied earlier in the text.

a. $\bar{X} = \dfrac{17 + 28 + 92 + 41}{4} = 44.5$

b. $P = \dfrac{8}{20} = .40$

c. $b = \dfrac{\Sigma xy}{\Sigma x^2} = \dfrac{\Sigma(X-\bar{X})(Y-\bar{Y})}{\Sigma(X-\bar{X})^2} = \dfrac{45}{180} = .25$

18-5 a. MME was closer -- just the luck of the draw.

b. With more and more simulations, it can be shown using statistical theory that the sampling distributions get closer and closer to the following probability distributions:

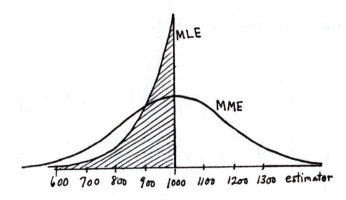

As we saw in part (a), occasionally the MME is closer. Yet on the whole, the graphs show MLE is closer. If we used some appropriate criterion such as MSE (mean squared error), we could express precisely how much closer (as in Problem 18-6d).

18-7   b does indeed satisfy these three properties. Specifically,

    (i),(iii)   By the normal approximation rule (12-4), b is unbiased and asymptotically normal.

    (ii)   Efficiency was not proved in this text, although it was hinted at in the Gauss-Markov theorem in Appendix 12-2 (which stated only that b was more efficient than any other <u>linear</u> combination of the Y values). Nevertheless, advanced texts do prove the efficiency of b.

18-9 a.   It is easiest if we first find the log of the given probability distribution (as in Example 18-2):

$$\log p(X|\theta) = \log(\theta\, e^{-\theta X})$$
$$= \log \theta - \theta X$$

Thus the log likelihood is just

$$\mathcal{L}(\theta) = \sum_{i=1}^{n} (\log \theta - \theta X_i) \tag{18-10}$$
$$= n \log \theta - \theta \Sigma X_i$$

We evaluate this at $\theta = .1$, for example:

$$\mathcal{L}(.1) = 5 \log(.1) - .1(15)$$
$$= 5(-2.303) - .1(15.0) = -13.0$$

Similarly, for $\theta = .2, .3, .4, .5$, we find $\mathcal{L}(\theta) = -11.0, -10.5, -10.6, -11.0$.

b. $\mathcal{L}(\theta)$ has a peak value of about -10.5 (all other values are more negative, and hence lower) at $\theta = .3$. A more detailed grid of values would show $\mathcal{L}(\theta)$ peaking at $\theta = .33$, as you can verify. That is,

$$\text{MLE} \simeq .33 \simeq .3$$

c.   Since $\theta = 1/\mu$, it is not surprising to find

$$\text{MLE of } \theta = 1/\overline{X} \quad (= 1/3.0 = .33 \text{ in this case})$$

This can be proved to be true, in general.

18-11 a.   The MME of the population mean of course is the sample mean $\overline{X}$. For a normal population, in (18-6) we stated that the MLE of μ is $\overline{X}$. In this case, $\overline{X} = 4.25$.

b.   The MME of π is P (Since π and P are just disguised means, or first moments). And in (18-5), we stated the MLE of π is P also. In this case, $P = 2/6 = 33\%$.

c.   The MME of N is given by $N = 2\overline{X} - 1$ (18-1)

$$= 2 \left(\frac{37 + 16 + 44 + 43 + 22}{5}\right) - 1 = 64$$

The MLE of N is given by

$$\text{largest observation} = 44 \tag{18-8}$$

This is likelier to be close to N.   That is, MLE has smaller MSE as we saw in Problem 18-6(d).

d.   Total = 310 x average
           So it is a question of how to estimate the population average μ.   Both the MME and MLE is:

$$\bar{X} = \frac{22 + 21 + \ldots + 27}{10} = 21.4$$

Thus total $\simeq$ 310 x 21.4 = 6,634

19-1 a. This is very similar to Example 19-2.

$$\text{posterior odds} = \text{prior odds} \times \text{likelihood ratio} \qquad (19\text{-}6)$$

Since 620 in every 100,000 children have the disease, 99,380 do not, and so the prior odds for the disease are 620/99,380 = .00624.
For the + reaction, the likelihood ratio is

$$\frac{\text{Pr}(+|\text{diseased})}{\text{Pr}(+|\text{healthy})} = \frac{495/500}{50/2000} = 39.6$$

We substitute these two quantities into the crucial equation (19-6) above:

$$\text{posterior odds} = .00624 \times 39.6 = .247 \simeq .24$$

To convert to probability,

$$\text{posterior prob.} = \frac{\text{odds}}{\text{odds} + 1} \qquad (19\text{-}3)$$

$$= \frac{.247}{1.247} = .198 \simeq 20\%$$

b. The likelihood ratio is now different, because the data is now a − reaction:

$$\frac{\text{Pr}(-|\text{diseased})}{\text{Pr}(-|\text{healthy})} = \frac{5/500}{1950/2000} = .0103$$

$$\text{posterior odds} = .00624 \times .0103 = .000064$$

$$\text{posterior prob.} = \frac{.000064}{1.000064} = .000064$$

c. With no error at all, the probabilities would be the ideal values of 1.00 and 0, respectively.

19-3 a. The prior probabilities, .10, .40, .50.

b. Since there are more than two machines, it is awkward to use odds. So we will just use Bayes' Theorem (Tree reversal) as in Example 19-1:

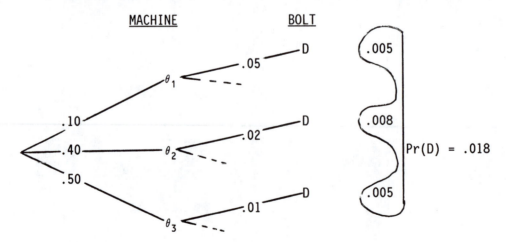

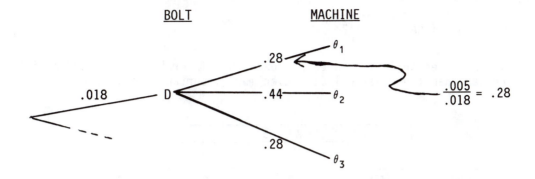

BOLT   MACHINE

$$\frac{.005}{.018} = .28$$

Alternatively, we could use a "Venn Diagram" like Figure 19-1:

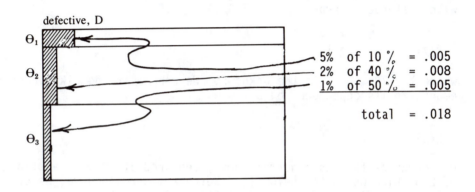

defective, D

5% of 10% = .005
2% of 40% = .008
1% of 50% = .005

total = .018

$$Pr\,(\theta_1|D) = \frac{.005}{.018} = .28, \text{ etc.}$$

19-5 **a.** **(i)** Based on more information, we expect the confidence interval to be narrower.

    (ii) Since the quasi-sample size $n_q = 5$ is relatively small, the Bayesian confidence interval will be little different from the classical confidence interval that ignores the quasi-sample entirely.

 b. $S^* = 1 + 30 + 1 = 32$

                       (19-17)

     $F^* = 4 + 20 + 1 = 25$

 Thus $n^* = 57$

                         (19-18)

 and $P^* = 32/57 = .56$

Thus the Bayesian 95% CI is

$$\pi = P^* \pm 1.96 \sqrt{\frac{P^*(1-P^*)}{n^*}} \qquad\qquad (19\text{-}19)$$

$$= .56 \pm 1.96 \sqrt{\frac{.56(.44)}{57}} = .56 \pm .13$$

Compare to the classical CI, using $P = 30/50 = .60$ and $n = 50$:

$$\pi = .60 \pm 1.96 \sqrt{\frac{.60\,(.40)}{50}} = .60 \pm .14 \qquad (8\text{-}29)$$

Thus the Bayesian CI is indeed narrower than in Problem 19-4, and a little narrower than the classical CI. Even more important, it is centered better:

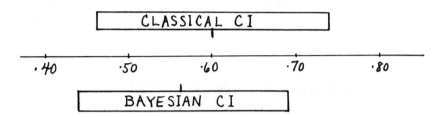

19-7 **a.** What is the likelihood of getting $\bar{X} = 70$? The distribution of $\bar{X}$ is normal, with a standard error $\sigma/\sqrt{n} = 17.3/\sqrt{48} = 2.5$. Thus

$$p(\bar{X}|\mu) \;\propto\; e^{-\frac{1}{2}\left(\frac{\bar{X}-\mu}{2.5}\right)^2} \qquad \text{like (19-20)}$$

where $\bar{X} = 70$, and μ is the unknown. We rename it the likelihood function to emphasize its dependence on μ:

$$L(\mu) \;\propto\; e^{-\frac{1}{2}\left(\frac{\mu-70}{2.5}\right)^2}$$

We recognize this as a normal curve, centered at 70 with a standard deviation of 2.5 which we sketch below (to sketch any normal curve, we draw about 2/3 of its area within one standard deviation of its center.)

b. The likelihood function is a maximum at $\bar{X} = 70$, which is called the maximum likelihood estimate (MLE).

c. The posterior distribution is normal, with its moments found as follows:

$$n_o = \frac{\sigma^2}{\sigma_o^2} = \frac{17.3^2}{10^2} = 3 \qquad (19\text{-}22)$$

$$\text{posterior mean} = \frac{n_o\mu_o + n\bar{X}}{n_o + n} \qquad (19\text{-}23)$$

$$= \frac{3(60) + 48(70)}{3 + 48} = 69.4$$

$$\text{posterior SE} = \frac{\sigma}{\sqrt{n_o + n}} = \frac{17.3}{\sqrt{3 + 48}} = 2.4 \qquad (19\text{-}24)$$

This normal posterior is also sketched below.

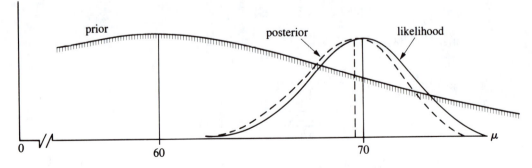

156

It lies between the prior and likelihood, but 16 times closer to the likelihood, because the sample size n = 48 is 16 times the quasi sample size n_o = 3.

d. Classical 95% CI:

$$\mu = \bar{X} \pm 1.96 \frac{\sigma}{\sqrt{n}} = 70 \pm 1.96 \ (2.5) \qquad \text{like (8-9)}$$

$$= 70.0 \pm 4.9$$

Bayesian 95% CI:

$$\mu = 69.4 \pm 1.96(2.4) \qquad \text{like (19-27)}$$
$$= 69.4 \pm 4.7$$

Note that the Bayes CI is very close to the classical CI, because the quasi-sample size n_o = 3 is very small relative to the sample size n = 48.

19-9 False: The Bayesian confidence interval is very similar to the classical when n is <u>large</u>. It is only when n grows <u>small</u> that the Bayesian confidence interval shows its real superiority to the classical.

19-11 a. In this problem, the unknown parameter is denoted by m instead of the usual μ. And everything is measured in %.

$$\mu_o = 15 \qquad\qquad \bar{X} = 13.8$$

$$\sigma_o = .5 \qquad\qquad \sigma = 1/5 = .2$$

$$n = 1$$

Hence $n_o = \dfrac{\sigma^2}{\sigma_o^2} = \dfrac{.2^2}{.5^2} = .16 \qquad (19\text{-}22)$

$$\mu = \frac{n_o\mu_o + n\bar{X}}{n_o + n} \pm 1.96 \frac{\sigma}{\sqrt{n_o + n}} \qquad (19\text{-}27)$$

$$= \frac{.16(15) + 1 \ (13.8)}{.16 + 1} \pm 1.96 \frac{.2}{\sqrt{.16 + 1}}$$

$$= 13.97 \pm 1.96(.186) = 13.97 \pm .36$$

b. We standardize the critical value of 14%, using the posterior mean and standard deviation (13.97 and .186) found in part (a):

$$Z = \frac{14 - 13.97}{.186} = .16$$

$$Pr \ (m < 14) = Pr \ (Z < .16)$$

$$= 1 - .436 = .564$$

19-13 a.

$$BE(\mu_1) = \frac{1}{F} \bar{\bar{X}} + (1 - \frac{1}{F}) \ \bar{X}_1 \qquad (19\text{-}35)$$

$$= (\frac{1}{8.3}) \ 52 + (1 - \frac{1}{8.3}) \ 49$$

157

$$= (.12)52 + (.88)49$$

$$= 49.36 \simeq 49.4$$

Similarly,

$$BE(\mu_2) = (.12)52 \pm (.88)56 = 55.52 \simeq 55.5$$

$$BE(\mu_3) = (.12)52 \pm (.88)51 = 51.12 \simeq 51.1$$

b.

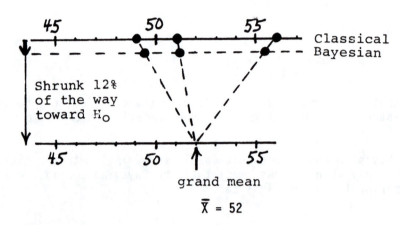

Shrunk 12% of the way toward H_0

Classical
Bayesian

grand mean
$\overline{\overline{X}} = 52$

c. (i) The graph in Figure 19-7 shows more shrinkage toward H_0.

(ii) Figure 19-7 also has more evidence that H_0 is true (larger p-value, from a smaller F).

19-15   To shrink, we first need F:

$$F = (\frac{b}{SE})^2 \qquad\qquad (19\text{-}38)$$

$$= (\frac{.024}{.010})^2 = 5.76$$

Thus Bayesian estimate $= (1 - \frac{1}{F})b$ $\qquad\qquad (19\text{-}37)$

$$= (1 - \frac{1}{5.76}) \quad (.024) = .020$$

19-17 a.

X_1	X_2	$D = X_2 - X_1$
73	79	6
61	67	6
60	68	8
70	75	5
76	81	5

Our calculator gives $\bar{D} = 6.0$ and $s_D = 1.225$. Thus the SE of $\bar{D}$ is:

$$SE = \frac{s_D}{\sqrt{n}} = \frac{1.225}{\sqrt{5}} = .548 \qquad\qquad \text{like (8-24)}$$

158

For the shrinkage estimate, we first need F:

$$F = t^2 \qquad\qquad\qquad\qquad \text{like (19-38)}$$

$$= \left(\frac{\text{estimate}}{SE}\right)^2 = \left(\frac{6.0}{.548}\right)^2 = 120 \qquad\qquad \text{like (9-17)}$$

$$\text{Thus Bayesian estimate} = \left(1 - \frac{1}{F}\right)\bar{b} \qquad\qquad \text{like (19-37)}$$

$$= \left(1 - \frac{1}{120}\right)6.0 = 5.95$$

For this Bayesian estimate, we assumed that before we collected the sample, the population improvement was about as likely to be negative as positive.

19-19 a.

	Red	White	Total	Comments
Peter	4	1	5	overwhelmingly red!
Paul	12	8	20	Not far from 50-50

Most people guess that Peter has the more decisive sample, that is, should feel more confident that he has the "largely red urn".

b. posterior odds = prior odds × likelihood $\qquad\qquad$ (19-6)

(i) We would get the same conclusion no matter what prior odds we used, so we will just use the given prior odds of 1/1 because they are reasonable, and simplify the arithmetic.

The likelihood ratio is

$$\frac{\text{Pr(1 red chip} \mid \text{"largely red urn")}}{\text{Pr(1 red chip} \mid \text{"largely white urn")}} = \frac{2/3}{1/3} = 2$$

Thus posterior odds $= \frac{1}{1} \times 2 = 2$

$\qquad\qquad$ = simply the likelihood ratio.

(ii) Again, the posterior odds will simply equal the likelihood ratio, which is now:

$$\text{L.R.} = \frac{\text{Pr(4 red chips} \mid \text{"largely red urn")}}{\text{Pr(4 red chips} \mid \text{"largely white urn")}} = \frac{(2/3)^4}{(1/3)^4} = 2^4 = 16$$

(iii) For the probability of drawing 4 red and 1 white, we use the binomial distribution (4-8):

$$\text{Peter's L.R.} = \frac{\binom{5}{4}\left(\frac{2}{3}\right)^4\left(\frac{1}{3}\right)^1}{\binom{5}{4}\left(\frac{1}{3}\right)^4\left(\frac{2}{3}\right)^1}$$

$$= \left(\frac{2}{1}\right)^4\left(\frac{1}{2}\right)^1 = 2^{4-1} = 8$$

(iv) $\qquad \text{Paul's L.R.} = \frac{\binom{20}{12}\left(\frac{2}{3}\right)^{12}\left(\frac{1}{3}\right)^8}{\binom{20}{12}\left(\frac{1}{3}\right)^{12}\left(\frac{2}{3}\right)^8} = \left(\frac{2}{1}\right)^{12}\left(\frac{1}{2}\right)^8 = 2^{12-8} = 16$

Note that Paul, not Peter, has the stronger evidence for a "largely red urn".

c. To generalize part (b), we can write out the full binomial probabilities:

$$\text{L.R.} = \frac{\binom{r+w}{r}\left(\frac{2}{3}\right)^r\left(\frac{1}{3}\right)^w}{\binom{r+w}{r}\left(\frac{1}{3}\right)^r\left(\frac{2}{3}\right)^w} = \left(\frac{2}{1}\right)^r\left(\frac{1}{2}\right)^w = 2^{r-w}$$

Or, we could just guess the pattern from part b(iv): Instead of 2^{12-8}, we have 2^{r-w}. In any case, we note that the L.R. (and hence the posterior odds) depends only on (ii), the excess number of red chips.

Remarks: This result is so contrary to our intuition in part (a) that it is worthwhile giving a simple explanation that will help to retrain our intuition:

It doesn't make any difference what order the chips are drawn. (This is formerly called "exchangeability"). For simplicity, therefore, let us imagine that Paul drew all 8 white chips first, then 8 red chips, and then paused. At this point, his evidence is completely useless --- it points equally strongly to both urns, and so leaves the prior odds unchanged. But then Paul goes on to gather the evidence that does matter -- the excess 4 red chips.

Peter's evidence is similarly analyzed. After the 1 white and 1 red chip, he is nowhere. But then Peter goes on to gather 3 excess red chips. But this isn't as strong evidence as Paul's excess 4 red chips!

19-21 a.

$$\mu = \overline{X} + t_{.025}\frac{s}{\sqrt{n}} \tag{8-11}$$

$$= 115 \pm 1.99\,\frac{21}{\sqrt{100}}$$

$$= 115 \pm 4.2$$

b. Each is making a correct inference from his or her available knowledge. It's just that Dr. B knows more. Once she informs C of the prior expert opinion, he might agree with her.

c.

$$n_o = \frac{\sigma^2}{\sigma_o^2} \simeq \frac{s^2}{\sigma_o^2} \qquad\qquad \text{like (19-22)}$$

$$= \frac{21^2}{3^2} = 49$$

$$\mu = \left(\frac{n_o\mu_o + n\overline{X}}{n_o + n}\right) \pm t_{.025}\frac{s}{\sqrt{n_o + n}} \qquad\qquad \text{like (19-27)}$$

$$= \frac{49(121) + 100(115)}{49 + 100} \pm 1.98\,\frac{21}{\sqrt{49 + 100}}$$

$$= 117.0 + 3.4$$

d. The overall mean is:

$$\overline{X} = \frac{n_2\overline{X}_2 + n_1\overline{X}_1}{n_2 + n_1} \qquad\qquad \begin{array}{l}\text{(2-7) repeated}\\ \text{like (19-27)}\end{array}$$

$$= \frac{50\,(121) + 100\,(115)}{50 + 100} = 117.0$$

$$\mu = \overline{X} \pm t_{.025}\frac{s}{\sqrt{n}} \tag{8-11}$$

$$= 117.0 \pm 1.98\,\frac{21}{\sqrt{150}} = 117.0 \pm 3.4$$

e. The estimates and confidence intervals in parts (c) and (d) are practically the same. Thus we see the prior was indeed equivalent to 50 observations (which is why we call it the "quasi-sample").

20-1

    a. Bayesian decision theory is a technique for making the best decision. By "best," we mean the one that [protects us from bad luck the best, exploits possible good luck the best, <u>weighs both good and bad luck in order to maximize expected profit</u>].

    b. When no current data are yet available for the states of nature, their prior probabilities alone [<u>can still</u>, cannot] be used to make a decision. When current data become available, then we can calculate the [prior, <u>posterior</u>, minimal] probabilities using [minimum expected loss, maximum expected profit, <u>Bayes Theorem</u>].

20-3 a.

$p(\theta)$	θ		a_1	a_2	a_3
.20	rain, θ_1		50	30	5
.80	shine, θ_2		15	30	35
average loss $L(a)$			22	30	29

minimum, best action is a_1

    b.   For the posterior probabilities, we apply Bayes Theorem:

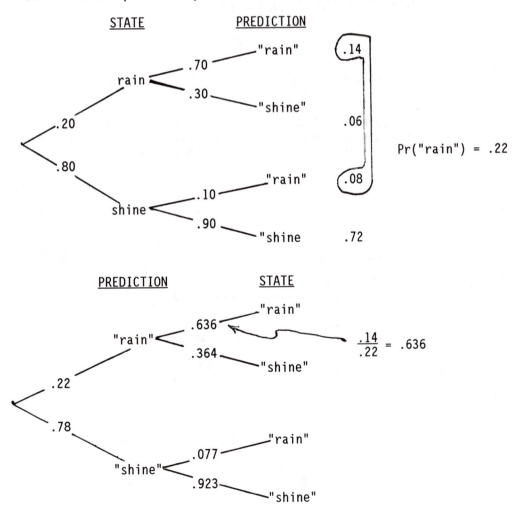

$$Pr("rain") = .22$$

$$\frac{.14}{.22} = .636$$

And so the decision becomes:

p(θ|"rain")	θ	a_1	a_2	a_3	p(θ|"shine")	θ	a_1	a_2	a_3
.636	θ_1	50	30	5	.077	θ_1	50	30	5
.364	θ_2	15	30	35	.923	θ_2	15	30	35
ave. loss L(a)		37.3	30	15.9	ave. loss L (a)		17.7	30	32.7

          ↑   ↑

        minimum   minimum

c. False. If John must decide before the weather report, he should choose a_1, which he should also choose if the prediction is "shine." He should choose a_3 if the prediction is "rain." This is not obvious, and requires an analysis--Bayesian analysis--to be sure of.

d. To find out how much the prediction is worth, we compare his average loss without prediction [22 in part (a)] with his average loss with prediction, calculated as follows [using part (b)]:

    average loss = (average loss, given "rain") Pr ("rain")
        + (average loss, given "shine") Pr ("shine")
        = 15.9 (.22) + 17.7 (.78) = 17.3

  Thus EVSI = \$22 - \$17.30 = \$4.70

    ENGS = EVSI - cost of sampling
      = \$4.70 - \$2.50 = \$2.20

20-5 We could solve this with a Table like Example 20-3. However, it is easier to exploit what we have learned already about symmetrical loss functions. If θ is the weekly sale, and a its estimate, then the loss function may be written as

   $l(a,\theta) = \$.40 \; |a-\theta|$

According to Figure 20-3, the best estimate will therefore be the median of the distribution, found as follows:

sales	rel. frequency
20	.10
25	.30
30	.20
35	.10
40	.10
45	.10
50	.05
55	.05

           .40

           median

           .40

Thus he should order 30 papers each week.

20-7 We must first find the relevant posterior distribution, as in Chapter 19. We are given:

    $\mu_0 = 220$ $n = 5$
    $\sigma_0 = 15$ $\bar{X} = (230 + 245+...)/5 = 240$
            $\sigma = 10$

Thus $\quad n_o = \dfrac{\sigma^2}{\sigma_o^2} = \dfrac{10^2}{15^2} = .44$

$$\text{posterior mean} = \frac{n_o \mu_o + n\bar{X}}{n_o + n}$$

$$= \frac{.44(220) + 5(240)}{44 + 5} = 238.4$$

Thus the posterior distribution is normal, and centered at 238.4. Since each of the given loss functions in (a), (b), and (c) is symmetric, the best estimate in each case will be the center of this symmetric normal distribution (238.4).

For those who feel uneasy about such a short argument, one can give more detail (although it really isn't necessary):

(a) This loss function is

$$\ell(a,\theta) \; \alpha \; |a-\theta|$$

Hence, according to Figure 20-3, we should use the median. In a normal distribution, this coincides with the mean, which was found to be 238.4

(b) This loss function is

$$\ell(a,\theta) \; \alpha \; (a-\theta)^2$$

Hence, according to Figure 20-3, we should use the mean, which was found to be 238.4

(c) This loss function is the 0-1 loss function. Hence, according to Figure 20-3, the best estimate is the mode, which coincides with the mean at 238.4

20-9 **b.** To simplify the exposition, without reducing the force of the argument, suppose there were just 5 values of θ (rather than a large shipment of bars), distributed as follows:

optimal estimate = MEDIAN?

If the estimate a were built anywhere but the median, for example, moved to the right slightly, then

- three times (1, 2 and 3) the estimate a would be further away from θ_i
- two times (4 and 5) the estimate a would be closer, by the same amount.

Accordingly, there would be a net increase in the total distance $\Sigma|a-\theta_i|$ or equivalently, the average distance $(1/5)\Sigma|a-\theta_i|$ -- which is just the average loss $\Sigma \ell(a,\theta_i)p(\theta_i)$

c. <u>FIRST, A SOLUTION WITH CALCULUS</u>
This problem is just a special case of the least squares problem of Appendix 11-2, when b = 0. The solution can be similarly found with calculus. We wish to minimize

$$f(a) = \Sigma(\theta_i - a)^2$$

Set the derivative equal to 0:

$$f'(a) = \Sigma 2(\theta_i - a)(-1) = 0$$

Then $\Sigma(\theta_i - a) = 0$

Then $\Sigma\theta_i - na = 0$

$$a = \frac{1}{n}\Sigma\theta_i = \theta$$

To prove this gives a minimum rather than an inflection point or maximum, there are several ways to proceed. The simplest way is to note that f(a) is a second degree polynomial in a that is always positive, that is, a parabola opening up.

ALTERNATIVE SOLUTION, WITHOUT CALCULUS
We wish to minimize the average, or equivalently, the total squared deviations:
$$f(a) = \Sigma(\theta_i - a)^2$$

This is a second degree polynomial in the unknown a, which we can write explicitly as:

$$f(a) = \Sigma(\theta_i^2 - 2\theta_i a + a^2)$$
$$= \Sigma\theta_i^2 - 2(\Sigma\theta_i)a + na^2 \qquad (1)$$

Now we draw on a general result about parabolas y = f(x) from high school algebra: The minimum y occurs,

$$\text{when } x = (-\frac{1}{2})\frac{\text{coefficient of } x}{\text{coefficient of } x^2}$$

In (1), the unknown is denoted by a instead of x, so this formula yields:
$$\text{optimal } a = (-\frac{1}{2})\frac{-2\Sigma\theta_i}{n} = \frac{\Sigma\theta_i}{n} = \bar{\theta}$$

d.   To minimize the average loss, we need to maximize the probability of getting 0 loss, that is, being _exactly_ right. So we should use the most probable value -- the mode.

20-11 a.   Correction: ... Then the best estimate is the _median_ of the _posterior_ distribution of V.

b.   Correction: ... Bayesian estimation _exploits_ prior distributions and losses.

21-1 a.

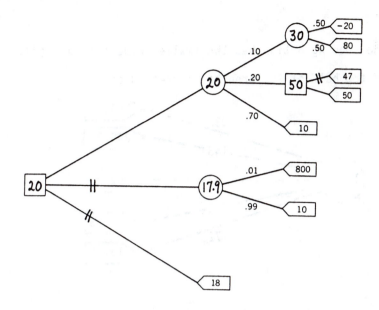

b. Now she would find selling even more attractive, because the venture's expected value of 20K was based on the assumption that she was risk neutral, and so exaggerates the value to a person who is risk averse.

   For example, at the very top branch, the 50-50 gamble was averaged out to give 30K. But a poor person would not find the gamble as attractive as 30K, because the gamble might leave her broke with no resources left to shoot for the long-run average.

21-3 a. Although a formal tree is hardly necessary in such a simple choice, it may help clarify the choice. In the top half of the tree, we add the .250 million cost of the seeding to the costs of the damage. And since the tree represents costs that we are trying to minimize, now the <u>smallest</u> number is chosen at each decision fork:

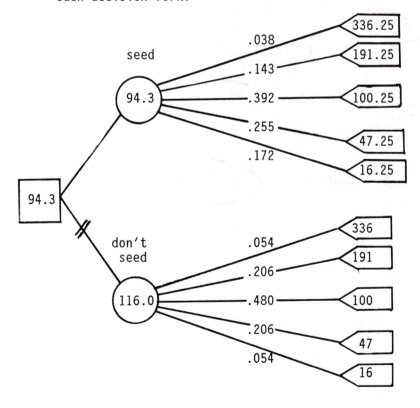

165

Thus the seeding option has the smaller expected cost (94.3 million).

b. Now the top half of the tree has increased costs.

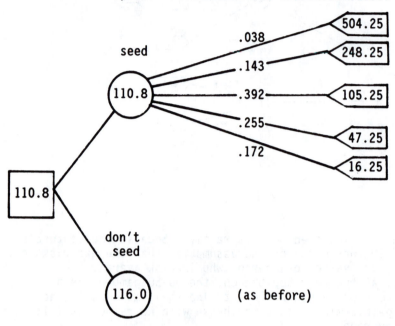

The seeding option still has the smaller cost (110.8 million).

21-5 a. First, we get the relevant posterior probabilities by tree reversal:

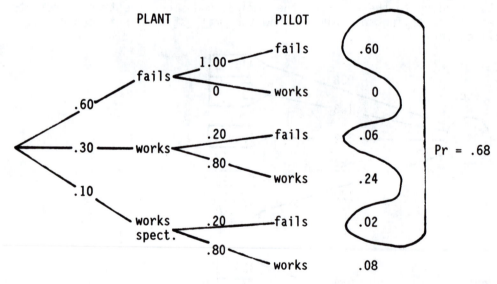

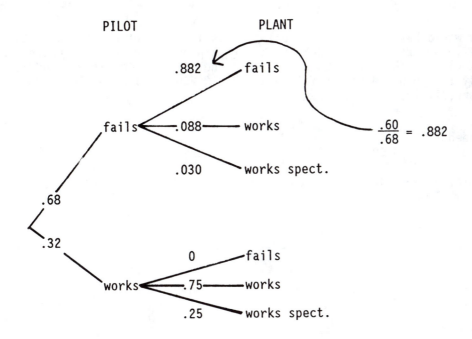

Then we use these posterior probabilities in the decision tree:

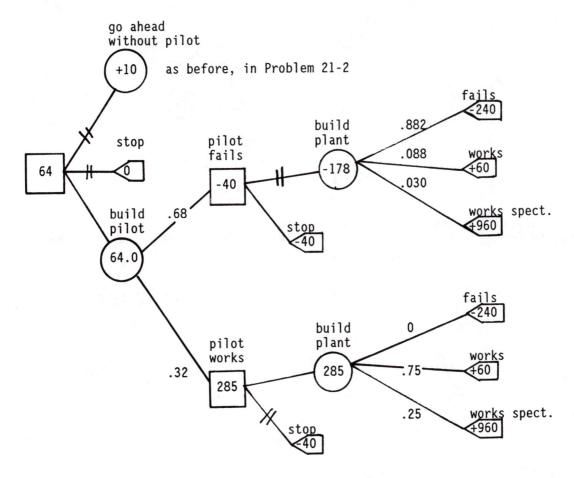

Thus they should go ahead with the pilot plant. As it fails or succeeds, of course, they should then stop or go ahead with the main plant.

b. The tree would have the same probabilities as in (a), but now the profits would be less. We must find 30% of the <u>gross</u> profits, before the expense of the 200K plant. This gives us 30% of 300K and 1200K, which is 90K and 360K respectively; then the net profits would be 90-200 = -110K and 360 - 200 = 160K respectively.

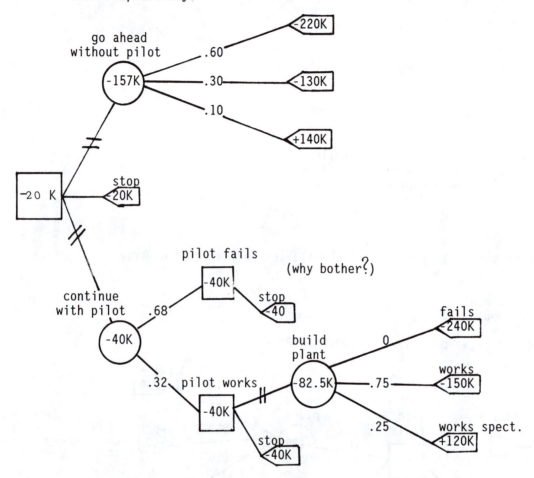

Thus they should stop and cut their losses. It would be a pointless waste of another 20K (even if the pilot plant worked, it would be foolish to build the main plant).

21-7 **a.** It's a little worse. The "perfect test" would predict perfectly, and have a table like this:

1	0	0
0	1	0
0	0	1

b. First of all, we get the relevant posterior probabilities by tree reversal:

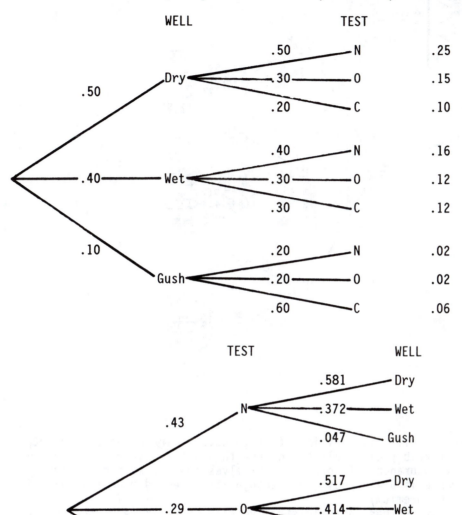

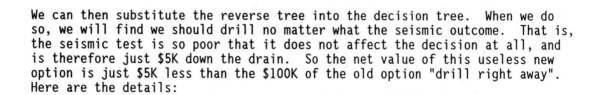

We can then substitute the reverse tree into the decision tree. When we do so, we will find we should drill no matter what the seismic outcome. That is, the seismic test is so poor that it does not affect the decision at all, and is therefore just $5K down the drain. So the net value of this useless new option is just $5K less than the $100K of the old option "drill right away". Here are the details:

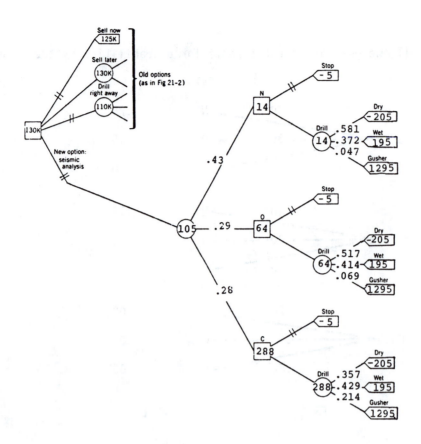

21-9 a. Many homeowners feel it is very important to have their own home, and yet would find it terribly difficult to achieve this after a large fire that was not covered by insurance. To protect themselves against such crippling losses, insurance is a wise buy (even though its expected monetary value is not equal to the premium).

Since insurance has an administrative cost, however (as discussed in part b), it might be better to buy insurance that covers only heavy losses, with small amounts deductible (as shown in part c). Then if a fire occurred, the homeowner could finance this small amount like a renovation--for example, out of savings, or a small mortgage.

b. Each given frequency was stated to be "fires per 100,000 homes, annually." For simplicity, suppose the insurance company insures 100,000 homes. To find out how much they would pay out, we just count each kind of fire appropriately, and sum:

damage x	freq. f	x f
$ 1,000	2100	$2,100,000
10,000	300	3,000,000
30,000	20	600,000
60,000	5	300,000
		$6,000,000

Since their income would be $115 x 100,000, the proportion paid for fires would be:

$$\text{proportion} = \frac{\$6,000,000}{\$115 \times 100,000} = .52$$

170

Alternatively, we would get the same answers from averages, of course: The average payout would be

$$\bar{X} = \frac{\Sigma xf}{n} = \frac{\$6,000,000}{100,000} = \$60$$

Hence the proportion paid for fires would be

$$\text{proportion} = \frac{\$60}{\$115} = .52$$

c. With $5000 deductible, the possible payments P are the following modification of part (b):

damage x	payment p	freq. f	pf
$ 1,000	0	2100	0
$10,000	$ 5,000	300	$1,500,000
$30,000	$ 25,000	20	$ 500,000
$60,000	$ 55,000	5	$ 275,000
			$2,275,000

As a proportion of the former loss, this is

$$\frac{2,275,000}{6,000,000} = .3792 = 38\%$$

The new premium would therefore be

37.92% of $115 = $43.60

21-11 a. Since the stakes are small, we can use the EMV criterion. First we must translate all time into money (60 min. = $12, so 1 min = $.20). Here is the solution if we ignore the return at the end of the day:

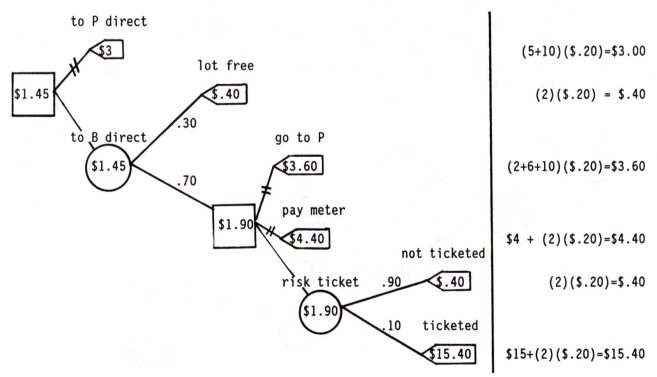

171

It would be better of course to take into account the time returning home at the end of the day too, which gives this tree:

to P direct

$6   2(5+10)($.20)=$6.00

lot free

$.80   2(2)($.20) = $.80

$1.85   .30

to B direct

$1.85   go to P

$6.60   (2+6+10+10+5)($.20)=$6.60

.70

$2.30   pay meter

$4.80 $4 + 2(2)($.20)=$4.80

not ticketed

risk ticket   .90 $.80   2(2)($.20)=$.80

$2.30

.10   ticketed

$15.80 $15+2(2)($.20)=$15.80

So he should go to B and park in the small lot there if it is free. Otherwise, he should park at a meter, but not feed it (risk the $15 fine). This strategy costs $1.85 including his time, on average (or $1.45, if the end of the day is ignored).

<u>Note</u> This assumes that money is the only criterion. If he feels any guilt about not feeding the meter or regret about getting a ticket, for example, then his decision might be different!

b.   Now the very bottom price tag would change. There is a 50% chance of getting hit with an additional cost of $40 + 60($.20) = $52. This raises the expected cost by .50($52) = $26, so the final price tag is $15.80 + $26 = $41.80. With this change, and taking account of the time at the end of the day, the tree now becomes:

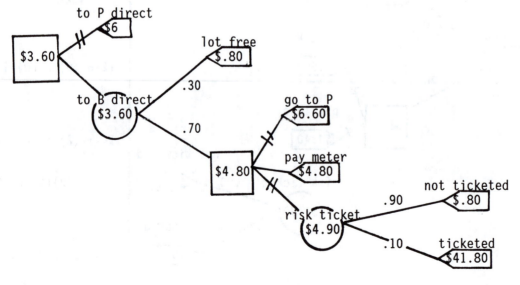

172

So he should go to B and park in the small lot there if it is free. Otherwise he should park at a meter. But now he should pay the meter, for an expected daily cost of $3.60.

(If we ignore the time to return home, we find a different optimal strategy: He should still go to B and park in the small lot there if it is free. Otherwise, he should now go over to P, for an expected daily cost of $2.64 -- as you could easily verify.)

21-13 a.

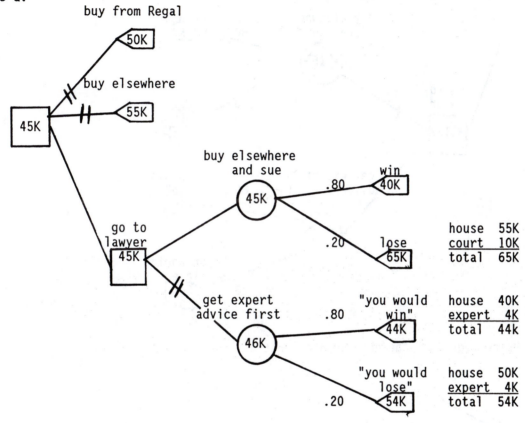

He therefore should buy elsewhere and sue--without consulting the legal expert. In taking his chances in court, he would have the smallest expected cost (45K).

b. Currently, the "expert route" costs 46K, which is 1 K higher than the best option costing 45K. If the expert reduced his price by 1K or more (to 3K or less), then his advice would be worthwhile.

c. Now we replace each price tag in part (a) with its disutility read off the given graph:

173

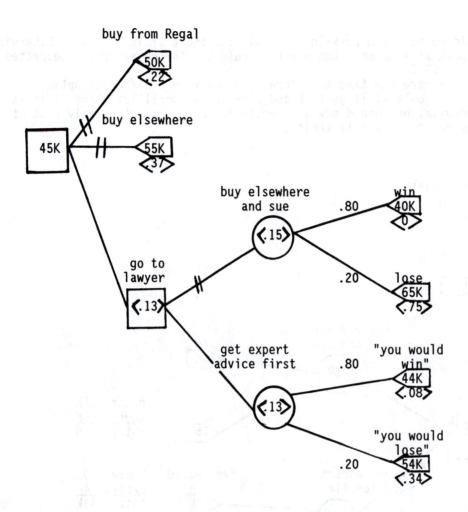

21-15 a. Price tags show the <u>change</u> in profit:

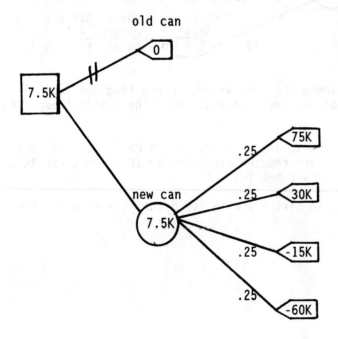

b. If information were perfect, then losses could be avoided by sticking with the old can under adverse conditions. Then the tree would have a third branch:

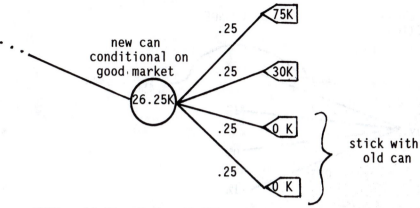

$$EVPI = 26.25 - 7.5 = 18.75K \simeq 19K$$

c.   (i)   Since perfect information is worth only 19K (as found in part b), imperfect information would be worth less. Thus 40K would be out of the question.

   (ii)   First we obtain the relevant posterior probabilities by tree reversal:

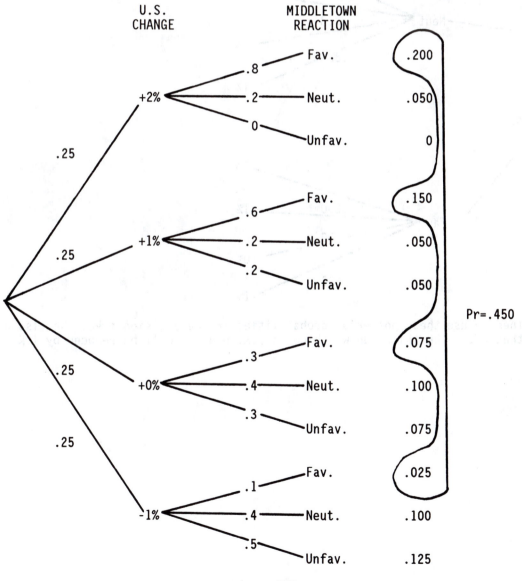

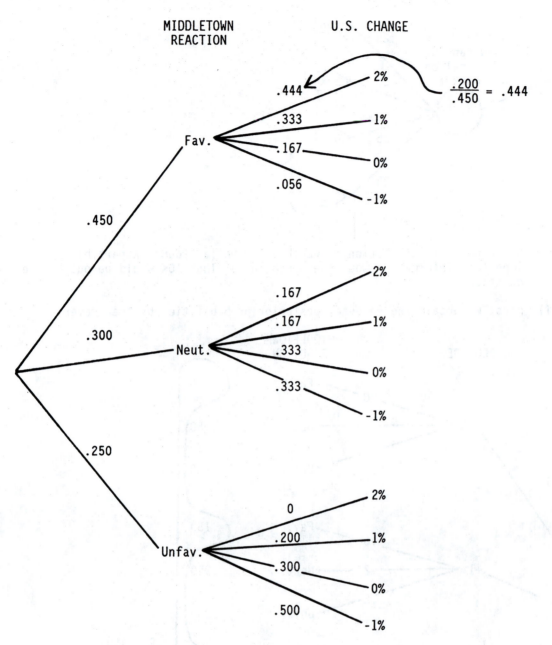

Then we use these posterior probabilities in the decision tree. We also note that after the third run which costs 10K, profits will be reduced by 10K:

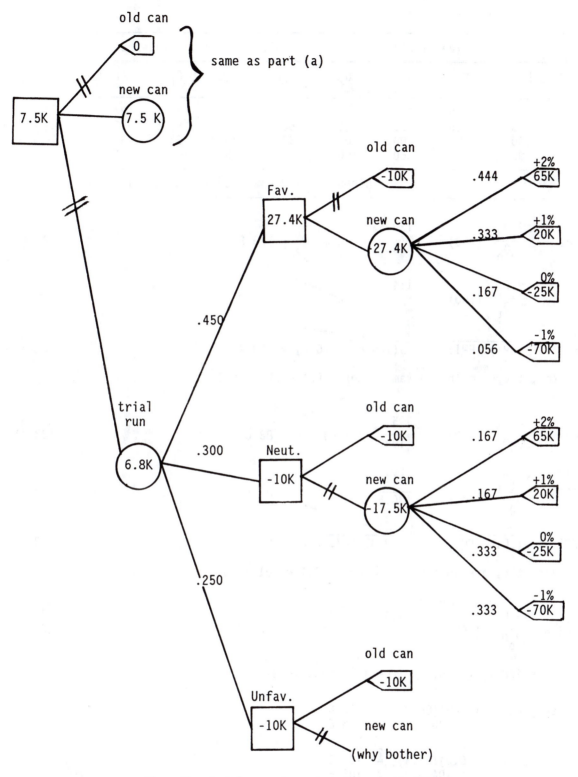

Thus the trial run is not quite worth it.

(iii) To find the price at which the trial run would be truly worthwhile, we saw in part (ii) that the trial run was just a little too expensive—it fell short of breaking even by 7.5K - 6.8K = 0.7K. We therefore would find it would break even, if we reduced its price to 10K - .7K = 9.3K. (Or, if we used more decimal places throughout, we would get the exact answer 9.375K.)

Item	Given Table				Calculations for Indexes			
	P_o	P_t	Q_o	Q_t	P_oQ_o	P_oQ_t	P_tQ_o	P_tQ_t
Flour	.25	.30	100	80	25	20	30	24
Eggs	1.00	1.25	50	40	50	40	62.5	50
Milk	.30	.35	100	100	30	30	35	35
Potatoes	.05	.05	60	100	3	5	3	5
				TOTALS	108	95	130.5	114

a.

$$\text{LPI} = \frac{\Sigma P_t Q_o}{\Sigma P_o Q_o} \ (100) \ = \ \frac{130.5}{108} \ (100) \quad = 120.8 \tag{22-4}$$

$$\text{PPI} = \frac{\Sigma P_t Q_t}{\Sigma P_o Q_t} \ (100) \ = \ \frac{114}{95} \ (100) \quad = 120.0 \tag{22-5}$$

$$\text{FPI} = \sqrt{(\text{LPI}) \ (\text{PPI})} \ = \ \sqrt{(120.8) \ (120.0)} = 120.4 \tag{22-6}$$

Yes, they are in the same order: $\text{PPI} \leq \text{FPI} \leq \text{LPI}$

b.

$$\text{LQI} = \frac{\Sigma Q_t P_o}{\Sigma Q_o P_o} \ (100) \ = \ \frac{95}{108} \ (100) \quad = \ 88.0 \tag{22-7}$$

$$\text{PQI} = \frac{\Sigma Q_t P_t}{\Sigma Q_o P_t} \ (100) \ = \ \frac{114}{130.5} \ (100) \quad = \ 87.4 \tag{22-8}$$

$$\text{FPI} = \sqrt{(\text{LQI}) \ (\text{PQI})} \ = \ \sqrt{(88.0) \ (87.4)} \ = \ 87.7 \tag{22-9}$$

Yes, they are in the same order: $\text{PQI} \leq \text{FQI} \leq \text{LQI}$

c.

$$\text{CI} = \frac{\Sigma P_t Q_t}{\Sigma P_o Q_o} \ (100) \ = \ \frac{114}{108.0} \ (100) \quad = \ 105.6 \tag{22-10}$$

$$(\text{Price index}) \ (\text{Quantity Index}) \ \overset{?}{=} \ \text{cost index} \tag{22-11}$$

Laspeyres: $(120.8)(88.0) \overset{?}{=} 105.6$
$\qquad\qquad\qquad 106.3 \quad > \quad 105.6$

Paasche : $(120.0)(87.4) \overset{?}{=} 105.6$
$\qquad\qquad\qquad 104.9 \quad < \quad 105.6$

Fisher : $(120.4)(87.7) \overset{?}{=} 105.6$
$\qquad\qquad\qquad 105.6 \quad = \quad 105.6$

From above it is clear that only the Fisher Index passes the factor-reversal test.

d. No difference, since the numerator and denominator would both be increased by exactly the same factor of 200 million.

22-3 a.

Item	Given table							
	P_0	P_1	P_2	P_3	Q_0	Q_1	Q_2	Q_3
Steak	1.00	1.20	1.40	1.20	40	50	70	50
Bread	.10	.20	.40	.20	80	100	110	100

Calculations for Indexes: Taking 1940 as Base Year										
P_0Q_0	P_0Q_1	P_1Q_0	P_1Q_1	P_0Q_2	P_2Q_0	P_2Q_2	P_0Q_3	P_3Q_0	P_3Q_3
40	50	48	60	70	56	98	50	48	60
8	10	16	20	11	32	44	10	16	20
48	60	64	80	81	88	142	60	64	80

$$\text{LPI for } 1950 = \frac{\Sigma P_1 Q_0}{\Sigma P_0 Q_0}\ (100) = \frac{64}{48}\ (100) = 133.3$$

$$1960 = \frac{\Sigma P_2 Q_0}{\Sigma P_0 Q_0}\ (100) = \frac{88}{48}\ (100) = 183.3$$

$$1970 = \frac{\Sigma P_3 Q_0}{\Sigma P_0 Q_0}\ (100) = \frac{64}{48}\ (100) = 133.3$$

$$\text{PPI for } 1950 = \frac{\Sigma P_1 Q_1}{\Sigma P_0 Q_1}\ (100) = \frac{80}{60}\ (100) = 133.3$$

$$1960 = \frac{\Sigma P_2 Q_2}{\Sigma P_0 Q_2}\ (100) = \frac{142}{81}\ (100) = 175.3$$

$$1970 = \frac{\Sigma P_3 Q_3}{\Sigma P_0 Q_3}\ (100) = \frac{80}{60}\ (100) = 133.3$$

$$\text{FPI for } 1950 = \sqrt{(133.3)\ (133.3)} = 133.3$$

$$1960 = \sqrt{(183.3)\ (175.3)} = 179.3$$

$$1970 = \sqrt{(133.3)\ (133.3)} = 133.3$$

Hence we have the following table:

Type of Price Index	1940	1950	1960	1970
Laspeyres	100	133.3	183.3	133.3
Paasche	100	133.3	175.3	133.3
Fisher	100	133.3	179.3	133.3

b. LPI is the simplest to calculate, since the denominator $\Sigma P_o Q_o$ remains the same every year.

By contrast, for the PPI the denominator $\Sigma P_o Q_t$ has to be revised every year. This means more calculation--a trivial matter for computers. It also means more measuring--updating the quantities consumed, Q_t. This is the overriding issue, that compels the government to use Laspeyres type indexes.

c.

			Using 1950 as Base Year				
P_o	P_t	Q_o	Q_t	$P_o Q_o$	$P_o Q_t$	$P_t Q_o$	$P_t Q_t$
1.20	1.40	50	70	60	84	70	98
.20	.40	100	100	20	22	40	44
			TOTALS	80	106	110	142

LPI for 1960 $= \dfrac{110}{80} (100) = 137.5$

PPI for 1960 $= \dfrac{142}{106} (100) = 134.0$

FPI for 1960 $= \sqrt{(137.5)\,(134.0)} = 135.7$

			Using 1960 as Base Year				
P_o	P_t	Q_o	Q_t	$P_o Q_o$	$P_o Q_t$	$P_t Q_o$	$P_t Q_t$
1.40	1.20	70	50	98	70	84	60
.40	.20	110	100	44	40	22	20
			TOTALS	142	110	106	80

LPI for 1970 $= \dfrac{106}{142} (100) = 74.6$

PPI for 1970 $= \dfrac{80}{110} (100) = 72.7$

FPI for 1970 $= \sqrt{(74.6)\,(72.7)} = 73.7$

Hence we have the following table:

Type of Price Index	1960 Index using 1950 Base	1970 Index using 1960 Base	Product of these indexes
Laspeyres	137.5	74.6	102.6
Paasche	134.0	72.7	97.4
Fisher	135.7	73.7	100.0

From above, it is clear that the time-reversal test is passed only by Fisher's Ideal Price Index.

22-5 a. It will help to show schematically what price and quantity changes we are given over the two decades (time periods):

Prices $\quad\quad P_o \quad\quad\quad P_t \quad\quad\quad P_o$ again

Quantities $\quad\ Q_o \quad\quad\quad Q_t \quad\quad\quad Q_o$ again

Over the first decade the Fisher price index is given by

$$FPI_1 = \sqrt{(LPI)(PPI)} \tag{22-6}$$

from (22-4) and (22-5),

$$FPI_1 = \sqrt{\frac{\Sigma P_t Q_o}{\Sigma P_o Q_o} \frac{\Sigma P_t Q_t}{\Sigma P_o Q_t}} \tag{1}$$

Now in the second decade, we <u>start out</u> with P_t and Q_t, and <u>end up</u> with P_o and Q_o. Thus the FPI is given by (1), with the subscripts o and t reversed:

$$FPI_2 = \sqrt{\frac{\Sigma P_o Q_t}{\Sigma P_t Q_t} \frac{\Sigma P_o Q_o}{\Sigma P_t Q_o}} \tag{2}$$

The product of (1) and (2) is therefore:

$$FPI_1\, FPI_2 = \sqrt{\frac{\Sigma P_t Q_o}{\Sigma P_o Q_o} \frac{\Sigma P_t Q_t}{\Sigma P_o Q_t}} \sqrt{\frac{\Sigma P_o Q_t}{\Sigma P_t Q_t} \frac{\Sigma P_o Q_o}{\Sigma P_t Q_o}}$$

All the factors above exactly cancel the factors below, leaving $FPI_1\, FPI_2 = 1$.

b. In part (a) we found

$$FPI = \sqrt{\frac{\Sigma P_t Q_o}{\Sigma P_o Q_o} \frac{\Sigma P_t Q_t}{\Sigma P_o Q_t}}$$

Similarly,

$$FQI = \sqrt{\frac{\Sigma P_o Q_t}{\Sigma P_o Q_o} \frac{\Sigma P_t Q_t}{\Sigma P_t Q_o}}$$

When we multiply them together, half the factors cancel, leaving:

$$\text{FPI FQI} = \sqrt{\frac{\Sigma P_t Q_t}{\Sigma P_o Q_o} \cdot \frac{\Sigma P_t Q_t}{\Sigma P_o Q_t}} = \frac{\Sigma P_t Q_t}{\Sigma P_o Q_o}$$

22-7 **a.** When our classes are polled, most students prefer the 1940 catalogue.

   b. Among our students, the subjective price index varies from about 70 to 400, being on the average about 250.

   c. The increase from 1940 to 1980 is by a factor of 100(246/42) = 586. Thus we see that the U.S. CPI overstates inflation, as felt by the average student in part (b).

   d. For an income of $500,000 the wide variety of goods available in 1980 looks especially attractive (such as electronics, sailboards, and medical care, in particular). Thus the subjective price index was well below 100. (The index varied from 10 to 100, being on average about 25.) Thus, the U.S. CPI grossly overstates inflation, as felt by the rich.

22-9

Item	Given Table				Calculations for Indexes			
	Q_o	P_o	Q_t	P_t	$P_o Q_o$	$P_o Q_t$	$P_t Q_o$	$P_t Q_t$
Beans	40	$.75	40	$.80	30	30	32	32
Milk	150	$.60	100	$.80	90	60	120	80
Gasoline	200	$1.80	250	$2.00	360	450	400	500
Shoes	3.5	$40.00	4.00	$50.00	140	160	175	200
TV	.05	$320.00	.10	$300.00	16	32	15	30
TOTAL					$636	$732	$742	$842

a.

$$\text{LPI} = \frac{\Sigma P_t Q_o}{\Sigma P_o Q_o}(100) = \frac{742}{636}(100) = 116.67 \approx 117$$

$$\text{PPI} = \frac{\Sigma P_t Q_t}{\Sigma P_o Q_t}(100) = \frac{842}{732}(100) = 115.03 \approx 115$$

$$\text{FPI} = \sqrt{(\text{LPI})(\text{PPI})} = \sqrt{(116.67)(115.03)} = 115.85 \approx 116$$

b.

$$\text{LQI} = \frac{\Sigma Q_t P_o}{\Sigma Q_o P_o}(100) = \frac{732}{636}(100) = 115.09 \approx 115 \qquad (22\text{-}7)$$

$$\text{PQI} = \frac{\Sigma Q_t P_t}{\Sigma Q_o P_t}(100) = \frac{842}{742}(100) = 113.48 \approx 113 \qquad (22\text{-}8)$$

$$\text{FQI} = \sqrt{(\text{LQI})(\text{PQI})} = \sqrt{(115.09)(113.48)} = 114.28 \approx 114 \qquad (22\text{-}9)$$

c.

$$CI = \frac{\Sigma P_t Q_t}{\Sigma P_o Q_o} \ (100) = \frac{842}{636} \ (100) = 132.39 \approx 132 \tag{22-10}$$

$$(\text{Price index}) \cdot (\text{Quantity Index}) \overset{?}{=} \text{cost index} \tag{22-11}$$

Laspeyres: $(117)(115) \overset{?}{=} 132$
$\qquad\qquad\quad 135 \quad > \quad 132$

Paasche : $(115)(113) \overset{?}{=} 132$
$\qquad\qquad\quad 130 \quad < \quad 132$

Fisher : $(116)(114) \overset{?}{=} 132$
$\qquad\qquad\quad 132 \quad = \quad 132$

This proves that only the Fisher Index passes the factor-reversal test.

22-11 We convert % increases to <u>factors</u> of increase: 30% means 1.30 times bigger, while 113% means 2.13 times bigger. Thus

overall factor of increase = $1.30 \times 2.13 = 2.77$

And the factor 2.77 means a 177% increase.

b. **(i)** $(1.02)(1.02)(1.02) \ldots 50 \text{ times} = (1.02)^{50} = 2.69.$

This is much more than doubling, because of the compounding effect. It is a rise of 169%.

(ii) $(1.02)^{35} = 2.00$

So it is 35 years that gives us a doubling -- a rise of 100%.

<u>Remarks</u> This is an example of the "rule of 70", that works for any sort of exponential growth -- whether it be a constant inflation rate r, money at a constant interest rate r, or biological growth at rate r:

$$\text{doubling time} = \frac{.70}{r}$$

For example, part b(ii) had R = .02, and this formula gives the correct answer:

$$\text{doubling time} = \frac{.70}{.02} = 35 \text{ years}$$

23-1 a.

$$\text{var }(\bar{X}) = \frac{\sigma^2}{n} \simeq \frac{s}{n} \qquad \text{like (6-6)}$$

$$= \frac{108^2}{5000} = 2.33$$

Then the 95% confidence interval for μ is:

$$\mu = \bar{X} \pm 1.96 \text{ SE} \qquad \text{like (8-8)}$$

$$= 53.2 \pm 1.96 \sqrt{2.33}$$

$$= 53.2 \pm 3.0$$

Finally, the total amount owed B is just the population size times the mean μ:

$$\text{total} = 100,000 \; (53.2 \pm 3.0)$$

$$= \$5,320,000 \pm \$300,000$$

b.

	Given			Pop. Prop.	Using (23-4)	Using (23-7)
N_i	n_i	$\bar{X}_i$ $\$$	s_i $\$$	w_i	$w_i \bar{X}_i$	$w_i^2 \dfrac{s_i^2}{n_i}$
50,000	2,470	16	32	.5	8.0	.104
20,000	1,020	29	51	.2	5.8	.102
20,000	990	67	86	.2	13.4	.299
10,000	520	251	202	.1	25.1	.785
100,000	5,000				$\bar{X}_s = 52.30$	var $\bar{X}_s$ = 1.29

We follow the same steps as in (a), using the stratified mean $\bar{X}_s = 52.30$ and its variance 1.29:

$$\mu = 52.30 \pm 1.96 \sqrt{1.29}$$

$$= \$52.30 \pm \$2.20$$

$$\text{total} = 100,000 \; (\$52.30 \pm \$2.20)$$

$$= \$5,230,000 \pm \$220,000$$

23-3 a.

$$\bar{X}_s = w_1 \bar{X}_1 + w_2 \bar{X}_2$$

$$= .20(36) + .80(11) = 16$$

b. $\bar{X}_1 = 36$, which is so biased it may be worse than useless.

23-5

				a.		b. Using (23-13)	c. Using (23-7)
Given				for C_o			
n_i	s_i $\$$	w_i	c_i $\$$	$c_i n_i$	$w_i s_i \sqrt{c_i}$	$n_i = k \dfrac{w_i s_i}{\sqrt{c_i}}$	$\dfrac{w_i^2 s_i^2}{n_i}$
540	4.50	.52	.25	135.0	1.170	220	.0249
330	12.10	.34	.36	118.8	2.468	322	.0526
130	31.60	.14	.64	83.2	3.539	260	.0752
1000				$C_o = 337.0$	7.177		.153

for part (b):

$$k = \frac{C_o}{\Sigma w_i s_i \sqrt{c_i}}$$

$$= \frac{337.0}{7.177} \quad = 47.0$$

c. In the last column, we find var X_s = .153 and hence SE = $\sqrt{.153}$ = .39. Compared to SE = $\sqrt{.20}$ = .45 found in Example 23-1 (b), this represents a reduction of .06, or 13%.

d. The most important step is the first, random sampling. Successive steps then give smaller and smaller gains (although still worth doing). Stratified sampling reduced the SE from .59 ($\sqrt{.35}$) to .45 ($\sqrt{.20}$), a reduction of 24%. Then optimal stratification reduced the SE another 13%, as shown in (c).

23-7

a. In the last stage, multistage sampling often observes everyone in the final sampling unit—or, as it's called by the Current Population Survey, the [USU, PSU]. Then it is called [cluster, systematic] sampling.

b. Cluster sampling—and multistage sampling—work best when each cluster is relatively [heterogeneous, homogeneous].

c. When testing an hypothesis H_0 against an alternative H_1, [systematic, sequential] sampling allows you to exploit the early results to determine whether it is necessary to continue sampling. Thus the sample size n will be very short when the early results are [overwhelming, indecisive], and longer otherwise. So n must be regarded as a [random variable, fixed parameter].

   The advantage of this kind of sampling is that the expected sample size will be [less, greater] than the sample size of the comparable simple random sample.

d. Systematic sampling [works best, may be disastrous] when there are unsuspected periodicities in the data. For example, to determine the average outgoing quality of automobiles from the Ford Ypsilanti plant, sampling each Friday afternoon would be [more biased, more fairly representative] than simple random sampling.

23-9 Simple random sample. We suppose there is some sort of student directory that contains a list of all the students. If they are serially numbered, from 1 to 8000, say, then a student can be randomly selected by drawing his serial number from Appendix Table I (using 4 digits at a time, and trying again if it exceeds 8000). By repeating this, a simple random sample of desired size can be obtained.

More likely, the students would not be serially numbered, and then an alternative scheme might be more feasible. For example, we could randomly select a student by using Table I to first draw a page at random, then a column, and finally a name within the column.

Stratified sample. Post stratification would be very simple and effective. Stratification by faculty, year, and/or sex might be helpful, depending on the issue.

Multistage cluster sample. First we could select a few regions at random (where a region is broadly defined as a dormitory, or section of the city, etc.) Then within a region--a dormitory for example--a floor or wing could be randomly chosen, and everyone in it sampled as the cluster.

23-11 This problem shows that a sample that is used to find the difference between two strata (two sexes) can also be used as a stratified sample to find the overall population mean or proportion.

a. $$(\pi_1 - \pi_2) = P_1 - P_2 + 1.96 \sqrt{\frac{P_1(1-P_1)}{n_1} + \frac{P_2(1-P_2)}{n_2}} \qquad (8\text{-}29)$$

$$= (.51 - .42) \pm 1.96 \sqrt{\frac{.51(.49)}{600} + \frac{.421(.58)}{600}}$$

$$= .09 \pm .056 \simeq 9\% \pm 6\%$$

b. As we saw in Section 6-1, a population proportion π is just a disguised population mean μ. And the population variance is then given by

$$\sigma^2 = \pi(1-\pi) \qquad (6\text{-}20)$$

$$\simeq s^2 = P(1-P)$$

Similarly, a sample proportion P is just a disguised sample mean $\bar{X}$. Our table of calculations therefore takes the form:

		Given		Using (6-20)	Using (23-4)	Using (23-7)
Stratum	n_i	$P_i = \bar{X}_i$	w_i	$s_i^2 = P_i(1-P_i)$	$w_i \bar{X}_i$	$w_i^2 \frac{s_i^2}{n_i}$
men	600	.51	.48	.250	.245	.000096
women	600	.42	.52	.244	.218	.000110
					.463	.000206

Thus the 95% confidence interval for μ (or π) is:

$$\mu \doteq \bar{X}_s \pm 1.96 \ SE$$

$$= .463 \pm 1.96 \sqrt{.000206}$$

that is, $\pi = .463 \pm .028$

186

24-1

	a.			b.			
	Predicted price $\hat{Y}$		Y	$(Y - \hat{Y})$		$(Y - \hat{Y})^2$	
	i	ii		i	ii	i	ii
	(using line)	("no change")					
1921	3.00	4.70	$4.10	1.10	-.60	1.21	.36
1931	2.80	2.40	$1.90	-.90	-.50	.81	.25
1941	2.60	1.90	$2.20	-.40	.30	.16	.09
1951	2.40	3.00	$3.20	.80	.20	.64	.04
1961	2.20	2.30	$2.40	.20	.10	.04	.01
					MSE ≈	2.86	.75

b. Using the naive "no change" rule is much better, giving only about ¼ as large an MSE as using the inappropriate regression line.

24-3 a. b.

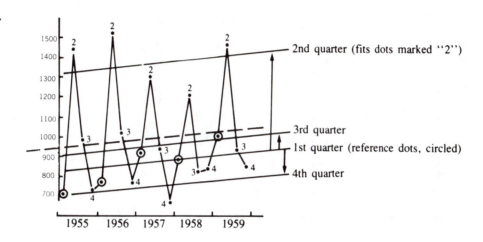

c.

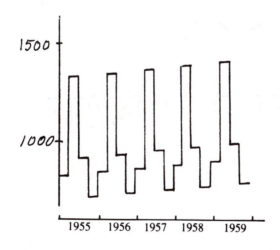

d. The distance of the second quarter above the first (on average) is found in either of the figures above to be about 500. That is, if we take the first quarter as our reference, the coefficients for the second quarter dummy Q_2 will be about 500. Similarly, for Q_3 and Q_4 the coefficients will be about 100 and -100, so that the regression equation would be:

$$\hat{Y} = a + bX + 500\ Q_2 + 100\ Q_3 - 100\ Q_4$$

Alternatively, of course, we could have used the fourth quarter, say, as our reference, and then obtain:

$$\hat{Y} = a + bX + 100\ Q_1 + 600\ Q_2 - 200\ Q_3$$

24-5 a. Just for good measure, we will show what happens for 20 (not just 10) time periods, and we will start at the beginning of Table II:

time t	from Table II, v_t	from equation (24-4), $e_t = .9\ e_{t-1} + v_t$
0		2 (given start)
1	.5	2.3
2	.1	2.2
3	2.5	4.5
4	- .3	3.7
5	- .1	3.2
6	.3	3.2
7	- .3	2.6
8	1.3	3.6
9	.2	3.5
10	-1.0	2.1
11	.1	2.0
12	-2.5	- .7
13	- .5	-1.1
14	- .2	-1.2
15	.5	- .6
16	-1.6	-2.1
17	.2	-1.7
18	-1.2	-2.7
19	0	-2.5
20	.5	-1.7

b.

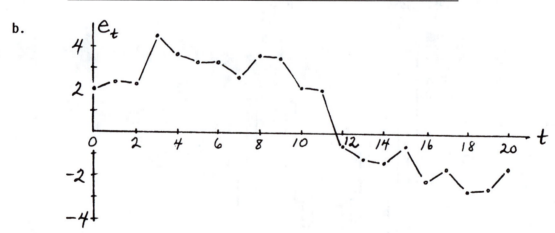

This shows random tracking, like Figure 24-5.

24-7 It would be easiest to run this through a standard computer program. If you do, you will get slightly different answers for Problems 24-7 and 24-9, due to the minor refinements the computer can easily make. [For example, the seasoned pattern S is slightly adjusted to average out to be 1.0000 exactly, instead of 1.0002 as in part (c) below.]

Also, with slightly different rounding you may get slightly different answers

Y	Moving Average	(a) Centered (M)	(b) Y/M	(c) Seasonal Calculated (S)	Seasonal Repeated	(d) Adjusted $Y^a = Y/S$
36					.654	55.0
44					.768	57.3
	57.75					
45		58.00	.776	.763	.763	59.0
	58.25					
106		58.50	1.812	1.816	1.816	58.4
	58.75					
38		59.00	.644	.654	.654	58.1
	59.25					
46		60.00	.767	.768	.768	59.9
	60.75					
47		61.25	.767		.763	61.6
	61.75					
112		62.12	1.803		1.816	61.7
	62.50					
42		62.62	.671		.654	64.2
	62.75					
49		63.50	.677		.768	63.8
	64.25					
48		64.25	.747		.763	62.9
	64.25					
118		64.38	1.833		1.816	65.0
	64.50					
42		64.88	.647		.654	64.2
	65.25					
50		65.25	.766		.768	65.1
	65.25					
51					.763	66.8
118					1.816	65.0

d.

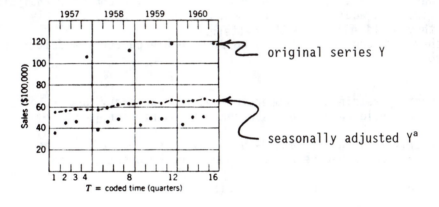

original series Y

seasonally adjusted Y^a

24-9

Y	Moving Average	(a) Centered (M)	(b) Y/M	(c) Seasonal Calculated (S)	Seasonal Repeated	(d) Adjusted $Y^a = Y/S$
508					.944	538
566					1.050	539
	542.0					
550		541.9	1.015 ——→	1.009	1.009	545
	541.8					
544		541.3	1.005	1.011	1.011	538
	540.8					
507		540.1	.939	.944	.944	537
	539.5					
562		541.1	1.039	1.050	1.050	535
	542.8					
545		541.8	1.006 ——		1.009	540
	540.8					
557		539.2	1.033		1.011	551
	537.8					
499		535.0	.933		.944	529
	532.2					
550		526.8	1.044		1.050	524
	521.2					
523		519.6	1.007 ——		1.009	518
	518.0					
513		515.0	.996		1.011	507
	512.0					
486		506.2	.960		.944	515
	500.5					
526		493.5	1.066		1.050	501
	486.5					
477					1.009	473
457					1.011	452

d.

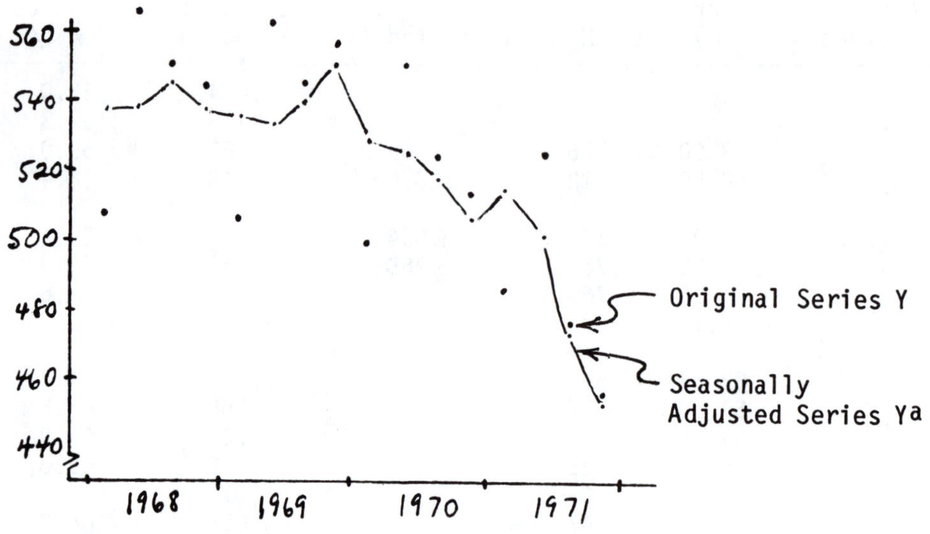

24-11 If there was much of a pattern, there are lots of avid computer analysts working at brokerage firms who would pick it out and use it to trade profitably. In trading this way, they would eliminate the pattern.

We therefore conclude there is no discernible pattern, and it is essentially white noise.

24-13 a. The monthly readings of temperature would rise every summer, of course. That is, there would be a strong seasonal component each <u>year</u>.

b. The hourly readings of temperature would rise most afternoons, of course. That is, there would be a strong periodic component each <u>day</u>.

c. Annual growth would show no periodic component.

d. The quarterly figure would likely show a seasonal component (such as Figure 24-2 does) each <u>year</u>.

25-1

a.

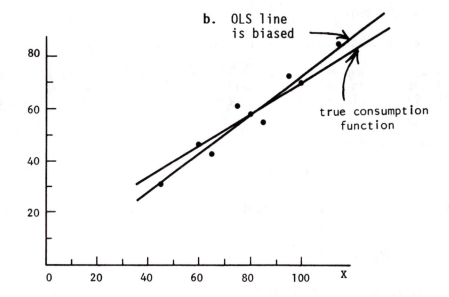

b. OLS line is biased

true consumption function

b.   For Problem 25-3

Y	X	I	$y=Y-\bar{Y}$	$x=X-\bar{X}$	xy	x^2	$i=I-\bar{I}$	iy	ix
46	60	14	-12	-20	240	400	-8	96	160
31	45	14	-27	-35	945	1225	-8	216	280
61	75	14	3	- 5	-15	25	-8	-24	40
58	80	22	0	0	0	0	0	0	0
43	65	22	-15	-15	225	225	0	0	0
73	95	22	15	15	225	225	0	0	0
70	100	30	12	20	240	400	8	96	160
55	85	30	- 3	5	-15	25	8	-24	40
85	115	30	27	35	945	1225	8	216	280
$\bar{Y}=58$	$\bar{X}=80$	$\bar{I}=22$	0 $\checkmark$	0 $\checkmark$	2790	3750		576	960

$$b = \frac{\Sigma xy}{\Sigma x^2} = \frac{2790}{3750} = .744$$

$$a = \bar{Y} - b\bar{X} = 58 - .744(80) = -1.5$$

Thus the OLS line is:

$$\hat{Y} = -1.5 + .744X$$

This is biased--like all OLS lines used in simultaneous equations.

25-3 a.   The calculations are shown in the last three columns of the table in Problem 25-1 above, and yield:

$$b = \frac{s_{IY}}{s_{IX}} = \frac{576}{960} = .60 \qquad\qquad (25-17)$$

$$a = \bar{Y} - b\bar{X} = 58 - .60(80) = 10$$

Thus the IV line is:

$$\hat{Y} = 10 + .60X$$

This coincides exactly with the true line given initially in Problem 25-1.

b. This is a lucky sample, because the errors e_i exactly cancel, yielding a perfect estimate in part (a). Usually we would not be so lucky, and we would find the IV estimate is exactly on target only for huge (infinite) samples.

25-5 a. The given equation is

$$Y = \beta_0 + \beta_1 X_1 + \beta_2 X_2 + e$$

Taking covariances of every variable in the given equation with respect to X_1, we obtain the analogue of (25-9):

$$s_{X_1 Y} = \beta_1 \, s_{X_1 X_1} + \beta_2 \, s_{X_1 X_2} + s_{X_1 e}$$

Since X_1 is predetermined, it is uncorrelated with e and hence

$s_{X_1 e} \rightarrow 0$. Thus

$$s_{X_1 Y} \simeq \beta_1 \, s_{X_1 X_1} + \beta_2 \, s_{X_1 X_2}$$

Similarly, applying X_2 as the IV, we obtain

$$s_{X_2 Y} \simeq \beta_1 \, s_{X_2 X_1} + \beta_2 \, s_{X_2 X_2}$$

b. When we solve the two approximate equations above, we obtain approximate answers for β_1 and β_2, that is, the IV estimates of β_1 and β_2.

c. The two IV equations we solved in (b) are essentially the same as the two OLS equations (13-5) and (13-6)--except for the constant divisor $n-1$. Thus the IV solution will be exactly the same as OLS.

25-7 a. The given first equation is

$$Y_1 = \gamma_2 Y_2 + e$$

To estimate γ_2, the first stage is to purge the regressor Y_2 of its dependence on e, by regressing it on all the exogenous variables (in this case, X_1):

given			deviation			products		For (b)
Y_1	Y_2	X_1	y_1	y_2	x_1	$x_1 y_2$	x_1^2	$x_1 y_1$
38	8	21	8	-4	3	-12	9	24
27	15	17	-3	3	-1	- 3	1	3
31	10	20	1	-2	2	- 4	4	2
21	18	14	-9	6	-4	-24	16	36
20	15	12	-10	3	-6	-18	36	60
43	6	24	13	-6	6	-36	36	78
30	12	18	0	0	0	-97	102	203

$$b = \frac{\Sigma x_1 y_2}{\Sigma x_1^2} = \frac{-97}{102} = -.95$$

Thus the purged instrument Y_2 is (in convenient deviation form)

$$\hat{y}_2 = -.95 \, x_1$$

For the second stage, we apply this instrument y_2 to the equation $Y_1 = \gamma_2 Y_2 + e$, that is, take covariances of $\hat{y}_2$ with respect to Y_1 and Y_2 (while the covariance with respect to e is small enough to drop):

From table above				products	
y_1	y_2	$\hat{y}_2 = -.95x_1$		$\hat{y}_2 y_1$	$\hat{y}_2 y_2$
8	-4	-2.85		- 22.80	11.40
-3	3	+ .95		- 2.85	2.85
1	-2	-1.90		- 1.90	3.80
-9	6	+3.80		- 34.20	22.80
-10	3	+5.70		- 57.00	17.10
-13	-6	-5.70		- 74.1	34.20
0	0	0		-192.85	92.15

Thus, when we apply the instrument $\hat{y}_2$ to the equation $Y_1 = \gamma_2 Y_2 + e$, we have (ignoring the divisor n-1):

$$s_{\hat{Y}_2 Y_1} \simeq \gamma_2 s_{\hat{Y}_2 Y_2}$$

that is, $-192.85 \simeq \gamma_2 (92.15)$

$$\gamma_2 = \frac{-192.85}{92.15} = -2.09$$

b.   The second equation is

$$Y_2 = \gamma_1 Y_1 + \beta_1 X_1 + e$$

Since the regressors (on the right side) are X_1 and Y_1, we will use as instruments X_1 and $\hat{Y}_1$. Using first X_1:

$$s_{X_1 Y_2} \simeq \gamma_1 \, s_{X_1 Y_1} + \beta_1 \, s_{X_1 X_1}$$

Ignoring the divisor (n-1) as usual, we find the required covariances in the last three columns of the initial table in part (a), so that:

$$-97 \simeq \gamma_1 (203) + \beta_1 (102)$$

Or, if we divide by n-1 = 5, we get

$$-19.4 = 40.6 \, \gamma_1 + 20.4 \, \beta_1 \tag{1}$$

Now consider the other instrument $\hat{Y}_1$, i.e. the fitted regression of Y_1 on X_1:

193

$$b = \frac{\Sigma x_1 y_1}{\Sigma x_1^2} = \frac{203}{102} = 1.99$$

Thus $\hat{y}_1 = 1.99\ x_1$. When we use this to take covariances, we get the same answers as using x_1, except for the factor 1.99 of course; that is, we get:

$$1.99 \times (-19.4 = 40.6\ \gamma_1 + 20.4\ \beta_1)$$

i.e., $-38.6 = 80.8\gamma_1 + 40.6\ \beta_1$ \hfill (2)

When we try to solve these two IV equations for the two unknowns γ_1 and β_1, what happens? To eliminate the first unknown γ_1, we would multiply the first equation by $80.8/40.6 = 1.99$ to get matching coefficients:

(1) x 1.99: \hspace{2em} $-38.6 = 80.8\gamma_1 + 40.6\ \beta_1$ \hfill (3)

Now when we subtract (3) from (2), we eliminate γ_1 as desired. But unfortunately, we eliminate everything else too:

$$0 = 0 + 0$$

Thus it is impossible to get a unique solution for this pair of IV equations, because one is just a restatement (multiple) of the other--what mathematicians call <u>linear dependence</u>.

Since there is too little information to get a unique solution, statisticians say the given equation $Y_2 = \gamma_1 Y_1 + \beta_1 X_1 + e$ is <u>underidentified</u> or just <u>unidentified</u>.

25-9

    a. In a system of mutually dependent variables, a regression equation may be badly biased if [IV, <u>OLS</u>] is used. This is because the error term is [<u>correlated</u>, uncorrelated] with the regressors. And OLS, in attributing as much as possible of the response to the regressors, attributes [<u>some</u>, none] of the error to the regressors.

    b. An instrumental variable should be [<u>highly correlated</u>, uncorrelated] with the regressors, and [highly correlated, <u>uncorrelated</u>] with the error term.

    c. OLS and 2SLS are both special cases of instrumental variables: OLS uses [mutually dependent variables, <u>the regressors themselves</u>] as IV, while 2SLS uses [mutually dependent variables, <u>linear combinations of the predetermined variables</u>] as IV.

PART II REVIEW PROBLEMS

Within each chapter, part A gives 5 or 10 review problems ordered roughly from easiest to most challenging.

In part B, themes are developed. They illustrate the insights that statistics gives to some of the great issues in social science -- ranging from experimental design,to Arrow's paradox, to evaluating the performance of a forecaster. At the same time, the student practices his skills learned in the chapter, just as in the Final Challenge at the end of each chapter in the text itself.

Problems based on starred optional sections of the chapter are themselves starred.

CHAPTER 1 - THE NATURE OF STATISTICS

On three successive nights a young man experimented with drinking his limit -- first scotch and soda, then rye and soda, finally bourbon and soda. As he recovered from his third raging hangover, he soberly concluded:

"I'll never drink soda again."

Drinkers' lore

PART A STANDARD PROBLEMS (EASIEST FIRST)

1-1   As the above quotation -- and the whole history of science -- vividly show, experimentation must be done carefully if confounding is to be avoided. Specifically, how can the treatment and control groups be created equal? How can they be kept equal (except for the treatment itself of course)? And how can they be evaluated fairly at the end?

1-2   Shortly before the 1988 Presidential election, a Gallup poll of about 1500 voters showed the following support for Bush among various groups:

        college educated, 58% (n = 440)   under age 30, 64% (n = 220)
        <u>less than college, 52% (n = 1060)</u>   <u>over age 30, 52% (n = 1280)</u>
        <small>Reconstructed from the Gallup Report, November 1988, p. 7.</small>

For each of the four groups, calculate a 95% confidence interval for the proportion supporting Bush.

1-3   An historical study of crime in American urban cores (Simon, 1981) shows that since 1950, the crime rate has tended to go up while the density has tended to go down. To what extent does this prove that low population density produces crime?

1-4   Give some historical examples of useless or even harmful "treatments" -- medical, social, educational, etc. -- that persisted for many years, because they were not evaluated properly.

1-5   Give some present-day examples of "treatments" that are perhaps useless or harmful, but still persist because they have not been evaluated well and nobody really knows their true effect.
      In which cases would it be relatively easy to evaluate the treatment properly? How? In which cases would it be extremely difficult to evaluate the treatment properly? Why?

1-6   A die was rolled 10,000 times and showed a single dot 1,720 times. Does that represent just random fluctuation from the "fair" number of 1,667, or would you say the die is biased? Answer as well as you can.

1-7   Between 1950 and 1975, many more people in the U.S. died from smallpox vaccinations (over 100) than from smallpox itself (none). [From Fischhoff 1986]. What does this say about the wisdom of the vaccination program?
    Explain briefly, and suggest what sort of additional evidence (if any) would be useful.

PART B DEVELOPING THEMES

B-1 HOW DOES RANDOMIZATION WORK?

1-8   To preserve confidentiality, suppose the 28 women in the infant-care experiment described in Section 1-2 of the text were lettered one by one as they entered the hospital, as follows (with single women denoted by capital letters):

        A a b B C   D c d e E   f F g h j
        k G m n p   H J q r s   t K u

One way to randomly assign them to treatment or control is to put all their names in a hat, and draw out half. Sometimes, however, the full list of subjects is not known initially; for example, subjects may just come in one by one until the researchers decide they have enough data. Then randomization has to be done differently. For example, as each subject enters the hospital, she could be assigned to treatment or control depending on whether a coin turns up heads or tails.

   a.   Actually flip a coin for each of the women lettered above to see how this randomization works. (Or use the table of random digits in Appendix Table I, letting an odd digit represent heads, and an even digit represent tails.) Circle the subjects who get "heads," and consequently go into the treatment group.

   b.   As already noted, the 10 capital letters represent the 10 women who are single. Does the randomization in part (a) leave them about evenly split into the treatment and control groups?

   c.   Suppose this experiment were repeated 10 times (or, equivalently, conducted on 10 times as large a scale). How evenly would you expect the single women to be split now?

   d.   To confirm your guess in part (c), actually repeat the randomized assignment 10 times and see whether the overall split is nearly 50-50. Does this show how randomization tends to even out confounding factors on average (in the long run)?

B-2 SAMPLE DESIGN AND EXPERIMENTAL DESIGN ARE SIMILAR -- AND CRUCIAL

1-9   a.   To make sure a sample is as representative as possible, that is, the individuals selected for the sample are like the individuals left behind in the population, we should make sure they [are drawn randomly, come forth voluntarily].

       b.   Similarly in designing an experiment, how can we ensure that the individuals who are selected for the treatment group are like the ones left behind as controls? That is, how can we get the treatment and control groups off to a fair start? We assign the individuals to the treatment group [randomly, by asking for volunteers so that those people who are reluctant to try the new treatment are not forced].

1-10   a.   From an ethical point of view, is it important that the people who are assigned to the treatment groups are volunteers, that is, are not forced to take the new treatment?

b.   Part (a) seems to conflict with the scientific requirements in Problem 1-9 (b) above. Is there any way to achieve good ethics <u>and</u> good science both? If not, which is more important?

1-11   In an experiment, simple randomized assignment creates treatment and control groups equal on average (in the long run). But in the short run, with the finite resources of real experiments, the two groups will be somewhat imbalanced. For example, suppose there are 10 diabetics who volunteered for the experiment, and the flip of a coin assigns them to treatment/control according to head/tail. Although 5-5 is the likeliest split, it might easily be 6-4 or even 7-3.

To prevent this imbalance, pairing can often be used. The 10 diabetics could be arranged in 5 pairs (matched in age too, as a bonus. For example, the two oldest diabetics form the first pair, then the next two oldest, until finally the youngest two form the last pair). Then in each matched pair, one diabetic is randomly assigned to treatment, and the other goes to control, to finally achieve the desired 5-5 balance.

a.   In the final step above, is it important that one diabetic from each pair be <u>randomly</u> assigned to treatment? Why?

b.   Unfortunately, when we form matched pairs, we cannot match for <u>all</u> the important variables, such as health, age, socio-economic status, sex, income, emotional health, and so on. That is why we randomize, to make sure the factors that were not matched are still split evenly in the long run -- and as evenly as possible in the short run.

Maybe further improvement can be made. Let us at least measure those variables that could not be matched, or were imperfectly matched. Could we include them in a multiple regression analysis of the data? What would this achieve?

1-12   a.   Could we not select a fairer sample, or a fairer treatment group for an experiment, by using expert judgement instead of randomization? What are the hazards of this?

b.   Is there any way to use expert judgement <u>and</u> randomization both?

CHAPTER 2 - DESCRIPTIVE STATISTICS

Everything should be made as simple as possible, but not simpler.

Albert Einstein

PART A - STANDARD PROBLEMS (EASIEST FIRST)

2-1   The number of incoming calls at a telephone exchange in each of 50 successive minutes were recorded as follows:

1,0,1,1,0,   0,2,2,0,2,   1,0,1,4,0,   3,0,1,0,2,   0,0,0,1,0,
0,1,2,1,0,   0,1,3,1,1,   1,1,4,0,1,   2,1,1,0,2,   0,0,1,2,1.

   a.   Tabulate and graph the relative frequency distribution.

   b.   On average, how many calls are there per minute?

   c.   Calculate the variance and standard deviation. (Counts of random events like these telephone calls, or fire alarms, or radioactive blips, etc., form a <u>Poisson</u> distribution. One of its characteristics is that the variance equals the mean for large n.)

2-2   The 50 American states have areas (in thousands of square miles) that range from 591 (Alaska) to 1.2 (Rhode Island). The median is 56.2 and the mean is 72.4. If possible, calculate the total area. If not possible, what further information would you need?

2-3   To estimate the lumber they could cut from a large stand of red pine, a Wisconsin mill took a random sample of 40 trees. The diameters (measured in feet, at waist height) were:

1.6, 2.8, 2.2, 2.5, 2.8   1.9, 2.2, 1.7, 1.8, 2.8
1.8, 1.8, 2.1, 3.1, 2.2   1.8, 1.5, 1.4, 1.5, 1.9
1.4, 1.5, 2.1, 2.5, 2.6   1.4, 2.5, 1.9, 1.9, 1.8
2.4, 1.6, 1.5, 2.0, 1.5   1.4, 2.4, 2.0, 2.4, 1.8

   a.   Without sorting into cells, graph the diameters as dots along an X axis.

   b.   What is the median? The interquartile range?

   c.   Draw the box plot.

2-4   Group the data of Problem 2-3 into cells, with midpoints 1.5, 2.0, ...

   a.   Graph the relative frequency distribution.

   b.   Calculate $\bar{X}$ and s and the relative standard deviation (or coefficient of variation) defined as CV = $s/\bar{X}$.

   c.   If the trees were measured in inches instead of feet, what would be $\bar{X}$, s, and CV?

2-5   (Precise definitions for the median and quartiles as used in MINITAB, for example.)
       If n is odd, the median is the very middle observation, that leaves an equal number
       of observations on either side. If n is even, there are two "middle" observations;
       then the median is defined as their midpoint (exactly halfway between).

       For the quartiles, we just cut each half of the data in half again. To define the
       lower quartile, for example, take the median of the lowest half of the observations
       (more precisely, the lowest n/2 observations if n is even, and the lowest (n+1)/2
       observations if n is odd).

       Do these definitions coincide with the informal advice given in Problem 2-3 in the
       text?

2-6   a.   Use the precise definition in Problem 2-5 above to find the median and quartiles
             of the following 20 Latin American populations in 1986 (which altogether
             contained 388 million people, excluding the Caribbean):

Brazil	143	Venezuela	18	ElSalvador	5	Costa Rica	3
Mexico	82	Chile	12	Honduras	5	Panama	2
Argentina	31	Ecuador	10	Paraguay	4	Guyana	1
Columbia	30	Guatemala	9	Uruguay	3	Surinam	0.4
Peru	20	Bolivia	6	Nicaragua	3	Belize	0.2

             (Stat. Abst. of U.S. 1987, p. 815)

       b.   Draw the box plot

       c.   Would you describe this distribution as symmetric or skewed? Therefore where
             would you expect to find the mean, in relation to the median?

       d.   Now calculate the mean population, to confirm your conjecture in (c). (Hint:
             Before you start calculating, read the opening sentence in part (a).)

2-7   Repeat Problem 2-6, for the 15 largest Latin American countries (deleting the smallest
       5).

2-8   In the following distributions, the mean, median, and mode are among the five little
       marks on the X-axis. Pick them out - without resorting to calculation.

       a.   b.

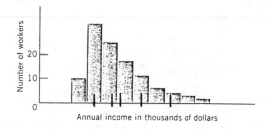

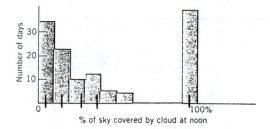

2-9 In Problem 2-8(a) suppose 2 zeros were mistakenly added to one of the incomes, making it 100 times too large. How would this affect the mean and median? Underline the correct choice:

a. The [mean, median] would erroneously be increased substantially.

b. The [mean, median] would be changed very little or not at all, depending on whether the one mutilated observation was originally below or above the [mean, median]. That is, the [mean, median] is resistant.

2-10 In Problem 2-8(b) suppose the right-most frequency was reduced slightly, to 3/4 of its present height. Although the distribution isn't changed much, one of the measures of center is drastically changed (lacks resistance). Which one is it: the mean, median, or mode?

2-11

Number of Children	frequency
1	30
2	50
3	10
4	10
	100

In a sample of 100 families, the number of children in each family was tabulated above.

a. For the 100 families, find the mean number of children per family.

b. For the 200 children belonging to these families, find the mean number of siblings that these children have. (A sibling is a brother or sister. Every child in a 5 child family, for example, would have 4 siblings.)

2-12 A random sample of 120 children from Mountsfield School were asked, "How many siblings do you have in this school?", and they gave the following answers:

number of siblings	frequency
0	18
1	60
2	18
3	24

All the families who had children in Mountsfield School were invited to discuss redistricting. To prepare their case, the School Board wanted to know what was their average family income, average family size, etc.
Since you are taking a Stats course, they have asked you to give them an unbiased estimate of average family size (more specifically, "family size" is the number of children attending Mountsfield School, and excludes the parents). What is it? (Hint: Do Problem 2-11 first)

B-1   GEE-WHIZ GRAPHS (SPECIAL SUPPLEMENT ON THE USE AND ABUSE OF GRAPHS)

Like Section 2-7 in the text, these "Gee Whiz" graphs in Part B will be drawn not from the dark corners of sleazy newsstands (where you might expect them), but from some of the best magazines and newspapers in the country.

2-13   For each of the following, suggest some improvements, and include them in a rough draft of a new graph.

a.

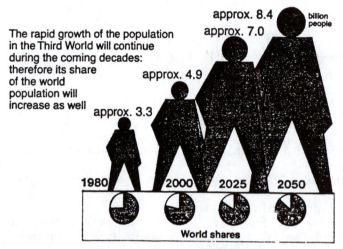

(1985 JRO Kartografische Verlagsgesellschaft mbl-1, D-8000 Munich)

b.

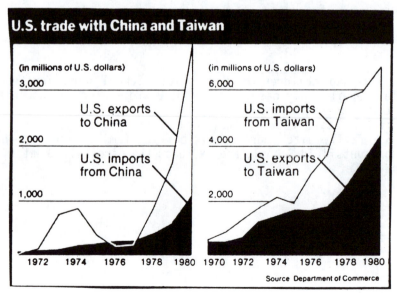

(New York Times, June 14, 1981, via Wainer 1984)

202

2-14 Now let us learn from some graphs that do it right, such as the one below.

    a.   At a glance, roughly determine:
           i)   By 1970 the farm population decreased to about _____ of the 1940 value.
          ii)   By 1970 the number of farms decreased to about _____ of the 1940 value.

    b.   Between 1940 and 1970, other sources show the amount of farm land changed hardly at all (increased very slightly). Calculate roughly the change in the <u>average</u> farm size.

    c.   From the graph, read off more careful values for (a) and (b).

    d.   Can you suggest any ways to improve the graph a little?

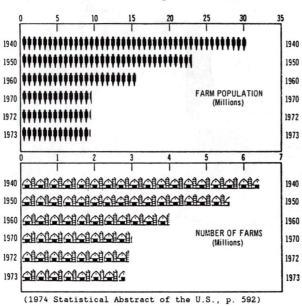

Changes in Farming: 1940 to 1973

FARM POPULATION (Millions)

NUMBER OF FARMS (Millions)

(1974 Statistical Abstract of the U.S., p. 592)

2-15 Whereas the ordinary maps of North and South America show the physical area of various countries, the map below gives a more interesting perspective -- the economic power, as measured by Gross Domestic Product (GDP). From it, at a glance you can estimate:

a. As a proportion of the United States, what is the economic power of Canada? of Mexico?

b. How does Portuguese-speaking Brazil compare with the Spanish-speaking rest of South America?

c. What percentage of the World's economic power is wielded by the United States? by Brazil? (Hint: the legend on the right shows how large an area represents 1%)

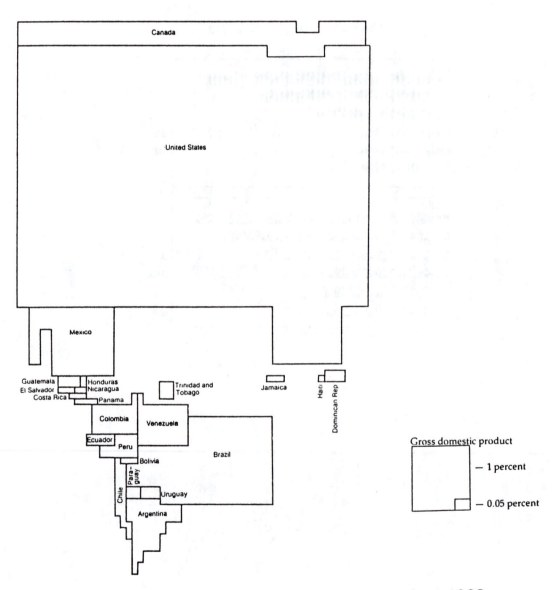

Distribution of product among selected countries, 1982

(World Bank 1984, World Development Report 1984, p. 14)

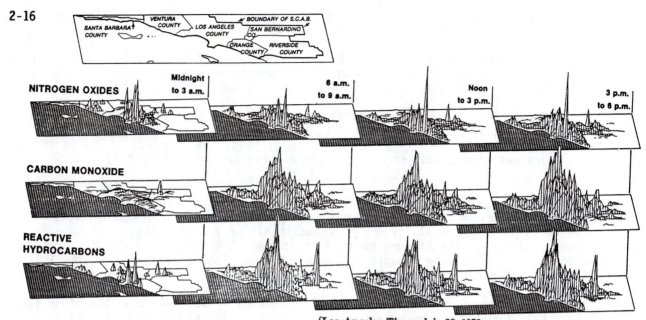

(**Los Angeles Times**, July 22, 1979;
based on work of Gregory J. McRae, California Institute of Technology. Via Tufte 1983, p. 42)

The above computer graph nicely illustrates that a "picture is worth a thousand words". It gives great impact to the main message, and still provides tremendous detail.

a.   Which time period is much cleaner than the others? Can you suggest why?

b.   Of the four southern counties (LA county and below), which county is much cleaner than the others?

c.   Now for some detail. In the dark hours of the night, where is the one small "hot spot" of carbon monoxide pollution? (It could be traced to Kaiser Steel's Fontana Plant). Does it produce the other two pollutants then too?

B-2 GEE-WHIZ WRITING

We must not forget the commonest form of communication. Even more important than graphs, the written word must tell a straight story too, as this special supplement will show.

2-17 (The disappearing base -- or no base at all.) When an expectant couple discover the tragic news that the fetus is seriously defective, they sometimes choose abortion over the birth of a deformed child. The emotional impact of this decision was described by Fuchs (1980):

> "In our study done at the University of California Medicine in San Francisco, depression developed in 92% of the women and 82% of the men in couples who elected to interrupt a pregnancy."

Those figures sound awfully high. What do they really mean about the couple's decision? Let us ask some probing questions:

a.   How severe was the "depression" that developed?

205

b.   Even if we grant the depression that developed was severe and too prolonged, can we conclude that in this regard, abortion was the wrong choice?

c.   The author continues (Fuchs 1980): "Yet most of the families studied would repeat the course of action and elect abortion over the birth of a defective child." Does this show that these families made the right choice?

d.   Do you agree with this summary? If there is any lesson in this, perhaps it is that statistics that <u>sound</u> important and precise may not really tell us anything, if they lack a <u>control or basis for comparison</u>. And they may give us a lot less insight than a good novel, that doesn't pretend to be scientific.

2-18   (Switching the base -- without mentioning it of course) "In the 1930's, the incidence of melanoma (severe form of skin cancer) among Canadians was about one in 10,000. Now, one Canadian in 135 will develop melanoma in his or her lifetime. ... Some medical experts attribute the phenomenon in part to the thinning of the earth's protective ozone layer." (Maclean's Magazine, Canada's Weekly Newsmagazine, June 13, 1988, p. 37. Brackets are ours.)

a.   After reading this article, my wife was terribly worried about the ozone layer. Let us see why. In just 50 years (since the 1930's) how much did the incidence of melanoma apparently increase?

b.   Now let us look more carefully at these astounding figures. <u>Incidence</u> is defined by medical statisticians as the number of new cases (per year, unless stated otherwise) relative to the number of people at risk (population). In the 1930's, Maclean's stated above that it was "about one in 10,000" (.0001).

Earlier in the MacLean's article, information was given that allows us to calculate the incidence in 1988: "This year in Canada, 2,200 (cases of skin cancer) will be melanomas." The 1988 population of Canada was 26,000,000.

Calculate the incidence of melanoma in 1988. How much did it actually increase in 50 years?

2-19   (Continuing Problem 2-18). The <u>lifetime</u> risk of melanoma -- rather than the annual risk or incidence above -- is an alternative way to measure its severity. It sounds deceptively the same, but mathematically it is vastly different. And maybe it will explain Maclean's sleight-of-hand above.

a.   How much higher will lifetime risk be, than annual risk, roughly? Using the 1988 annual risk (incidence) found in Problem 2-18(b), therefore, roughly estimate the lifetime risk in 1988.

b.   How does your answer in (a) compare to the 1988 lifetime risk of "one Canadian in 135" given by Maclean's in Problem 2-18?

c.   We have clarified how Maclean's "switched horses in midstream" without warning us. Some famous humorist -- Mark Twain perhaps? -- gave a similar example of this scam long ago: "In 1870 oranges cost 20¢ each. By 1880, the price of a dozen oranges had skyrocketed to $2.40."
          To make the analogy clear, fill in the blanks of this paraphrase of the quotation from Maclean's at the start of Problem 2-18: "In the 1930's, the annual risk of melanoma was about one in 10,000. Now the lifetime risk over [75, 20] years has skyrocketed to about [75, 20] in 10,000, that is, about 1 in 135 ... Some statisticians attribute the phenomenon in part to [the thinning of the ozone layer, skulduggery]."

CHAPTER 3 - PROBABILITY

Gambling -- the sure way of getting nothing for something

Wilson Mizner

3-1   I kept extensive records of my favourite baseball pitcher, and this is what I found
       for those batters who took three pitches (or more). Three strikes in a row were
       pitched 15% of the time. And for every possible sequence of strikes and balls, here
       are all the relative frequencies (approximate probabilities):

Sequence of first 3 pitches	probability
SSS	.15
SSB	.15
SBS	.10
SBB	.10
BSS	.10
BSB	.10
BBS	.15
BBB	.15

Suppose we are interested in the following events:

E: 2 or 3 strikes
F: all pitches the same (all strikes, or all balls)
G: 2 or 3 balls
H: some pitches different

Find the following probabilities:

a.   Pr(E), Pr(F), Pr(E or F), Pr(E and F)

b.   Pr(G), Pr(H), Pr(G or H), Pr(G and H)

c.   Verify that the formula (3-12) for Pr(G or H) holds true in both (a) and (b).

3-2   In Problem 3-1, consider three more events:

E_1:   first pitch is a strike
E_2:   last two pitches are strikes
E_3:   all three pitches are strikes

a.   Are E_1 and E_2 independent?

b.   Are E_1 and E_3 independent?

3-3   Repeat Problem 3-2, except now flip a coin three times instead (marking the two sides
       S and B instead of head and tail). Answer in two ways:

       i)   Intuitively (would knowledge of the first event affect your betting on the
             second?)
       ii)   More formally, draw up the sample space and calculate the relevant
             probabilities.

3-4 Two transmissions are randomly sampled from a supply of ten -- three of which are faulty. What is the chance of getting

a. Both faulty?

b. Both okay?

c. One faulty, and one okay?

3-5 As quality control manager of a camera firm, you have found that 70% of the cameras coming off the line are satisfactory; 20% have fixable flaws; and 10% are so defective that they are worthless. A sample of two cameras is drawn. What are the chances that:

a. Both are satisfactory

b. Both are worthless

c. Exactly one has fixable flaws

3-6 The long experience of a clinic is that 1/10 of its patients have disease A, 2/10 have disease B, and 7/10 have neither. Of those with disease A, 9/10 have headaches; of those with disease B, 1/2 have headaches; and of those with neither disease, 1/20 have headaches.
   If a patient in this clinic has headaches, what is the probability that he has disease A? Disease B? Neither?

3-7 Use Venn diagrams to determine which of the following statements are true:

a. $\overline{E \text{ or } F} = \overline{E} \text{ or } \overline{F}$

b. $\overline{E \text{ or } F} = \overline{E} \text{ and } \overline{F}$

c. $\overline{E \text{ and } F} = \overline{E} \text{ and } \overline{F}$

d. $\overline{E \text{ and } F} = \overline{E} \text{ or } \overline{F}$

Incidentally, the true statements are known as De Morgan's Laws.

3-8

Region of Canada	Proportion of Canadians living in the region	Proportion who speak French*
Atlantic Provinces	10%	14%
Quebec	29%	81%
Ontario	34%	7%
Prairie Provinces	18%	4%
British Columbia and North	9%	2%

*French as their first language. 1961 Census

a. What proportion of Canadians speak French?

b. I happened upon a Canadian yesterday in Hong Kong. What is the chance she is from Quebec,

   i) before I knew anything else about her?

ii) if I found out she spoke French?
iii) if I found out she did <u>not</u> speak French?

c.   What assumptions did you make in part (b)?

3-9   A high-precision milling machine recently has not been working right, so that 10% of its output is defective. A new machine was purchased, which worked at twice the speed, with flawless output. But until back orders were filled, both machines were used.

I sampled a package of four items produced by one of the machines. The first three items were found flawless. Now what is the chance the fourth is flawless?

3-10   A poker hand (5 cards) is drawn from an ordinary deck of cards. What is the chance of the following events?

a.   The first 4 cards are the aces?
b.   The first 2 cards and the last 2 cards are the aces?
c.   The 4 aces are somewhere among the 5 cards ("4 aces")?
d.   "4 of a kind" (4 aces, or 4 kings, or 4 queens, ..., or 4 deuces)?

3-11   Discuss critically the following:

In the 3-year period that followed the murder of President Kennedy in 1963, fifteen material witnesses died - six by gunfire, three in motor accidents, two by suicide, one from a cut throat, one from a karate chop to the neck, and two from natural causes. An actuary concluded that on the day of the assassination, the odds against this particular set of witnesses being dead within 3 years were one hundred thousand trillion to one. Since all these things couldn't have just happened, they must reflect an organized coverup of the assassination.

3-12   A millionaire devised the following "sure-fire" sequential scheme for netting $1000 eventually by betting on the right color (black or red) at roulette, where the probability of each color is nearly 1/2.

The first time, bet $1000. If you win, stop. If you lose, double your bet to $2000.

If you win this second time, stop. If you lose, double your bet again, to $4000. Continue betting this way -- stopping if you win, doubling the bet if you lose. When you finally stop, you will have a net win of $1000.

As proof that this actually worked, he pointed out that he had made it successfully five times already, to give him five "free" weekends in Las Vegas.

This is a very old idea, actually. Is it a good one? Why?

CHAPTER 4 - PROBABILITY DISTRIBUTIONS

> If you bet on a horse, that's gambling. If you bet you can make three spades, that's entertainment. If you bet cotton will go up three points, that's business. See the difference?
>
> Blackie Sherrod

PART A - STANDARD PROBLEMS (EASIEST FIRST)

4-1   The Swedish population of men's heights is approximately normally distributed with a mean of 69 inches and standard deviation of 3 inches. Find the proportion who are:

    a.   Under 5 feet (60 inches).

    b.   Over 6 feet (72 inches).

    c.   Between 5 and 6 feet.

4-2   The mathematics Scholastic Aptitude Test (SAT, math) gives scores that range from 200 to 800. They are approximately normally distributed about a mean of 470, with a standard deviation of 120 (for the population of U.S. college-bound seniors in 1978).

    Graph this distribution, and then calculate and illustrate the following:

    a.   What percentage of the scores are between 500 and 600?

    b.   What score is the 75th percentile (upper quartile)?

    c.   What score is the 25th percentile (lower quartile)?

    d.   What is the interquartile range?

4-3   a.   If the moments of X are $\mu = 5$ and $\sigma = 10$, what are the moments of:

        i) $U \equiv 2X + 3$
        ii) $V \equiv .4X - .7$
        iii) $Z \equiv X - 5/10$

    b.   If X has mean μ and standard deviation σ, what are the moments of

$$Z = \frac{X - \mu}{\sigma}$$

    c.   In part (b), if X has a distribution that is normally shaped, what will be the shape of the distribution of Z?

4-4   To test whether a drug has an effect, a group of 10 matched pairs of volunteers are used. In each pair, one is selected at random to be treated with the drug while the other is treated with a placebo as a control. At the end of the experiment, a doctor examines each pair and declares which of the two is healthier. (She is forced to declare a decision -- no ties allowed). Then she counts up X, the number of pairs in which the treated patient was declared healthier than the control. Of course, the random variable X could be any integer from 0 to 10.

a. If the drug was ineffective (neither good nor bad), what would be Pr(X ≥ 8)?

b. Suppose now that the drug was so effective that for each matched pair, the probability is 90% that the treated patient will be declared healthier. What would be Pr(X ≥ 8) now?

c. Should the doctor who makes the diagnosis know who has been treated and who has not, or should she be kept "blind" about this? Why?

4-5 In a behavior modification experiment, the time T required for a rat to run a maze is a random variable with the following probability distribution:

t	5	6	7	8	9	10
p(t)	.1	.1	.3	.2	.2	.1

a. Find the average time, and variance.

b. Suppose that the rat is rewarded with 1 biscuit for each second faster than 9. (For example, if he takes just 7 seconds, he gets a reward of 2 biscuits. Of course, if he takes 9 seconds or longer, he gets no reward.) What is the rat's average reward?

c. Suppose that the rat is punished by getting a shock that increases sharply as his time increases - specifically, a shock of T^2 volts for a time of T seconds. What is the rat's average punishment? Calculate two ways:

   i)   using (4-32)
   ii) using (4-36)

4-6 Tom and Gary play a tennis match, best 2 out of 3. That is, the first player to win 2 games wins the match. The chance of Gary winning any game is .60, and the games are statistically independent.

a. What is the chance that Gary wins the match?

b. If it is the best 5 out of 9, what is the chance now that Gary wins?

4-7 A TV network selling prime time to advertisers claims that the number of homes reached each afternoon by its soap opera "San Francisco" has a mean of 2.6 million homes and a standard deviation of 0.4 million. (Assume a normal distribution.)

a. Assuming their claim is true, what fraction of the afternoons does "San Francisco" reach fewer than 2.0 million homes?

b. If two afternoons are randomly sampled, what is the chance that "San Francisco" will reach fewer than 2.0 million homes both times?

c. When a TV rating service carried out the random sampling in (b), they found this event did indeed occur. Would you believe the TV networks claim? Explain briefly.

4-8   A shoe repair shop has one large motor supplying power to 8 workers. Each worker needs the power for 24 minutes every hour on average, so that his chance of needing power at any given moment is 24/60 = 40%. And each worker works independently of the other workers. That is, at any given moment his chance of drawing power does not depend on whether his co-workers happen to be drawing power.

   a.   At any moment, what is the chance that all 8 workers would happen to need power? And what is the average number who need power?

   b.   If the motor's capacity is limited to 3 workers drawing power at once, what proportion of the time will it be overloaded?

   c.   Management wants this overload to occur only 5% of the time, at most. To what level must they increase the capacity of the motor [i.e., how many workers should the motor allow to draw power at once]?

4-9   a.   Suppose a secretary spills 3 different letters and their envelopes. She scrambles them so hopelessly that, in despair, she stuffs each letter into an envelope at random and then mails them. Let S = number of people who receive the right letter; thus S = 0, 1, 2, 3. Find the mean of S.

   b.   Repeat part (a) if there are just 2 letters.

   c.   Guess what the answer would be in general for n letters.

4-10   The owner of a small motel with 10 units has 3 videos that he rents for $2 per night. Long-run past experience shows that only 20% of his guests request a video, so he hopes his supply of 3 videos will ordinarily be adequate.

   Considering just those nights when all 10 units of the motel are rented:

   a.   On what proportion of the nights will the requests exceed the available supply of 3 videos?

   b.   What is the average number of videos requested?

   c.   What is the average number of videos actually rented?

   d.   What is the average revenue per night from video rentals?

   e.   What assumptions did you make?

PART B - DEVELOPING THEMES

B-1 AN INVENTORY DECISION

4-11   Expecting to sell about 400 copies of a hot new novel, the owners of a bookstore order 500 just to be sure. If they have any left over after six months (when the paperback will come out), they will have to sell them at a loss of $10 each. Yet if they don't have enough, they may not be able to reorder; they expect a loss (opportunity loss) of $5 on each book they could have sold, but didn't have in stock. All this makes them wonder how successful their order of 500 books will be.

To answer this question, they first looked at past records of best sellers to make up a schedule of possible sales over the next six months, as shown in column 1 of the table below. Then they made a shrewd guess in column 2 at the chance of each -- their personal probability p(x).

For each possible level of sales x, they listed their loss c(x) in the last column. (For example, if sales x = 200, they would have 300 copies left over; at $10 each, this is a loss of $3000. At the other extreme, if sales x = 900, they would be 400 copies short; at $5 each, this is a loss of $2000.)

possible sales x	personal probability p(x)	loss (from mismatching order of 500) c(x)
200	.10	$3000
300	.30	$2000
400	.20	$1000
500	.20	0
700	.15	$1000
900	.05	$2000

a.   Calculate the expected number that will be sold. Is it about 400 as stated?

b.   Make a table of possible costs c (in the usual increasing order), and tabulate their corresponding probabilities p(c).

c.   Then calculate the expected cost, and the standard deviation of cost.

d.   Alternatively, calculate the expected cost from the given table in one step: just weight the costs c(x) in the last column with their probabilities p(x) in the previous column, and add, as in (4-28).

4-12   In Problem 4-11, suppose books have to be ordered in 100 unit lots.

a.   Would 400 be a better number to order than 500? (Hint: Calculate the expected cost for ordering 400, by calculating the new c(x) column, and then proceed as as before.)

b.   Guess what might be an even better number than 400 to order. Then calculate how small it makes expected cost.

c.   Suppose you work in an MBA program as a small-business consultant. Write a very short note to the bookstore manager explaining what the best number to order is, and why it is less than the expected sales E(X).

213

B-2 A LIE DETECTOR TO PROTECT THE INNOCENT

4-13 The following scheme, called a guilty-knowledge test, has been proposed (Lykken, 1975) to help the police free innocent suspects, and so narrow down the list of possible suspects to a crime. Suppose, for example, that a savings and loan company has been robbed, and that a suspect is being interrogated. The police officer reads him the following multiple-choice question:

> "Before showing his gun, the robber pretended to take out a loan for a certain purpose. If you're the guilty man, you will know whether that purpose was to buy a car, to pay doctor bills, to buy stocks, to pay for a vacation, or to buy a color TV. I'm going to name each of these five possibilities in order, and I want you to sit quietly and just repeat what I say."

The suspect is hooked up to a polygraph (lie detector) that graphs his responses, and indicates which of the 5 choices produces the strongest reaction. If the suspect is guilty, it is likely that his strongest reaction will be to the correct answer. If he is not guilty, however, his strongest reaction may be to any of the 5 possibilities, equally likely.

Suppose the suspect answers 10 guilty-knowledge questions of this type. (For example, one question might be: The name of the Savings and Loan Company that was robbed was First Federal, Citizens Guarantee, Hartford National, Connecticut Western, or Middlesex?) Finally suppose, as a rule of thumb, that the suspect is immediately released if he shows guilty knowledge (answers "correctly") for 5 or fewer of the 10 questions; but he continues to be held if he answers 6 or more questions correctly.

a. The lie-detector test often requires the operator to make a very skilful judgment based on all the various graphs (hence the name "polygraph"). In view of the judgment required, should the polygraph operator herself know which answer is "correct"? Should the police officer who reads the statement to the suspect know?

b. What is the chance that an innocent man would incorrectly continue to be held? [This is called Type I error.]

c. Answer True of False; if False, correct it (quoted from Lykken, 1975):

   i) "With 10 guilty-knowledge questions of this type, there is only about one chance in 10 million that an innocent suspect will react strongest to the correct alternative in all 10 questions."

   ii) "And if a suspect shows guilty knowledge in 6 or more out of 10 questions, the chances that he is innocent are only 1 in 1000."

B-3 BIDDING: NONLINEAR MODELS

4-14 Suppose that you are bidding on a cottage, where the probability of your bid B successfully buying the cottage increases nonlinearly as given in the second column below:

Possible Bid B	Probability of Successful Bid, P(B)	Gain if Bid is Successful	Expected Gain
$40,000	0		
$41,000	.10		
$42,000	.30		
$43,000	.50		
$44,000	.80		
$45,000	.90		
$46,000	.96		
$47,000	1.00		

a. Suppose the cottage is worth $46,000 to you. If a bid of $42,000 succeeded, what would be your gain? What is your expected gain for a bid of $42,000? Enter these in the appropriate line in the table above.

b. Similarly fill out all the table, and so find your optimal bid.

*4-15 a. What answer to Problem 4-14 is obtained from the formula (4-39) in the text?

b. Why does the formula (4-39) give only an approximately correct answer?

B-4 BIDDING AND NEGOTIATION: SUMMARY

4-16 Underline the correct choice:

a. The optimal one-shot bid derived in Problem 4-14 is a careful trade-off between too [low, high] a bid that leaves too small a profit, and too [low, high] a bid that leaves too small a chance to make any profit at all.

b. The advantage that extended negotiation has over a one-shot bid is that if my initial offer is turned down, I can still try to strike a bargain that leaves me with some profit, rather than nothing at all. This is particularly important for many of the high-stake negotiations where the participants have no viable alternatives, so that failure to achieve some sort of agreement may entail very high losses -- for example, negotiations for labor contracts, for trade agreements, and for [peace treaties, buying a major item like an automobile]. In all these cases, it is crucial for the negotiators to keep their heads, and not let [altruism, bitterness] get in the way of striking a bargain.

4-17 Comment on how a couple of historical examples illustrate your answer to Problem 4-16(b):

    a.   In World War I (1914-18), 30 or 40 million people died in the futile struggle. And Europe's total exhaustion and bitterness led to the rise of Hitler in Germany (1933), and eventually the equally catastrophic World War II (1939-45). From all this bloodshed, what have we learned? Many historians feel that an unwillingness to negotiate and compromise was one of the major causes of this war starting, and then continuing to the point of brutal exhaustion. Then the victors' unwillingness to negotiate a compassionate peace was a major cause of the rise of Hitler.

    b.   One major light can be discerned in the gloomy history of war in the first half of this century. After World War II, the U.S. was astoundingly generous to the vanquished, especially with the Marshall Plan (1947-), which rehabilitated friend and foe alike. This helped to produce viable democracies in all three of the major vanquished countries -- West Germany, Italy, and Japan.

CHAPTER 5 - TWO RANDOM VARIABLES

If the only tool you have is a hammer, you tend to see every problem as a nail.
                                                                    - Abraham Maslow

PART A - STANDARD PROBLEMS (EASIEST FIRST)

5-1   The students in a large class wrote two exams, obtaining a distribution of grades with the characteristics shown in the table below.

	Class Mean μ	Standard Deviation σ
1st exam, X_1	50	20
2nd exam, X_2	80	20
a. Average, $\bar{X}$	?	?
b. Weighted Average, W	?	?
c. Improvement, I	?	?

If the covariance of the first and second exam grades was 50, fill in the table for the following three cases:

a.   The instructor calculated a simple average of the two grades:

$$\bar{X} = (X_1 + X_2)/2$$

b.   The instructor thought the second exam was twice as important, so she took a weighted average:

$$W = \frac{1}{3} X_1 + \frac{2}{3} X_2$$

c.   The instructor wanted to find how much X_2 was an improvement over X_1:

$$I = X_2 - X_1$$

5-2   Repeat Problem 5-1,

i.   If the covariance is now -200. How might you interpret such a negative covariance? What has it done to the variance of the average grade? And the variance of the difference I?

ii.   If the covariance finally is 0.

5-3   In planning a new shopping mall, the developer has to allow for two consecutive stages: time for buying the land (B), and then for construction (C). Based on past experience, the developer feels that these times will be uncertain, with the distributions given below (in years). He also feels that B and C are statistically independent (since a delay in buying the land does not change the betting odds on the construction time).

b	p(b)	c	p(c)
1	.10	1	.50
2	.30	2	.40
3	.30	3	.10
4	.20		
5	.10		

The developer will enjoy a big tax advantage if he can finish in 4 years or less. What is the chance of this?

5-4   Answer Problem 5-3, under the following alternative assumptions about the distributions of B and C:

    a.   Assume B and C are independent, with distribution given by the following formulas (geometric distributions):

$$p(b) = .4(.6)^{b-1}, \quad b = 1,2,3,\ldots$$
$$p(c) = .7(.3)^{c-2}, \quad c = 2,3,4,\ldots$$

    b.   Assume B and C are independent and normally distributed, with means of 2 and 1.5 years, and standard deviations of .3 and .4 years, respectively. (Hint: As we will see in Chapter 6, the sum B + C will be normally distributed too.)

    c.   Assume B and C are as in part b, except that now they are correlated: If B is especially long, the developer will work hard to shorten C, so that B and C have a negative correlation, $\rho = -.40$.

5-5   Each student from a large class took a test X before a three-week review session, and another test Y immediately after. The marks were normally distributed, with these parameters:

$$\mu_X = 60 \qquad \mu_Y = 75$$
$$\sigma_X = 12 \qquad \sigma_Y = 10 \qquad \rho = .80$$

The improvement or difference D = Y − X was then calculated for each student.

    a.   What proportion of the students showed an actual improvement (positive D)?

    b.   Who tends to show the most improvement, the students who start out weakest or strongest? [Hint: To answer this, you need to know whether the correlation of D with X is positive or negative. Calculate the covariance as $E(DX) - E(D)E(X)$, where $E(DX) = E(Y-X)X = E(XY) - E(X^2)$. Finally, use equation (4-36) for $E(X^2)$, and (5-11) for $E(XY)$.]

    c.   Does your answer to (b) bear out the folklore, "If you start low enough, you've got nowhere to go but up"? More formally, this is called "regression to the mean", and is studied extensively in Chapter 11 and 15.

PART B - DEVELOPING THEMES

B-1   SAMPLING THEORY

5-6   (Sampling with replacement) A bowl contains three chips numbered 2, 6 and 7. One chip is selected at random, replaced, and then a second chip is selected at random. Let X_1 and X_2 be the first and second numbers drawn.

   a.   Tabulate the joint distribution of X_1 and X_2.

   b.   Tabulate the (marginal) distribution of X_1, and of X_2.

   c.   Are X_1 and X_2 independent? What is their covariance?

   d.   Find the mean and variance of X_1, and of X_2.

   e.   Find the mean and variance of $\overline{X} = (X_1 + X_2)/2$ from the formulas for linear combinations. Then find the distribution of $\overline{X}$ and verify directly.

   f.   How would your answers above be different if the bowl contained 1,000 chips of each kind?

   g.   Is this a correct conclusion from part (f)? If not, correct it: In sampling with replacement, the important issue is the <u>relative</u> frequency of the various kinds of chips. The <u>absolute</u> frequency is immaterial.

5-7   Continuing Problem 5-6, if ten chips are sampled with replacement, what are the mean and variance of $\overline{X}$?

5-8   (Sampling without replacement.) Repeat Problem 5-6 with the following change: The first chip is kept out when the second is drawn. (Equivalently, the two chips could be drawn simultaneously).

B-2 ARROW'S PARADOX

5-9   After 100 contests in bowling, the 100 final scores of the Ypsilanti Yeomen showed the following distribution (relative frequency, or approximate probability):

Yeomen's score y	p(y)
10,000	.30
20,000	.40
30,000	.30

In this same league are two other teams, the Xenons and the Zebras, with even simpler distributions of final score:

Xenons' score, x	p(x)	Zebras' score z	p(z)
12,000	.40	15,000	.60
24,000	.60	25,000	.40

Whenever two teams play against each other, they play in separate lanes and are completely indifferent to each other, so that the two teams' scores are statistically independent. The winner, of course, is the team with the higher score that day.

a. When the Yeomen play the Xenons, who is usually the winner? With what probability?

b. When the Yeomen play the Zebras, who is usually the winner? With what probability?

5-10 a. To summarize Problem 5-9, is it fair to say that X usually beats Y, and Y usually beats Z? Which team would you say is the strongest? And the weakest?

b. Then what do you suppose will usually happen when X plays Z?

c. To confirm your conjecture in (b), go through the appropriate calculations. What do you find?

5-11 What happened in Problem 5-10 is embarrassing. We couldn't declare an unambiguous winner in terms of who usually beats whom. This is technically called "intransitivity", and is an example of "Arrow's Paradox". In more serious applications, such as some voting procedures, it shows that there are real difficulties in unambiguously declaring a winner.

a. In this bowling example, however, there is a simple alternative rule to declare the league winner unambiguously. Let each team play the other two teams equally often. Then which team will win most often -- and be unambiguously declared the league winner?

b. As an alternative to (a), suppose the league changes the rules, and declares the team with the highest average score the winner. Now which team would be declared the winner?

5-12 It is easy to imagine the teams in Problem 5-11 squabbling about the league rules: While the Zebras love the first rule (winning most often) the Yeomen prefer the second rule (the highest average score).

a. Finally, you are hired by the league president to settle the dispute. Which rule would you use?

b. The Yeomen make the following argument on behalf of the second rule (the highest average score): "Averages are not only easy to calculate and understand. They also are proportional to totals, and total points seem like a good criterion.
"Now what can we say about the first rule (winning most often)? If there were only two teams in the league, the Zebras and the Yeomen, it would declare the Yeomen the winner. But if the league is expanded to the present 3 teams, this first rule embarrassingly enough has to declare the Zebras the winner. If a further expansion to 4 or 5 teams occurred, the declared winner could switch again! How can we trust a rule so fickle, that lets the rivalry between two teams be decided by the size of the league?
"Note that the second rule (the highest average score) is not so fickle. No matter what other teams are in the league, the Yeomen will consistently be declared the winner, because their average score of 20,000 exceeds the Zebras' average score of 19,000."
Is this right? Comment.

220

CHAPTER 6 - SAMPLING

I returned, and saw under the sun, that the race is not to the swift, nor the battle to the strong, neither yet bread to the wise, nor yet riches to men of understanding, nor yet favor to men of skill; but time and chance happeneth to them all.

Bible, Ecclesiastes 9:11

PART A - STANDARD PROBLEMS (EASIEST FIRST)

6-1   A union organizer takes a random sample of 25 workers in a large plant, and calculates their mean weekly income $\bar{X}$. He realizes that if he had sampled another 25 workers, $\bar{X}$ would have been different, and this uncertainty worries him.

Then he remembers his stats course, and the Monte Carlo studies. Samples had been drawn over and over again, in a classroom exercise that was easy and quick (a privilege not available in real life, where one sample of 25 workers is all he could afford). When the many possible values of $\bar{X}$ were arrayed·in a sampling distribution, he had seen the pattern clearly:

a. $\bar{X}$ fluctuated about the [sample mean, population mean] in a [normal, flat, multivariate] distribution.

b.   The typical deviation of $\bar{X}$ from its target μ was called the [population standard deviation σ, standard error SE], which turned out to be much [more, less] than the typical deviation [σ, SE] of an individual observation.

6-2   In a campaign to improve the freshness of its dairy products, a large supermarket chain conducted a random sample of 100 of its stores. In each store, a carton of milk (among other things) was randomly drawn from the shelf and the number of days X remaining until its "due date" was recorded.

In the whole population of milk cartons in all the stores, suppose X has a mean of 5.6 days and a standard deviation of 2.7 days. What is the chance that the <u>sample</u> mean will be quite close to the population mean -- specifically, between 5.4 and 5.8 days?

6-3   In Problem 6-2 above, suppose among the whole population of milk cartons, the proportion that are past the due date is 6%. What is the chance that among the 100 sampled, more than 10 will be past the due date?

6-4   An instructor wanted to draw a random sample of 5 students from her class of 30 students. She noticed that the classroom consisted of 9 rows, each having 8 chairs.

To choose the first student, she drew from Table I two random digits for the row and chair -- which turned out to be 4 and 3. So she went to the 4th row, and counted across to the 3rd chair. It happened to be empty so she drew a new random digit for the chair, 9. No student there, of course, since the last chair was number 8. The next random digit was 2, and in the 2nd chair of the 4th row at last was a student -- her first observation.

She continued to draw all 5 observations in this way -- the first random digit gave the row, the next digit (or digits, if required) gave the student within the row.

a.   Imagine doing this in your own classroom. Would it give a <u>random</u> sample? Why?

b.   Would it give unbiased estimates? Why?

6-5   A narrow slot 15.20 cm long is to be filled with 5 cylinders fitted end to end. These 5 cylinders are randomly drawn from a production run that has a mean of 3.00 cm and a standard deviation of .09 cm. What is the chance that the 5 cylinders will be too long to fit in?

6-6   Suppose the breaking strength of a rope is the sum of its 9 component strands of hemp; these strands are drawn at random from a large supply, whose mean breaking strength is 50 pounds and standard deviation is 12 pounds. What is the chance that a rope will hold a 400-pound load without breaking?   •

6-7   Suppose that X, the number of fast-food meals eaten in the past 14 days, has this distribution for the 200,000 adults in a target city being surveyed:

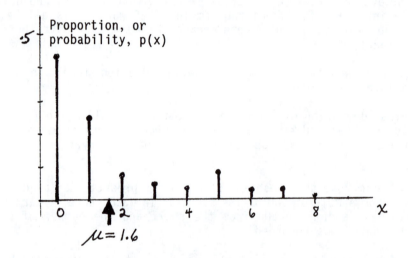

a.   Suppose a random survey of 10 residential phone calls is made on a Tuesday afternoon, but only 4 adults were at home to answer. Sketch on the graph where this sample of 10 might be typically located, and then the 4 replies. Where would the average reply be? And how close to the target μ?

b.   Repeat, for a random sample of just 4 to begin with, carefully followed up to obtain a 100% response rate. Would $\bar{X}$ be closer or further from μ?

6-8   Recall that probability was defined as limiting relative frequency. That means, for example, that if a fair die is thrown a million times, the relative frequency of aces (or proportion P) will likely be very close to 1/6. To be specific, calculate the probability that P will be within .001 of 1/6 (correct to about 3 decimal places).

6-9   When polarized light passes through α-lactose sugar, it is rotated by an angle of exactly 90°. The observed angle, however, is somewhat in error; suppose it is normally distributed around 90° with a standard deviation of 1.2°. A sample of 4 independent observations is taken. What is the chance:

a.   That the first observation exceeds 91°? (Since another sugar, D-xylose, rotates polarized light by 92°, the observer might then mistakenly think the α-lactose was D-xylose.)

b. That the average of the four observations exceeds 91°?

c. That all four observations exceed 91°? [Before you calculate the chance, can you say how it will compare to parts (a) and (b)?]

6-10 In a large East-coast city, 45% of the eligible jurors were women. If a jury of 12 is picked fairly (at random), what is the probability that there would be 3 or fewer women?

6-11 The 500 skiers on the slopes of Jay Peak on a sunny March afternoon had weights distributed as follows:

Weight	frequency
100	100
150	200
200	100
250	100
Total	500

a. The tram to the top carries 25 skiers, and has a load limit of 2½ tons (5000 lb). What is the chance that 25 skiers will overload it?

b. What assumptions did you make in (a)? Give a plausible example of where they might fail.

*6-12 (Monte Carlo) The number of fan belts ordered from a large auto supply fluctuates from day to day, with the following distribution:

daily order	proportion
15	.01
20	.05
25	.22
30	.33
35	.26
40	.10
45	.03

a. Supposing that successive days are independent, simulate a sample of 5 daily orders (a week's orders). Then calculate the sample average $\bar{X}$.

b. If the sampling experiment in (a) was repeated millions of times, what would the sampling distribution of $\bar{X}$ look like? Graph it.

Mark on this distribution the $\bar{X}$ you found in (a). Would you say it is a typical value of $\bar{X}$?

c. If the number ordered in a week exceeds 200, there is a problem with restocking. Find the chance of this occurring, using the distribution found in (b).

6-13 The number of completed years of college had the following distribution, in a large class of statistics students:

223

x = Number of Completed Years	p(x) = Relative Frequency
0	.30
1	.30
2	.40

a. Find the mean and variance of X.

b. If a random sample of 10 students were taken, what is the chance that $\bar{X}$ is .40 or less?

c. The instructor looked up the background of the 10 best students in the class. He found that 6 were freshmen and 4 were sophomores, so that their average number of completed years of college was $\bar{X}$ = .40. This led the instructor to claim that the younger students were doing unusually well. The dean replied that instead, it was just "small-sample fluctuation". How would you settle the dispute?

6-14 a. A farmer has two wheat fields of equal size, whose two yields (in tons) are independent random variables -- each with mean 30 and standard deviation 7, and normally distributed.

What is the chance he will get a total yield of 75 tons or more (the amount required to completely pay off his combine)?

b. Repeat part (a), now assuming more realistically that the yields of the two fields are correlated, because they share the same weather conditions, weed control, etc.; in fact the correlation is ρ = .70. (Hint: equation (5-18)).

c. Answer True or False; if False, correct it:

When there is positive correlation among the components of a sample mean $\bar{X}$, there is a tendency for high yields to occur with other high yields, rather than having highs and lows cancel. This makes a very high value of $\bar{X}$ itself more likely.

6-15 From an industry employing 123,000 workers, a random sample of 5,000 is drawn in order to estimate the number N that earn less than $15,000 annually. If N is actually 38,000, what is the chance the estimate will be fairly close, specifically, between 36,000 and 40,000?

PART B - DEVELOPING THEMES: A SIMPLE TREATMENT OF DUMMY VARIABLES

6-16 Of the 3000 professors at Elora University, 30 had earned a second doctorate, as shown in the last line of this distribution:

x = Number of PhD's earned by professor	frequency	proportion p(x)
0	870	.29
1	2100	.70
2	30	.01
	3000	1.00

The Carnegie Commission on Higher Education drew a random sample of 25 professors. What is the chance that their average number of doctorates will exceed 1/2 (the minimum standard)?

6-17 (Dummy Variables) In Problem 6-16, the 30 professors with the double doctorate moved on, and were replaced with young instructors without a doctorate yet. This produced as short a table as one can get and still have _some_ variability (a "dummy" variable):

x = Number of PhD's earned by professor,	proportion p(x)
0	.30
1	.70

a. What is the population mean? How is it related to the proportion of professors who have a doctorate?

b. In a random sample of n = 25, what is the chance that the proportion of doctorates will exceed 50% (the average number $\bar{X}$ will exceed 1/2)?

CHAPTER 7 - POINT ESTIMATION

The race is not always to the swift, nor the battle to the strong, but that's the way to bet.

Damon Runyon

PART A - STANDARD PROBLEMS (EASIEST FIRST)

7-1   In Chapter 1 we saw how nonrandom samples can be biased. In Chapter 6 we studied biased estimates more formally. Let us see how these two ideas are related, with a simple example. A week's production of galvanized nails was of uneven quality, due to a midweek adjustment of the coating process. In fact, the thickness of the coating was of two sizes:

       .12 mm for 70% of the nails
       .10 mm for 30% of the nails

    a.   Calculate the mean thickness μ.

    b.   To estimate μ, a haphazard sample of 100 nails was drawn without proper stirring. Since the nails with the thick coating tended to settle to the bottom, there was only a 50-50 chance that each nail drawn would have a thick/thin coating, rather than the fair 70-30 chance. As an estimator of μ, what is the bias of this haphazard sample mean?

7-2   The May 1989 issue of Working Mother magazine summarized 2015 responses to a questionnaire included in an earlier issue. Among other things, they reported a mean family income of $48,000 (roughly reconstructed from an Associated Press release reported in the London Free Press, 8 May 1989, p. C8).

    a.   The U.S. mean family income was actually about $30,000 (with a standard deviation of about $20,000. These figures are like those calculated in Problem 6-6 of this workbook, adjusted for the four-year time difference). What is the error in Working Mother's estimate? Then square it to get the squared error.

    b.   Suppose a <u>random</u> sample of 2015 families had been drawn, to obtain an unbiased estimate $\overline{X}$. What is the mean squared error (MSE) of this estimate? How does this compare to the answer in (a)?

    c.   Working Mother's questionnaire covered a lot of issues besides family income. How trustworthy do you think it was for making inferences about the whole U.S. population? Or about the population of working mothers?

7-3   a.   Using Table II, draw a random sample of 5 observations from a normal population with $\mu = 0$, $\sigma = 1$. Calculate the mean and median to estimate the population center. Which provides the best point estimate in your specific sample?

    b.   Which estimate would outperform the others if this sampling experiment were repeated many times?

7-4   Repeat Problem 7-3, with one twist: The last observation inadvertently has its decimal point dropped (so that it is actually multiplied by 10, and can be viewed as coming from a population with $\mu = 0$ and $\sigma = 10$).

7-5 A producer of audio equipment wants to estimate the proportion of defectives (π) in a large shipment of microchips. So he takes a random sample of n chips, and takes the sample proportion P as his natural estimate. He also needs to estimate a couple of other parameters, but is unsure whether the "natural estimate" is unbiased. Give him his answer, by filling out the last column:

	parameter	estimator	expected value	bias
a.	π (proportion defective)	P		
b.	π^2	P^2		
c.	$\dfrac{\pi(1-\pi)}{n}$ (variance of P)	$\dfrac{P(1-P)}{n}$		

7-6 A normally shaped population is to have its central value estimated with a random sample of size n. Peter takes a sample of n = 200 observations; he is fortunate to know that the shape of the distribution is normal, and so uses $\bar{X}$ as his estimator.

Paul does not know the shape of the distribution, and uses the sample median as his estimator. How large should Paul's sample be in order to get the same expected accuracy as Peter?

7-7 The voters in Perth County are 80% urban and 20% rural; 70% of the urban voters, and only 25% of the rural voters, vote for D in preference to R. In a straw vote taken just before the election, a rural voter has 6 times the chance of being selected as an urban voter. This bias in the sampling will cause the sample proportion to be a biased estimator of the population proportion in favor of D.

How much is this bias? Is it large enough to cause the average sample to be wrong (in the sense that the average sample "elects" a different candidate from the one the population elects)?

7-8 In Problem 7-7, if we consider the viewpoint of the pollster, realistically we cannot suppose that the population proportion π favoring D is known. However, we can suppose that the 80%-20% urban-rural split in the population is known - through census figures, for example. Suppose that the pollster then obtains the following data from a biased sample of 700 voters:

	Vote		
Location	For D	For R	Totals
Urban	210	92	302
Rural	80	318	398
Totals	290	410	700

The simple-minded and biased estimate of π is the sample proportion 290/700 = 41%. Now calculate an unbiased estimate of π instead. Incidentally, a technique like this, which is based on several population strata (such as urban/rural) whose proportions are known and allowed for, is an example of stratified sampling.

*7-9 (Requires Section 6-5) A random sample of 1000 students is to be polled from a population of 5000 students. Judging on the grounds of efficiency, is it better to sample with replacement, or without replacement? How much better?

PART B - DEVELOPING THEMES

B-1   HOW TO KEEP THE WEATHERMAN (OR MARKET FORECASTER) HONEST

7-10   The weatherman is asked to predict whether or not it will rain tomorrow. Since he never knows for sure, however, it has been found more informative if he states his <u>probability</u> that it will rain. Thus, for example, suppose he observes conditions such as a clear sky, moderate temperatures, and low humidity -- the sort of day that is followed by rain only 10% of the time, in his experience. Then he would predict, "The probability of rain for tomorrow is .10."

Now suppose there are two competing forecasts, whose records for a week are as follows.

Day	Weather Office's Forecast (W)	Old Fisherman's Forecast (F)	Actual Rain Indicator (θ)
May 1	.30	0	0
2	.60	1	0
3	.80	1	1
4	.30	0	1
5	.40	0	0
6	.10	0	0
7	.90	1	1

The old fisherman just took the forecast from the weather office, and rounded it to 0 or 1; that is, he removed the element of uncertainty that seemed to confuse his crew, and simply forecast "It won't rain" for May 1, or "It will rain" for May 2, etc.

In the last column the actual weather is tabulated for comparison (where 0 = no rain, 1 = rain). Thus, on the first day, the old fisherman made a better forecast -- his error was F - θ = 0 - 0 = 0, while the weather office's error was .30 - 0 = .30. But on the second day, the old fisherman did worse -- his error was 1 - 0 = 1.00, while the weather office's error was only .60 - 0 = .60.

a.   To judge overall performance, calculate the mean absolute error MAE $\equiv \Sigma|W - \theta|/n$ for the weather office. Then calculate the MAE for the old fisherman. According to this criterion of MAE, who is making the better forecasts overall?

b.   Repeat, using mean squared error MSE $\equiv \Sigma(W - \theta)^2/n$ instead of MAE. Then summarize your answers by filling in the following table:

Criterion	Weather Office	Old Fisherman	Winner
MAE			
MSE			

7-11   Let us see how well the forecasting procedures of Problem 7-10 work on a very familiar problem -- trying to predict whether or not "ace" will occur when a die is thrown. The two competing forecasts, along with the actual results, were recorded for a few throws, as follows:

228

Trial Number	Forecast of Weather Office	Forecast of Old Fisherman	Actual Throw
1	1/6	0	0 (no ace)
2	1/6	0	0
3	1/6	0	1 (ace)
4	1/6	0	0

Answer the same questions as in Problem 7-10. Also state what would happen in the long run, after many, many throws. Summarize your answers in the following table:

Criterion	Weather Office	Old Fisherman	Winner
MAE (4 trials)			
MSE (4 trials)			
MAE (many trials)			
MSE (many trials)			

7-12 a. To draw some conclusions now, answer True or False; if False correct it:

    i) The old fisherman is a worse predictor than the weather office, because he is less informative -- he does not give any information about the probability of an "ace", except that it is less than 1/2.

    ii) If we want a criterion that correctly judges that the weather office is a better predictor than the old fisherman, we have to use the MSE criterion rather than the MAE criterion.

b. Suppose the weather office is thinking of using a new computer system for forecasting. Its forecasts, along with the forecasts of the old system, for a trial run of 5 randomly chosen days, were as follows:

Day	Forecast of New System	Forecast of Old System	Actual Rain Indicator
June 1	.2	.1	0
22	.7	.8	1
July 3	.6	.6	1
19	.4	.7	0
28	.3	.1	0

Which system forecasts better in the trial run of 5 days? (Use the criterion chosen in (a), of course).

B-2 EFFICIENCY OF RANDOMIZED RESPONSE

7-13 In Problem 3-46 of the text, you may recall that we found out how randomized response works in the long-run: The proportion π_A who actually committed an illegal act (such as inside trading) can be found from the proportion π_Y who answered yes to the questionnaire, as follows:

$$\pi_A = 2\pi_Y - .50$$

In a small sample of size n, how do we deal with sampling uncertainty? Let P_Y denote the corresponding sample proportion who answer yes -- the only available statistic. Then by analogy with the equation above, the unknown π_A is estimated by

$$P_A = 2P_Y - .50$$

Let us see how reliable an estimate this is -- assuming there are no refusals, mistakes, or lies in the responses.

a.   What is the bias of P_A?

b.   What is the standard error of P_A?

c.   Now let us compare P_A with the risky alternative -- asking the question directly and receiving a lot of lies. In fact, suppose the true proportion who have done inside trading is $\pi_A = 20\%$, but only 6% will admit to it, even when reassured of strict anonymity. The remaining 14% lie. (We assume there is still a 100% response rate, since a refusal to respond might be regarded with suspicion). This gives a biased sample proportion P_B.

Now find the relative efficiency of P_A relative to P_B

i)   For a sample of n = 100

ii)   For a sample of n = 500

d.   (Requires Chapter 8) Suppose that in a sample of n = 1200 executives, 408 answered "yes". Construct a 95% confidence interval for the target proportion π_A who had actually engaged in inside trading.

CHAPTER 8 - CONFIDENCE INTERVALS

The only way to save yourself from the pain of lost illusions is to have none.
Charles Marriott

A. STANDARD PROBLEMS (EASIEST FIRST)

8-1   In a target city of 80,000 households, 800 were randomly sampled in a marketing survey by a Korean auto manufacturer extending their penetration of the North American market. To see how typical this city was, some preliminary statistics were collected: The average number of cars per household was 1.32, while the standard deviation was 0.8. As well, 11% of the households had no cars at all. For the whole city, construct a 95% confidence interval for:

   a.   The average number of cars per household

   b.   The percentage of households with no car.

8-2   An analysis was carried out (Gilbert and others, 1977) on 44 research papers that used randomized clinical trials to compare an innovative treatment (I) with a standard treatment (S), in surgery and anaesthesia. In 23 of the papers, I was preferred to S (and in the other 21 papers, S was preferred to I).

   a.   Assuming the 44 papers constitute a random sample from the population of all research papers in this field, construct a 95% confidence interval for the population proportion where I is preferred to S.

   b.   Do you agree with their interpretation?

   "... When assessed by randomized clinical trials, innovations are successful only about half the time. Since innovations brought to the stage of randomized trials are usually expected by the innovators to be sure winners, we see that ... the value of the innovation needs empirical checking."

8-3   In a 1974 poll (New York Times, June 2, 1974, p. E6), 1650 Americans were asked for an answer to this question:

   "The U.S. Supreme Court has ruled that a woman may go to a doctor to end pregnancy at any time during the first three months of pregnancy. Do you favor or oppose this ruling?"

   A week later, an independent sample of 1650 Americans were asked the same question, except that the words "to end pregnancy" were changed to "for an abortion". The responses now were different:

Wording	in Favor	Opposed	No Opinion
"To end pregnancy"	46%	39%	15%
"For an abortion"	41%	49%	10%

a. Let the proportion of voters in favor be denoted by π_1 for the first wording ("to end pregnancy") and by π_2 for the second wording ("for an abortion"). Construct a 95% confidence interval for the difference $\pi_2 - \pi_1$

b. Repeat (a) for the proportion of voters who had an opinion. Now, for example, $P_1 = .46/(.46 + .39) = .54$

c. Would you agree with the conclusion, "If you want to know what Americans really think about abortion, you have to ask them about abortion."

8-4 A psychologist runs 6 people through an experiment on work stress, and collects the following data on heart rate:

Heart Rate

Subject	Before Experiment	After Experiment
Smith	71	84
Ng	67	72
Gunther	71	70
Wilson	78	85
Pestritto	64	71
Seaforth	69	80

Calculate a 95% confidence interval for the effect of the experiment on heart rate.

8-5 A Gallup poll of 1500 Americans just before the 1988 Presidential election showed the following approximate breakdown by age (Reconstructed roughly from the Gallup Report, Nov. 1988, p. 7):

vote	under 30	over 30	totals
Bush (R)	140	670	810
Dukakis (D)	80	610	690
totals	220	1280	1500

a. Construct a 95% confidence interval for the proportion of voters for Bush,
   i)   in the whole population
   ii) in the population under 30
   iii) in the population over 30
   iv) for the difference in Bush support between those under 30 and those over.

b. Just by looking at the table (without peeking at your calculations above), which confidence interval in (a) should be most precise? And least precise? Now look at the calculated answers, to confirm your guess.

8-6 A professor was evaluated on a five-point scale by 15 students randomly selected from one class, and 40 students from another, with the following results:

	Frequencies	
Scale Value	10:30 a.m. Class	3:30 p.m. Class
1 (terrible)	0	4
2	0	7
3	4	13
4	7	9
5 (excellent)	4	7
	n = 15	n = 40

a. Graph the frequency distributions of the two samples.

b. Calculate the two sample means and standard deviations, and show them on the graph.

c. The registrar wanted to know whether the difference in the two samples was just a sampling fluke, or reflected a real difference in the classes. In fact, she suspected it showed a real difference, because it was customary for late classes to be restless and give their professors rather low ratings.
Answer her with an appropriate confidence interval.

8-7 To estimate the speed of postal service, a consumers' group timed how many days it took for 100 letters to go from Toronto to San Francisco. To see whether service had improved or worsened, the results were compared with a similar experiment two years earlier (hypothetical data, modelled after a real survey conducted by Marketplace, a program of the Canadian Broadcasting Corp.).

number of days	frequencies	
	1989	1987
2	27	24
3	46	41
4	15	14
5	6	7
6	1	8
7	3	2
8	0	4
9	2	0

a. Assuming these letters were mailed at random times, find a 95% CI for the mean time in 1989, and also for the improvement since 1987.

b. People who post letters may be more interested in reliability than averages. For example, they may not be concerned if letters take, on average, 3 rather than 2 days to deliver, so long as letters do not take more than 5 days to deliver.

What is the chance of a letter taking more than 5 days? Calculate the appropriate 95% CI for the chance in 1989, and also for the improvement since 1987.

8-8 (Monte Carlo)

a. Take a sample of five random normal numbers from Appendix Table II. Then find a 95% confidence interval for the mean of the population. Assume $\sigma = 1$ is known.

b. Repeat part (a) if σ is not known, and has to be estimated with s.

c. Since you know $\mu = 0$, you can see whether or not your confidence intervals are correct. Have the instructor check the proportion of the confidence intervals that are correct in the class. What proportion would be correct in a very large class (in the long run)?

d. Answer True or False; if False, correct it:
The confidence intervals in part (b) based on the t distribution are always wider than those in part (a) based on the normal z distribution. This represents the cost of not knowing σ.

8-9 In one of the very earliest immunization experiments, 280 people were inoculated in the Boston smallpox epidemic of 1721. Compared to the 11,720 people who were not inoculated, here are the results (Langer, 1976).

	Not Inoculated	Inoculated
lived	10,882	274
died	838	6
Totals	11,720	280

Assume (contrary to fact) that this was a well-controlled experiment. That is, suppose that the 280 individuals to be inoculated were drawn at random from the Boston population. In this population, denote by π_1 and π_2 the proportions who would have died (among the not inoculated and inoculated, respectively). In order to see how much larger the death rate is with no inoculation,

a. Calculate the estimate of the difference $\pi_1 - \pi_2$

b. Calculate the estimate of the ratio $R = \pi_1/\pi_2$

c. Calculate a 95% confidence interval for $\pi_1 - \pi_2$

8-10 In Problem 8-9, which estimate is better, (a) or (b)? It depends on the question, of course. For example, suppose another inoculation is known to have $\pi_1-\pi_2=.04$, and $\pi_1/\pi_2 =3.0$. Use whichever of these numbers is appropriate to calculate:

a. If an epidemic hits a city of 70,000 inhabitants, how many lives would be saved by inoculation?

b. If an epidemic left 12,000 people dead in a city where everyone was innoculated, how many would have died with no innoculation?

8-11 Do men and women agree on the ideal number of children in a family? To answer this question, a Gallup poll of 750 men and 750 women in 1980 gave the following reply.

| | Relative Frequency of Reply | |
Ideal Number of Children	Men	Women
0	1%	1%
1	3%	3%
2	52%	49%
3	21%	20%
4	11%	13%
5	2%	2%
6	2%	3%
no opinion	8%	9%
Total	100%	100%

Summary Statistics of Those With an Opinion		
Mean	2.57	2.65
Median	2	2
Range	6	6
IQR	1	1
$\Sigma(X - \bar{X})^2 f$	755	880

a. Verify the very first summary statistic ($\bar{X} = 2.57$).

b. Of those who have an opinion, what difference is there between mean and women in the whole population? Construct a 95% confidence interval.

8-12 A sample survey of home owners, correctly carried out, concluded: "We estimate that 13% have recently insulated their homes (spending at least $500 within the past 3 years). In fact, the 95% confidence interval is 13% ± 3%.

Imagine this survey was independently repeated over and over (same sample size and same population) and a 95% confidence interval calculated each time. Then how often would the following occur? Fill in the blanks with the appropriate answer (95%, more than 95%, or less than 95%):

a. _____ of such intervals will cover the midpoint, 13%

b. _____ of such intervals will cover the population percentage

c. _____ of such intervals will completely cover the given interval (10% to 16%)

d. _____ of such intervals will partially cover the given interval (10% to 16%)

8-13 Of the 453 boys released from a detention home for delinquents, there were 150 boys for whom sufficient information was available, both for the period before and the period after detention. The behavior record of these 150 boys was as follows (Abridged from the Oxford University examinations, Trinity term, 1964).

Before Detention	After Detention			Totals
	Good	Fair	Bad	
Good	18	9	2	29
Fair	49	33	15	97
Bad	10	4	10	24
Totals	77	46	27	150

a. We would like to know, on the average, how the stay at the detention home changes behavior. One possible way to analyze the data is, for each boy, to ascribe to bad behavior the value 0, to good behavior the value of 1, and to fair behavior

235

some intermediate value, say ½. For each boy, therefore, a numerical improvement can be calculated. The 150 improvements may be considered a sample from a population; calculate a 95% confidence interval for the mean of this population. (Although this coding is somewhat arbitrary, it allows a simple and powerful analysis that can't be too far wrong.)

b.   In what way does your analysis in part (a) show, or fail to show, how the detention home changes behavior?

PART B - DEVELOPING THEMES - BOOTSTRAPPING TO MAKE   A COMPLEX PROBLEM MANAGEABLE

*8-14 To show how bootstrapping can give an idea of sampling error in a very complex situation, consider contour maps. For example, the contours in Figure 1 mark various levels of acidity in rainfall in the Eastern U.S. (Diaconis and Efron, 1983). The contour where pH is at the lowest level (4.2) marks off the shaded region where "acid rain" is worst, for example. These contours were drawn by a powerful computer, to give the best fit to some 2000 data points. (On average, over 2000 rainfalls were sampled at each of the 9 weather stations named on the map.) As an estimate, this map is already a tribute to the computer's effectiveness.

But does the map give any idea of reliability? What if different weather stations and different rainfalls had been sampled? What we really would like is the "true map", based on an unlimited number of stations and rainfalls in this region.

Fortunately, bootstrapping can give some idea of the range in which this true map might lie. Figures 2, 3, and 4, for instance, give several "bootstrap" maps -- an illuminating glimpse of what the true map might be.

The interesting feature of this example is its complexity: a whole map has been bootstrapped instead of a single number like $\bar{X}$. Thus the bootstrap maps cannot be summarized in a simple confidence interval. Nevertheless, by displaying several bootstrap versions alongside the best estimate (the original contour map), the uncertainty of where the true map lies can be appreciated.

a.   Figure 1 shows Rockport Indiana as a hot spot of acid rain. Just how low is the true average pH there? Answer with a rough estimate, ± a very rough confidence allowance.

b.   Figure 1 estimates that Michigan (the state north of Roanoke Indiana) is pretty clean (with pH > 4.4). Is this really true, or is it just a sampling fluke?

c.   Figure 1 estimates that the four southern states are about as clean as Michigan. Is this really true, or just a sampling fluke?

Figure 1. Acid rain in the Eastern U.S. The average levels of pH are marked by level curves, with the region of lowest pH (highest acidity) shaded. (Diaconis and Efron, 1983).

Figure 2, 3, 4. Three typical bootstrap versions of Figure 1, showing roughly the range where the true (population) map might lie.

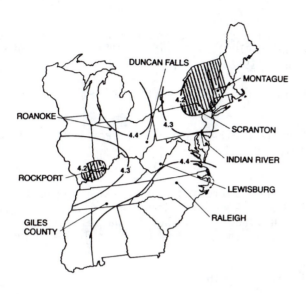

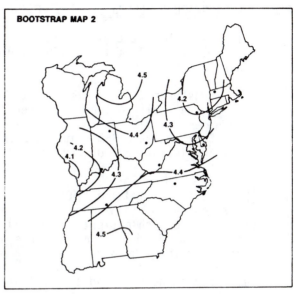

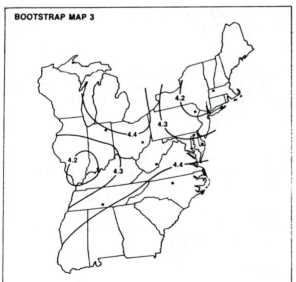

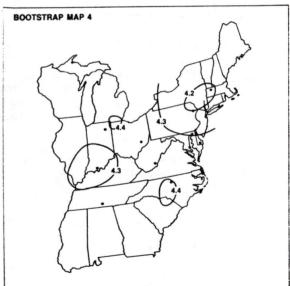

CHAPTER 9 - HYPOTHESIS TESTING

Between two evils I always pick the one I never tried before.

Mai West

PART A - STANDARD PROBLEMS (EASIEST FIRST)

9-1 "Thinking about the last time you got into a car, did you use a seat belt or not?" In a Gallup poll of about 1500 Americans in 1984, 25% answered "yes". In 1986, 52% answered "yes" (Gallup Poll Public Opinion 1986, p.98).

    a. Construct the 95% confidence interval for the proportion of Americans who used a seat belt in 1984, and then in 1986.

    b. Construct the 95% confidence interval for the improvement from 1984 to 1986. Is the improvement discernible at level $\alpha = 5\%$?

9-2 With current treatment, 40% of all patients suffering from a rare tropical disease improved (within a year), and 60% did not. A new treatment was given to a random sample of 8 such patients, in a pilot study to see whether it was effective. It was agreed that if 6 or more patients improved, the new treatment would be judged more effective than the old.

    a. State the null and alternative hypotheses, in symbols.

    b. State the region where H_o is to be rejected, in symbols.

    c. Use the binomial tables to find α.

    d. Suppose in the long run (unknown to the researchers, of course) that 70% of the patients given the new treatment would improve. What is the chance that the pilot study will miss finding this treatment more effective than the old? What is this number called, by statisticians?

*9-3 In evaluating a dam, suppose government officials want to estimate μ, the mean annual irrigation benefit per acre. They therefore take a random sample of 25 one-acre plots and find that the benefit averages $8.10, with a standard deviation of $2.40.

To promote the dam, they want to make a statement of the form, "μ is at least as large as...." And to avoid political embarrassment, they want 99% confidence in this statement. What value should they put into the blank?

*9-4 (Interpreting the p-value) A manufacturing process has produced millions of TV tubes with a mean life $\mu = 1200$ hours, and standard deviation $\sigma = 300$ hours. A new process is tried on a sample of 100 tubes, producing a sample average $\overline{X} = 1265$ hours. (Assume σ remains unchanged at 300 hours.) Will this new process produce a <u>long-run</u> average that is better than the null hypothesis $\mu_0 = 1200$?

    a. Specifically, is the sample mean $\overline{X} = 1265$ discernibly better than the H_0 value of 1200, if $\alpha = 5\%$? Answer by seeing whether the one-sided 95% confidence interval excludes $\mu_0 = 1200$.

    b. Repeat, for $\alpha = 1\%$

    c. Repeat, for $\alpha = 0.1\%$

d. As α decreased above, note that discernibility changed into indiscernibility. Estimate the critical level α at which the changeover occurs. How does this critical level compare to the one-sided p-value?

e. Answer True or False; if False, correct it:
The p-value can be regarded as the lowest that we could push the level α and still claim discernibility (barely) -- as stated earlier in equation (9-28) in the text.

9-5 In 1980 a Gallup Poll asked Americans to give their opinion of their country on a numerical scale from +5 (very favorable) to -5 (very unfavorable). The following table gives the frequency of reply, for two contrasting groups: Americans from big cities (over one million) and Americans from rural areas (including villages up to 2,500 inhabitants).

Reply	relative frequency of reply	
	big city	rural
+5 (favorable)	60%	68%
+4	21%	16%
+3	8%	8%
+2	5%	3%
+1	3%	3%
0 (don't know)	1%	2%
-1	0%	0%
-2	1%	0%
-3	0%	0%
-4	0%	0%
-5 (unfavorable)	1%	0%
Total	100%	100%
Sample size	285	420

a. Graph the two contrasting distributions.

b. Were the samples large enough to discern a real difference between big-city and rural America? If so, how would you appropriately express the difference?

9-6 In a 1965 court case (Kaye, 1982) the defense argued that the grand jury had racially discriminated. Although 25% of the men in the jurisdiction were black, only 17% (177 out of 1050) of the men called for jury duty had been black. The null hypothesis of a fair draw (selection of jurors) may be stated as H_0: The 1050 men called for jury duty constituted a random sample of men drawn from the jurisdiction.

a. Calculate the p-value for H_0.

b. The judge said the evidence was not sufficient to establish that discrimination had occurred. Do you agree?

9-7 In Problem 9-6, let us take a closer look. The law stated that only literate males were eligible for jury duty. And past discrimination had left many more blacks than whites illiterate (52% vs 17%). To see whether there was discrimination on the part of the court itself:

a. Of the eligible population, what proportion was black? (Hint: Bayes Theorem in Chapter 3.)

b.   Now let us define the null hypothesis as H_0: The 1050 men called for jury duty constituted a random sample from the <u>eligible</u> population. Calculate the p-value for H_0.

c.   Do you think there was racial discrimination?

d.   What do you think was the real problem -- the selection of jurors, the eligibility rule, or something else?

9-8   In the Gallup poll in Problem 9-1 above, do you think that every respondent answered correctly? Then how would you revise your answer in part (a)? In part (b)?

B   DEVELOPING THEMES

B-1   IMPROVING QUALITY CONTROL

9-9   A large producer of industrial solvents found that about 15% of the time they were being supplied sulphuric acid contaminated with a trace impurity. Since each contaminated batch caused $12,000 to clean up later, it was important to catch the trouble at the start.

Unfortunately, the impurity was very difficult to test for. In the contaminated batches where the impurity was present, their test gave a reading that varied widely -- with a standard deviation of 85 -- around a mean value $\mu = 280$. For clean batches free of the impurity, the readings were equally varied, but now around a mean value $\mu = 220$. Thus readings in the range between 220 and 280 were very ambiguous, and very common.

Management decided to split the difference: If a batch gave a reading that exceeded the critical value C = 250 (midway between the two possible means) they would clean the batch up (whether it actually needed it or not) at a cost of $900.

a.   What proportion of the clean batches are unnecessarily discarded with this rule? (This chance of a "false alarm" is customarily denoted by what?)

b.   What proportion of the contaminated batches are inadvertently let through with this rule? (This chance of a missed alarm is customarily denoted by what?)

c.   For their bottom line, management needs to add up all the costs. In a thousand batches, what would be the total cost of this mess? What therefore is the average cost per batch?

9-10   A consultant suggested changing the critical value C so as to make $\alpha = 5\%$. To see how good an idea this is:

a.   What value of C would achieve this?

b.   Then what would β be?

c.   What would be the average cost per batch for this mess now?

9-11   From your intuitive understanding of this problem, suggest an even better value for C. Then calculate the new values of:

a. α.

b. β.

c. Average cost per batch. Is it indeed lower?

B-2 FORMULATING AS WELL AS TESTING SOME HYPOTHESES

9-12 When 287 mothers were observed on how they held their newborn babies, most held them on the left side. This was true of both left and right-handed mothers, as the following breakdown shows. (From Salk, 1973, via Nemenyi and others, 1977.)

Mother is:	She Holds Baby on:		Totals
	Right Side	Left Side	
Right-handed	43	212	255
Left-handed	7	25	32
Totals	50	237	287

Assuming these 287 are a random sample:

a. Calculate a 95% confidence interval for the proportion of mothers in the population who hold their babies on the left side. Is this proportion statistically discernible from the 50-50 split you would expect from sheer chance?

b. Calculate a 95% confidence interval for the difference between the right and left-handed mothers. Is the difference statistically discernible?

c. Would you care to guess why there is a strong preference for the left side?

9-13 In Problem 9-12, Dr. Salk conjectured that the mother holds the baby on the left instinctively, so that the baby can better hear the reassuring beat of the mother's heart. To test this hypothesis, he randomly divided newborns into two groups: The treated group of 45 babies had a tape of an adult heartbeat played into the nursery; the control group of 45 babies had no heartbeat tape, but otherwise were treated the same. For each baby, the weight increase from the first to the fourth day was recorded, and graphed as follows (again, from Salk, 1973).

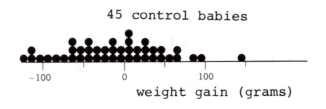

45 treatment babies

weight gain (grams)

45 control babies

weight gain (grams)

241

Note that on the whole, the treatment babies gain weight, while the control babies lose slightly. Specifically, here are the calculated sample statistics:

	Sample Mean $\overline{X}$	Squared Deviations $\Sigma(X - \overline{X})^2$
Treatment	37	158,000
Control	-17	186,000

Assuming these babies were a random sample from a population:

a. Calculate the 95% confidence interval for the mean difference that the treatment makes.

b. At the 5% level, can the null hypothesis be rejected, that is, is the difference in means statistically discernible?

9-14 Let us look more closely at the assumption made in Problem 9-13 that the 90 babies were "a random sample from a population." In fact they were not. Like most researchers, Dr. Salk found it completely impractical to take a random sample from the whole U.S. population. Instead he merely studied whatever babies were convenient, in a New York City hospital nursery.

Although the samples were not randomly drawn, nevertheless the really important randomization was done: The division of the babies into treatment and control groups was randomized, to ensure that it was fair and unbiased. What sense does it make to talk about an underlying population? A confidence interval? A p-value?

CHAPTER 10   ANALYSIS OF VARIANCE

If at first you don't succeed, you're just about average.

Bill Cosby

10-1   A random sample of 50 American workers in each of several selected industries in 1980 showed the following differences in average hourly wage:

Industry Group	sample size n	mean $\bar{X}$	squared deviations $\Sigma (X - \bar{X})^2$
Construction	50	$9.50	156
Manufacturing	50	$7.00	92
Retail trade	50	$4.80	107

(Reconstructed from the Stat. Abst. of U.S. 1981)

a.   Calculate the ANOVA table, including the p-value for H_0.

b.   Calculate the simultaneous 95% confidence intervals for the differences in mean wage.

10-2   Repeat Problem 10-1(a), if the samples had been of different sizes--50, 30, and 40 respectively.

10-3   To compare prices of bread from the four leading bakeries in a large city, a random sample of three supermarkets was taken, and the following prices (in cents) recorded:

bakery	Supermarket A	B	C	Averages
I	139	135	134	136
II	134	128	125	129
III	128	126	124	126
IV	131	123	121	125
Averages	133	128	126	

Calculate the ANOVA table to test whether the bakery prices are equal on average.

*10-4   In Problem 10-3, calculate the simultaneous 95% confidence intervals for the the differences in bakery prices.

10-5   In Problem 10-3, if data had instead been obtained from three different supermarkets for each bakery, for a total of 12 supermarkets, what difference (if any) would it make to the analysis and conclusions?

10-6   The sales manager of a large hardware chain proposed two different promotional campaigns, and needed to evaluate how effective they would be. Fifteen stores were therefore randomly selected and assigned to one of three groups: campaign A, campaign B, and no campaign at all as a control C. Then the sales over the week of the campaign were recorded for each store (y). It was also suggested that the sales for the previous week be recorded for comparison (x):

Sales before (x) and during (y) the promotional campaign ($000)

	Campaign A		Campaign, B		Control C	
	x	y	x	y	x	y
	24	24	27	35	23	18
	28	30	27	31	33	32
	38	39	44	55	39	33
	42	41	38	43	36	35
	24	27	32	44	20	18
average	31.2	32.2	33.6	41.6	30.2	27.2
variance	69	56	54	86	69	72
average of (y - x)	1.0		8.0		-3.0	
variance of (y - x)	2.5		12.5		5.5	

a. Using the y values, calculate the ANOVA table (Hint: Within each sample of 5 observations, how can the sum of squared deviations be found from the variance? See equation (2-11) in the text if necessary.)

b. Similarly calculate the ANOVA table using the improvements (y-x).

c. Which analysis is better, (a) or (b)? Why?

10-7 In Problem 10-6, construct the appropriate 95% simultaneous confidence intervals.

10-8 a. (Monte Carlo) Simulate 5 observations from a normal population with σ = 10 and μ = 50 and call it Sample A (Hint: Take 5 numbers from Table II, multiply by 10, and add 50---as justified by (6-29) in the text.) Then simulate a second and third sample (B and C) from the same population.

b. From the array of 15 observations, calculate the ANOVA table to test whether these three samples are from the same population.

c. Can you conclude the 3 samples are discernibly different at level α = 5%? Is your conclusion correct?

10-9 a. Have the instructor record from every student the F statistic found in Problem 10-8. Graph the resulting distribution of F. Does the graph resemble Figure 10-2 in the text?

b. What proportion of the F values exceed the tabulated value $F_{.05}$ = 3.89 and hence are found statistically discernible? What proportion would exceed this value if the class were very large?

10-10 Repeat Problem 10-8, except that the three underlying populations now are different, with means μ_1 = 50, μ_2 = 60, and μ_3 = 70 (while σ remains at 10).

10-11 Repeat Problem 10-9 for the case of three different means in Problem 10-10.

CHAPTER 11   FITTING A LINE

Figures don't lie, but liars will figure.

Charles Grosvenor

11-1   In a series of 6 experimental runs (statistically independent), the yield of a chemical process was found to depend on the temperature as follows:

Temperature (°C)	Yield (%)
1000	11
1200	13
1400	12
1600	15
1800	17
2000	16

a.   Graph the data.

b.   What would you predict would be the yield if the process was run again at a temperature of 1400°C?

11-2   The U.S. income tax schedule is progressive, that is, higher incomes pay a higher proportion of their income in taxes. But tax shelters and other benefits available primarily to the rich work in the opposite direction (regressive). To determine the overall effect, a sample of 6 incomes showed the following taxes paid:

I = net income ($000)	T = taxes paid ($000)
50	6
10	1
20	3
40	8
100	13
80	16

For each individual, calculate what percentage P of his net income is being paid in taxes. Then regress P against I.

11-3   How can the volume of wood in a tree be conveniently estimated, before cutting it down? The trunk diameter (in feet, at chest height) is easily measured. Then, if all trees were the same shape and differed only in their relative scale, the volume of wood would be exactly proportional to the diameter cubed.

Actual trees of course differ individually, as the following random sample of 5 hardwood trees indicates:

diameter cubed ($C = D^3$)	actual volume of wood (V)
0.8	15
1.1	18
2.0	36
2.1	41
4.0	65

a.   To show how the individual trees vary, graph V against C for the 5 given trees.

b.   Calculate and graph the least-squares regression line for predicting V from C.

c.   What is the predicted V for a tree that is 1.5 feet in diameter? (Hint: First, what is the cube of this?)

11-4 Consider a random sample of 4 pine trees:

diameter (D)	actual volume of wood (V)
.8	12
1.2	18
1.6	46
1.7	52

Using the technique of Problem 11-3, estimate the volume of a pine tree of diameter 1.3 feet.

CHAPTER 12 - SIMPLE REGRESSION

There are no whole truths; all truths are half truths.

A.N. Whitehead

12-1 For each of Problems 11-1 and 11-2,

a. Calculate the 95% confidence interval for the underlying population slope.

b. At level α = 5%, is the population slope discernibly different from 0?

12-2 In Problem 11-1(b), hedge your prediction with an interval that you are 95% certain will be right.

12-3 A study is done on 6 expectant mothers to determine whether there is a linear relation between X = number of cigarettes smoked per day during pregnancy, and Y = weight of the baby (pounds).

X	0	0	0	10	20	30
Y	8.0	7.0	7.6	7.1	6.0	6.3

a. Calculate the least squares regression of Y against X.

b. Graph the data and the line in (a).

c. Construct a 95% confidence interval for the population slope. (Assume the 6 women were a random sample, and the computer gave the residual standard deviation s = 0.46)

d. Would it be fair to conclude that, "at level α = 5%, smoking during pregnancy reduces the weight of the baby"? Why?

12-4 To estimate overall performance in assembling a newly designed thermostat, 25 workers were randomly sampled from the assembly line. Their performance scores averaged $\bar{Y}$ = 87.4 with s_y = 8.6

Since the plant was only 8 months old, the experience of the labor force was quite limited. (For these 25 workers, their experience X in months had a maximum of 8, a mean of 5.4, and standard deviation of 3.4). Nevertheless, to test whether even limited experience might be helpful, a regression of Y against X was computed, that left a residual s = 6.2:

$$\hat{Y} = 78.2 + 1.71 X$$

a. Construct a 95% confidence interval for the population slope β.

b. Is the dependence of performance on experience statistically discernible at level α = 5%?

12-5 In Problem 12-4, construct a 95% confidence interval for the following mean performances:

a. The mean of all workers.

247

b. The mean of all workers with 6 months experience.

12-6 In Problem 12-4, find a 95% prediction interval for:

a. The production of a worker drawn at random, using an equation analogous to equation (12-20):

$$Y = \bar{Y} \pm t_{.025} \, s_y \, \sqrt{1/n + 1}$$

b. The production of a worker drawn at random, if his experience turns out to be 6 months.

c. Which interval is wider, (a) or (b)? Why?

CHAPTER 13 - MULTIPLE REGRESSION

The man in the ticket-office said:

"Have an accident insurance ticket, also?"

"No," I said, after studying the matter over a little. "No, I believe not; I am going to be travelling by rail all day to-day. However, tomorrow I don't travel. Give me one for tomorrow."

The man looked puzzled. He said: "But it is for accident insurance, and if you are going to travel by rail-"

"If I am going to travel by rail I sha'nt need it. Lying at home in bed is the thing I am afraid of."

I hunted up statistics, and was amazed to find that after all the glaring newspaper headings concerning railroad disasters, less than three hundred people had really lost their lives by those disasters in the preceding twelve months.

By further figuring, it appeared that between New York and Rochester the Erie ran eight passenger trains each way every day - 16 altogether; and carried a daily average of 6,000 persons. That is about a six million in six months - the population of New York City. Well, the Erie kills from 13 to 23 persons out of its million in six months; and in the same time 13,000 of New York's million die in their bed! My flesh crept, my hair stood on end. "This is appalling!" I said. "The danger isn't in travelling by rail, but in trusting to those deadly beds. I will never sleep in a bed again."

You will excuse me from taking any more chances on those beds. The railroads are good enough for me.

And my advice to all people is, Don't stay at home any more than you can help; but when you have **got** to stay at home a while, buy a package of those insurance tickets and sit up nights. You cannot be too cautious.

Mark Twain

13-1 Suppose a random sample of 5 families yielded the following data (in thousands of dollars):

Family	Annual Saving S	Annual Income X	Assets W
Hobb	2	30	10
Doherty	4	10	0
Oakley	0	20	10
Nosko	12	60	0
Sansom	2	30	10

a. Calculate the simple regression of saving S against income X.

b. The multiple regression of S against X and W is

$$\hat{S} = 2.33 + .16X - .53W$$

On the (S, X) plane, graph the following:

   i) The 5 given points, each one tagged with its value of W.
   ii) The simple regression line.
   iii) The 2 lines you get from the multiple regression, by setting W = 0 and 10

c. Explain why the simple and multiple regression equations have different coefficients of X.

d. Suppose the Graham family has an annual income of 30 thousand dollars and assets of 5 thousand dollars. What would you estimate is their annual saving?

e. Compared to the Graham family, the Buck family has the same assets, but an annual income of 3 thousand dollars more. Estimate how much more their annual saving would be.

f. Compared to the Graham family, the Carducci family has an annual income of 5 thousand dollars more, and assets of 2 thousand dollars less. Estimate how much more their annual saving would be..

13-2 The computer output for Problem 13-1 is as follows:

THE REGRESSION EQUATION IS
Y =   2.33 + 0.162 X1 - 0.532 X2

	COLUMN	COEFFICIENT	ST. DEV. OF COEF.
	--	2.3291	0.2691
X1	C2	0.16203	0.00620
X2	C3	-0.5316	0.0212

For the coefficient of X_1 (income) and then X_2 (assets)

a. Calculate the 95% confidence interval for the population coefficient β.

b. Is it discernibly different from zero, at level $\alpha = 5\%$? Why?

13-3 The University of Oregon wanted to determine which applicants should be admitted in the future to a graduate program. On the basis of all 111 students who had been admitted in the past, the following multiple regression was computed (Dawes, 1971):

$\hat{Y} = -.50 + .0006 \text{ GRE} + .76 \text{ GPA} + .25 \text{ QI}$

where GRE = graduate record exam score of the applicant

GPA = his undergraduate grade-point average

QI = the quality of his undergraduate institution

Y = student's graduate performance, as rated by the faculty after several years in the graduate program [Y = 1 for failure, up to Y = 5 for outstanding].

a. If the admissions committee decided that anyone who had a predicted performance level Y greater than the cutoff value 3.0 would be admitted, which of the following applicants would be admitted by this rule?

	GRE	GPA	QI
Judy Silver	610	3.2	5
Rod Singh	680	3.6	2

b. Chris Russell and John Foster graduated from Haverford together, and then applied to Oregon for Graduate work. Chris had a better GPA at Haverford (better by 0.3 points) while John had a better GRE score (better by 30 points). According to this model, can you predict who would do better at Oregon? Explain briefly.

13-4 The admissions committee doesn't understand the equation in Problem 13-3. To help them out,

a. Explain briefly what one of the coefficients means, for example, the coefficient of GPA.

b. Draw a graph showing how students with the same GRE (650, let us say) have a predicted performance $\hat{Y}$ that improves with their GPA and their QI. Specifically Graph $\hat{Y}$ against GPA, for three different levels of QI (QI = 1, 2, and 3).

13-5 For each of 25 years, an experimental farm in Oregon recorded total spring rainfall R (inches), mean spring temperature T (degrees centigrade), and the corresponding yield of a standard variety of wheat Y (bushels/acre). The summary statistics were

$$\bar{R} = 13, \qquad \bar{T} = 12 \qquad \bar{Y} = 47$$
$$\Sigma r^2 = 160, \qquad \Sigma t^2 = 30, \qquad \Sigma y^2 = 4300$$
$$\Sigma rt = -50, \qquad \Sigma ry = -320, \qquad \Sigma ty = 215$$

The multiple regression was computed:

$$\hat{Y} = -55 + .50 \ R + 8.0 \ T$$

a. Will the <u>simple</u> regression coefficient of Y against T be positive too? And Y against R?

b. Verify the three following simple regressions:

$$\hat{Y} = -39 + 7.2 \ T$$
$$\hat{Y} = 73 - 2.0 \ R$$
$$\hat{T} = 16 - .31 \ R$$

13-6 Using the data in Problem 13-5, fill in the blanks and choose the correct words in brackets:

a. If irrigation added a total of 2 inches more water, the estimated [increase, decrease] in yield is _____ bushels per acre -- assuming irrigation water has the same effect as rain water.

b. If we know that a season has a rainfall R that is 3 inches below average, but temperature T is unknown, the estimated yield is _____ bushels per acre [above, below] average.

c. If we know that a season has a temperature T that is 2° above average, but rainfall R is unknown, the estimated yield is _____ bushels per acre [above, below] average.

d. If we know that a season has a rainfall R that is 2 inches below average, and a temperature T that is 3° above average, the estimated yield is _____ bushels per acre [above, below] average.

*13-7 In Problem 13-5 suppose the summary statistics were lost, and so was the second simple regression ($\hat{Y} = 73 - 2.0 \ R$).

a. Is there any way to reconstruct this simple regression slope from the remaining information in Problem 13-5, that is, from the other regression equations? If so, do it. If not, state what else you need to know.

b. Does the negative coefficient of R in this simple regression equation mean that more rainfall hurts the crops? Explain.

CHAPTER 14 - REGRESSION EXTENSIONS

"The cause of lightning," Alice said very decidedly, for she felt quite sure about this, "is the thunder - no, no!" she hastily corrected herself, "I meant it the other way."

Lewis Carroll

PART A - STANDARD QUESTIONS (EASIEST FIRST)

14-1 To see how movie prices were related to several factors, a study of urban theaters yielded the following regression (Lamson, 1970):

$$P = 5.8L - 8.2A - 7.7D + ...$$

where P = price of admission to the theater (adult evening ticket, in cents)
L = location dummy = 1 for suburbs, 0 for city center
A = age dummy = 1 if theatre older than 10 years, 0 if newer
D = drive-in dummy = 1 if outdoor theater, 0 if indoor

a.   What would you predict is the difference in the admission price if, other things being equal:

i)   the theater is in the suburbs instead of the city center?
ii) the theater is old instead of young?
iii) the theater is young and outdoors, instead of old and indoors?

b.   At what sort of theater would you predict the admission price to be highest?

14-2 To help determine what makes schools good, 2500 elementary schools in Michigan were studied (Klitgaard and Hall, 1977). The average grade 4 math score in each school (Y) was then found to depend on the average socio-economic status (SES) of its students, according to the following simple regression equation:

$$\hat{Y} = 27 + .46 \text{ SES}$$
$$\text{(SE)} \quad (.019)$$

The urban-rural dimension was also important, and was measured by 5 categories:

1.   urban core
2.   city (10,000 - 50,000)
3.   town (2500 - 10,000)

4.   urban fringe
5.   rural

To distinguish these five categories, four dummy variables were introduced (C_1 C_2 C_4 C_5), leaving the middle category as a reference. Thus the multiple regression was computed as follows:

$$\hat{Y} = 29 + .41 \text{ SES} - 0.8 C_1 + 0.2 C_2 - 0.8 C_4 + 0.1 C_5$$
$$\text{(SE)} \quad (.014) \quad (.22) \quad (.25) \quad (.19) \quad (.19)$$

a.   For each coefficient, calculate
i)   the 95% confidence interval
ii) the t-ratio
iii) the p-value for H_0. Star the coefficients that are statistically discernible at level $\alpha = 5\%$

b. Plot $\hat{Y}$ against SES, for the 5 different categories of urbanization. Do these 5 categories seem to fall into two clusters?

c. For all four dummy coefficients, the SE (or confidence allowances) are roughly the same. Show this 95% confidence allowance roughly on the graph in (b). What does it say about the two clusters in (b)?

14-3 The authors' main reason for computing the multiple regression equation in Problem 14-2 was to help them locate unusually effective schools among the 2500 tested. The 2500 residuals were therefore of even greater interest than the multiple regression equation itself, and are reproduced below in histogram form:

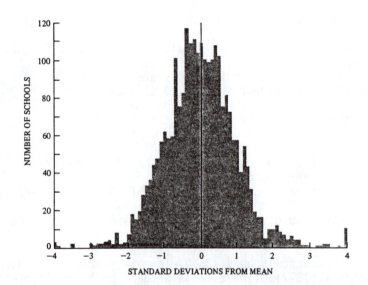

a. Circle the 10 or 15 schools in this histogram of residuals that are particularly effective, that is, that do much better than comparable schools (with the same SES, degree of urbanization, etc.)

b. The 15 most effective schools overall (not merely in the grade 4 reading test above) were carefully looked over to see if they shared any characteristics that might provide guidance on how to excell. The authors (Klitgaard and Hall 1977, p. 71) found these outstanding schools had a strong tendency to be rural.
     Looking for guidance for the urban majority of schools, the authors did a similar search for excellence among the 2000 urban schools, with the 500 rural schools deleted. They found the outstanding schools "tended to have smaller classes, more teachers with five or more years of experience, and more teachers earning $11,000 or more annually".
     Do these results confirm or contradict your prior expectation about what makes schools good?

*14-4 How is a nation's road system related to its wealth and population density? To answer this question, the following variables were deemed reasonably relevant and accessible for each of 113 countries in 1968 (Glover and Simon, 1975):

    R = road mileage (number of miles of paved roads per square mile of land)
    P = population per square mile
    I = income per capita (U.S.$)

The logarithmic multiple regression was then computed to be

$$\log R = -6.43 + 1.17 \log P + 1.10 \log I$$
$$(SE) \qquad\qquad (.053) \qquad\quad (.070)$$

a. Does it make sense for both coefficients to be positive? Why?

b. Are both coefficients discernibly positive (at level $\alpha = 5\%$)? Why?

c. What would be the expected difference in R for:

    i) a country that had 5% higher population density than another of the same per capita income?

    ii) a country that had 5% higher population density and 10% lower per capita income than another country?

*14-5 In a 1964 study of how personal income was related to education, IQ, race and other variables, the following multiple regression was computed from a sample of 1400 U.S. veterans (Griliches and Mason, 1973):

$$LINC = .046E + .0010\ AFQT + .17\ WHITE + \text{other variables}$$
$$(SE)\ (.007)\ \ (.0004) \qquad\quad (.05)$$

where LINC = log of the veteran's weekly income
        E = number of years of additional education (during and after military service)
    AFQT = the veteran's percentile rating on the Armed Forces Qualification Test Score, which was used as a rough measure of IQ
   WHITE = dummy variable for race, being 1 for whites and 0 otherwise
Other variables = age, amount of military service, amount of schooling before military service, father's education and occupation status, and degree of urbanization of his childhood home.

Other things equal, on average it was estimated that back in 1964:

a. A veteran with 1 more year's additional education earned _____% more income.

b. A veteran who was white earned _____% more income than one who was not.

c. A veteran who rated 20 points higher on the AFQT (e.g., who was in the 70th percentile instead of the 50th percentile) earned _____% more income.

d. A non-white veteran who scored in the 80th percentile in the AFQT earned _____% more income than a white veteran who scored in the 50th percentile.

*14-6 In order to be 95% certain of being correct in Problem 14-5, by how much should you hedge your estimate in part (b)? In part (c)?

14-7 The manager of a delivery service decided to conduct a critical examination of the costs of his fleet of 28 vans (maintenance and repairs). He therefore selected 12 vans of comparable size (1 ton load) to see if their records would give him some insight:

VEHICLE MAKE	AGE (YEARS)	COST ($00, ANNUALLY)	MAKE	AGE	COST
F	0	12	G	1	18
F	2	17	G	3	22
F	1	20	G	4	22
F	1	14	G	2	14
G	2	15	G	3	18
G	4	22	G	3	16

a.   His analysis led him to the following conclusions, which he has asked you to verify. (In each case, check both his arithmetic and his reasoning, and make constructive suggestions):

   i)   "The average cost for the new vans (0 and 1 years old) is $1600; and for the old vans (2, 3 4 years old) is $1825. Since age makes little difference to annual costs, and since new vans depreciate much more, I should keep the old vans rather than trade them in."

   ii) "The average repair cost for make F is $1575, and for make G is $1838. Clearly my next purchase should be F rather than G."

b.   The data was run through a multiple regression program, with cars coded D = 1 for make F, and 0 for make G:

   $$COST = 12.4 + 2.18\ AGE + 1.20\ D$$
   $$(SE) \qquad\quad (.89) \qquad (2.28)$$

   Interpret what this means to the manager. Since he hates computers but loves pictures, include graphs.

14-8   Verify the regression equation in Problem 14-7(b), using a computer.

*14-9

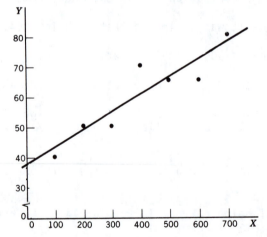

The simple regression of wheat yield against fertilizer gave the graph above (reproduced from Figure 11-4). To check whether this model is adequate, let us look at the yields with the largest residuals, and see whether they show any distinguishing factor.

a.   Circle the two points with the largest positive residuals, and the three points with the largest negative residuals.

256

b. A couple of other factors being considered as possibly relevant were total spring rainfall and average spring temperature. For the 7 data points, their values were found to be as follows; for simplicity, they are indicated as being higher (+) or lower (-) than average:

Yield (Y)	fertilizer (X)	temperature	rainfall
40	100	62	10-
50	200	60-	20
50	300	64+	10-
70	400	62	30+
65	500	64+	20
65	600	60-	20
80	700	60-	30+

On the graph, tag the circled extreme points with a + or - sign, according to the value of temperature. Then repeat for rainfall. Do you see any patterns?

c. Suggest a better model than the simple regression, to reduce residual variation and subsequently improve prediction. What other benefits would the better model give?

14-10 Continuing Problem 14-9, in practice the search for a better model does not always have to start with residuals. We could simply try out the relevant factors like temperature, rainfall, etc. in a multiple regression, to see which factor reduced the residual variance the most (had the most explanatory power). This takes only a moment to compute, and is such a common technique it has a standard name: "stepwise regression".

Which regressor -- temperature or rainfall -- would stepwise regression choose as having most explanatory power in this case?

14-11 Suppose the variation in milk prices (¢ per quart) was observed over 5 regions of the country, and 3 levels of urbanization. For each of these 15 combinations, 4 random observations were sampled, giving 60 observations in all.

The ANOVA table started out as follows:

Source	SS	df	MS	F	p-value
regions	464				
urbanization	102				
interaction	109				
residual					
Total	1862	59			

Fill in the d.f. column as follows:

a. How many dummy variables would be required to handle the 5 regions? This is the df for regions.

b. Similarly obtain the df for urbanization.

c. For interaction, each region dummy is multiplied by each urbanization dummy. How many regressors does that produce? This is the df for interaction.

d. The residual is the variation within the 15 cells; since each cell has 4 observations, or 3 df, this totals 15 x 3 = 45 df for the residual.
   Finally, make sure all the df add up to the total.

257

14-12   (Continuing Problem 14-11) Finish the ANOVA table, including the p-values. Star the discernible sources of variation in milk prices (at level α = 5%)

14-13   (Continuing Problem 14-11) Suppose we also wished to study the relation of milk prices to another important variable X = the degree of competition, as measured by some standard formula involving number of producers and their market shares.

Could a multiple regression be computed with this additional numerical regressor? Would it still be called ANOVA?

CHAPTER 15 - CORRELATION

Correlation is not causation.

R.A. Fisher

PART A - STANDARD PROBLEMS (EASIEST FIRST)

15-1 A random sample of 10 baseball players was drawn, out of all the National League players who came to bat at least 100 times in both the 1979 and 1980 season. Their batting averages (rounded) were as follows (a batting "average" is just the proportion of times a player gets a hit when he comes to bat):

Player and team	1979 (X)	1980 (Y)
Boroughs (Atlanta)	.220	.260
Schmidt (Pittsburgh)	.250	.290
Foote (Chicago)	.250	.240
Scott (St. Louis)	.260	.250
Cedeno (Houston)	.260	.310
Milner (Pittsburgh)	.270	.300
Kennedy (St. Louis)	.280	.250
Cruz (Houston)	.290	.300
Mazzilli (NY)	.300	.280
Henderson (NY)	.310	.290
Average (approx.)	.270	.280
Standard deviation	.027	.025

a. Graph the 10 points on the X-Y plane.

b. By comparison with Figure 15-2 in the text, guess what r is roughly. Then calculate r.

c. Calculate the regression line of Y on X. Graph it.

15-2 (Continuing Problem 15-1.) Without looking at the data, would you guess the worst two players in 1979 will improve in 1980? And the best two players in 1979? Why?

Now look at the data to confirm your guess.

15-3 a. (Continuing Problem 15-1.) Predict the 1980 average of a player who batted .290 in 1979, in the National League.

b. Predict the 1979 average of a player who batted .240 in 1980.

15-4 a. (Continuing Problem 15-1.) Find the 95% confidence interval for ρ.

b. Find the 95% confidence interval for β. [Hint: s^2 is easiest to get from (15-17), or (15-30) to be exact].

c. Do (a) and (b) give the same consistent answer to the question, "Is there a discernible linear relation between X and Y?".

15-5 In each part of Problem 15-3, calculate an interval wide enough that you have 95% confidence in it.

15-6 In Problem 15-1, split the data into two subsamples of five each -- drawing the line halfway down the list, after Cedeno.

    a.   As you glance at the graph of the data, guess how the two correlations in the subsamples compare to the original correlation for the whole sample.

    b.   Now calculate the two subsample correlations to confirm your guess in part (a)

    c.   Answer True or False; if False, correct it:
In Figure 12-4 (a) in the text, where the values of X are less spread out, there is less "leverage" to estimate the true linear relation, and hence a smaller coefficient of determination r^2. Splitting a sample into two likewise reduces the leverage, and hence r^2.

15-7 Referring to the regressions for Michigan schools given earlier in Problem 14-2, the simple correlation was r = .44, and the multiple correlation was R = .72.

    a.   For each regressor in the multiple regression, calculate its partial correlation with Y.

    b.   Repeat (a) for the simple regression. How does this partial correlation compare to the simple correlation coefficient r = .44?

15-8 a.   (Continuing Problem 15-7)   What proportion of the SS (variation) in Y is explained by
i)   the simple regression?
ii)   the multiple regression? How much more is this than (i)?

    b.   The standard deviation of the Y values from their mean (before any regression was done) was s_Y = 4.2. What was the residual standard deviation s of the Y values from the regression equation after
i)   simple regression?
ii)   multiple regression?

    c.   What would you predict is the score Y of a school with SES = 45? Include a 95% prediction interval (Hint: equation (12-21) in the text footnote).

    d.   Repeat (c), if you knew the school was rural, and so the multiple regression could be used.

PART B - DEVELOPING THEMES

B-1 "ATTENUATION": HOW MULTIPLE REGRESSION CAN DECEIVE

The text has illustrated how multiple regression is a vast improvement over simple regression or other statistical techniques that disregard confounding variables. But it is still far from perfect. This theme will show how crucial some regression assumptions can be. In particular, if X as well as Y is randomly disturbed, OLS regression can give a misleading result called attenuation, or under-adjustment, that is particularly vexing to the courts as they wrestle with discrimination (Finkelstein 1980, p. 747).

15-9 (IDEAL WORLD AS A BENCHMARK) The graph below shows how salary in a large corporation might hypothetically be related to productivity -- if there were absolutely no error in assigning salary. For simplicity, men and women fall into two distinct groups.

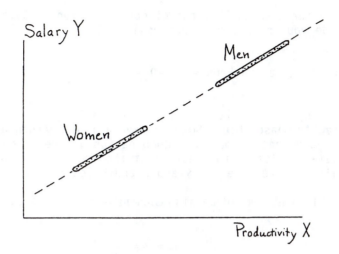

a. Let us start with two very simple but basic questions:
   Do men and women earn the same salaries on average?
   Is there any sex discrimination?

b. Now let us define the usual dummy variable to distinguish the sexes (M = 1 or 0, depending on whether the employee is male or female). Then a regression of salary against productivity and sex could be computed:

$$Y = b_0 + b_1 X + b_2 M$$

This is equivalent to fitting two parallel lines for the two sexes. Sketch these two lines so that you can answer (c) below.

c. What would be the coefficient of M? If a court interpreted this coefficient as the amount of discrimination against women, would they be correct?

15-10 (MORE REALISTIC WORLD) Let us make the model above more realistic. Suppose actual salaries are randomly disturbed, according to the usual regression model. Then the pattern of (X, Y) points would be spread out in the Y direction, roughly as follows:

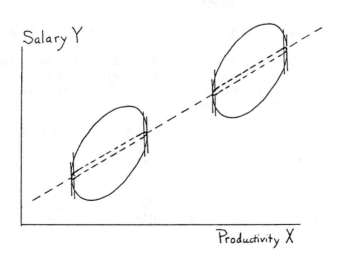

We have outlined the scatter with an "ellipse of concentration." Some vertical lines are also added, to guide you in sketching regression lines as in Figure 15-7 in the text.

Now answer the same questions as in Problem 15-9

15-11 (EVEN MORE REALISTIC WORLD) To make our model more realistic, we must recognize that productivity is not exactly measurable. Some "proxy variable" (such as education, or seniority, or personal judgement, or maybe a combination of these) has to be used by management to assign salary. Assume the best, that the proxy variable is an unbiased estimate of productivity, scattered equally above and below the true value.

Now the pattern of (X, Y) points would be also spread out in the X direction, roughly as follows:

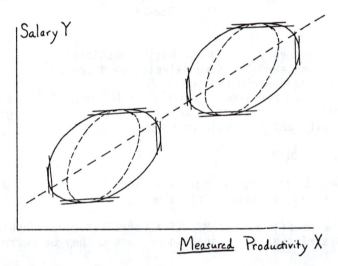

Again answer the same questions as in Problem 15-9.

15-12 So far we have kept the scatter of women's salaries separate from the men's, in order to clarify the argument. In practice, of course, the two scatters would overlap. But the logic and conclusions would be exactly the same.

To review what these conclusions are, chose the correct alternative in brackets:

a.   In OLS regression of Y against X and M, the coefficient of M is commonly interpreted as how much salary a [man, woman] earned more than a [woman, man] of the same productivity -- that is, the estimate of [how much more productive women are than men, sex discrimination against women].

b.   This common interpretation will be correct, however, only if [X, Y] is without error, while the other variable can randomly fluctuate -- that is, if the variables [satisfy the regression model (13-3), are all dummy variables].

15-13 Professor Harry Roberts (Finkelstein 1980, p. 747) has suggested a way of detecting the problem of "attenuation" described above, without graphing (since graphing may be impractical when there are many variables): Do a "reverse" regression of X against Y and M.

a. Now what is the common interpretation of the coefficient of M?

b. Would the coefficient of M be positive, negative, or zero for the data in Problem 15-11?

c. Now underline the correct choice:

When there is no sex discrimination at all, the regression of Y against X and M shows discrimination against [men, women], whereas the reverse regression of X against Y and M shows discrimination against [men, women].

Thus the conflicting message of reverse regression has warned us that [only the original, neither] regression should be trusted.

CHAPTER 16 - NONPARAMETRIC AND ROBUST STATISTICS

Grown-ups love figures. When you tell them that you have made a new friend, they never ask you any questions about essential matters. They never say to you, "What does his voice sound like? What games does he love best? Does he collect butterflies?" Instead, they demand: "How old is he? How many brothers has he? How much does he weigh? How much money does his father make?" Only from these figures do they think they have learned anything about him ....

They are like that. One must not hold it against them. Children should always show great forbearance toward grown-up people.

Antoine St. Exupery, in The Little Prince

PART A - STANDARD PROBLEMS (EASIEST FIRST)

Unless otherwise specified, use a nonparametric statistic rather than a classical one.

16-1   To see whether a new personnel policy reduces absenteeism, a random sample of 8 employees were recorded for the 12 months before it took effect, and the 12 months after:

Days Absent	
Before	After
3	1
9	6
8	6
0	7
13	4
9	7
8	4
3	5

a.   The personnel manager had claimed that the new policy would reduce the annual absenteeism to a median level of 3 days. Is this claim credible? Calculate its p-value using the sign test.

b.   A skeptic in the finance department claimed that the new policy did not really reduce the median level of absenteeism at all. Calculate the p-value for this claim.

16-2   a.   Calculate an appropriate confidence level for the median reduction in absenteeism that the new policy makes in Problem 16-1. Use a level of confidence around the customary 95%.

b.   What assumptions did you make in part (a)? Are they important? Were they made in Problem 16-1 too?

16-3   The 1980 family incomes (in thousands of dollars) were randomly sampled from two different locations in Minneapolis, with the following results:

Core	Suburbs
37	40
22	26
16	34
23	61
30	31

a. What is the null hypothesis?

b. Calculate its p-value.

16-4 a. What is a robust estimator?

b. What is the trimmed mean? Is it more or less robust than the ordinary mean? When is it a better estimator than the ordinary mean? When is it worse?

*16-5 a. What is the biweighted mean? What are its advantages and disadvantages relative to the trimmed mean?

b. What is biweighted regression?

PART B - DEVELOPING THEMES

INDUSTRIAL LEAD POISONING: THREE DIFFERENT VIEWS

In this sequence we will use the same data to illustrate three different statistical methods: Exploratory Data Analysis (EDA), nonparametric tests, and classical t-tests.

16-6 The data (Morton and others, 1982) is lead levels (Y) in the blood of 33 children who were exposed to lead via their parents working in a battery factory. For each child, an unexposed child matched for the same age and neighborhood was also measured (X). The 33 pairs of lead levels, plotted along the Y and X axis in the central square below, give a "scatter plot" of 33 points shown as little crosses (Rosenbaum 1989).

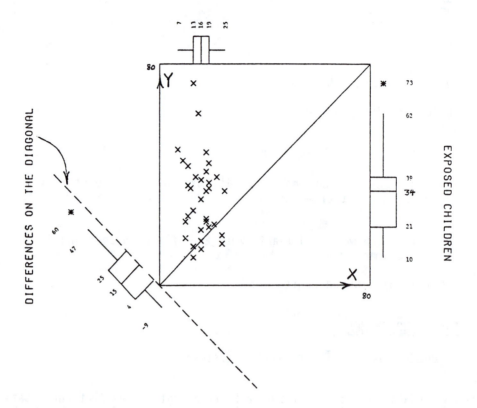

UNEXPOSED CHILDREN

If the points are projected to the right, they give the boxplot there that shows a median lead level of 34 for the exposed children. Similarly if the points are projected to the top, they give the boxplot there that shows a much lower median of 16 for the unexposed children.

The diagonal drawn through the square of course shows where Y=X, that is, where the difference D=Y-X is zero (no difference between the exposed and unexposed child). The point furthest from the diagonal -- at the very top of the scatterplot -- is where the difference D is greatest.

To show in general how large is the difference D, the dashed diagonal line is drawn below the square to the left. If the 33 points are projected onto it, they give the boxplot there that shows a median difference of 15.

To make sure this is clear, look again at the top-most point (little cross) in the scatterplot. Its projection to the right gives the outlying star on the boxplot there, showing it was the most extreme level of all the exposed children. Its projection to the top, however, shows that the unexposed child in the matched pair was fairly typical, appearing near the lower quartile of 13. Thus the difference that exposure makes in this matched pair is large -- as shown by the projection onto the dashed diagonal, where it appears as the outlying star once more.

a. Now from the first two box plots, what can be concluded? Relative to the control children, the exposed children have blood lead levels that are [lower, higher], and [less, more] spread out, and [skewed, symmetric].

266

b. The third box plot, on the dashed diagonal, shows the difference that exposure makes. The median difference is [15, 18], with [half, nearly all] the differences lying in the range from 4 to 25.

16-7 Is the exposure to lead harmful overall? The sample seems to indicate so, but will a formal test bear this out? Use the sign test to calculate the p-value for H_0 (exposure makes no difference in the population, or more precisely, the median population difference is zero).
(Hint: Since n = 33 exceeds the binomial tables, use the normal approximation.)

16-8 Calculate the classical p-value for H_0 (the mean population difference is zero), using the following statistics: $\bar{D} = 17$, $s_D = 16$, n = 33.

16-9 Which test do you think is more appropriate -- the sign test or the t-test? (Hint: Should an outlying difference like the star in the boxplot be counted heavily as in the t-test, or should it count no more than any other difference, as in the sign test? That is, in terms of human health, how serious is it?)

16-10 Here are some summary statistics:

	Mean	Median
Y (exposed)	33	34
X (unexposed)	16	16
Y−X (difference)	17	15

a. Note that the difference of the means (33−16) is just the mean of the difference (17). Is this just a fluke, or must it always be so?

b. Do the medians behave like the means in (a)? Does this indicate there is a mistake in the table?

16-11 a. In general, what is the benefit from using matched pairs instead of two independent samples?

b. Is this benefit achieved in this particular data? (Include the evidence for your answer, too.)

CHAPTER 17 - CHI SQUARE TESTS

The age of chivalry is gone; that of sophisters, economists and calculators has succeeded.

Edmund Burke

17-1 The following table of monthly births in Sweden in 1935 gives some detail missing in the aggregated data of Table 17-2 in the text.

Monthly Detail on Births			
Jan	7,280	July	7,585
Feb.	6,957	Aug.	7,393
Mar.	7,883	Sept.	7,203
Apr.	7,884	Oct.	6,903
May	7,892	Nov.	6,552
June	7,609	Dec.	7,132
		Total	88,273

a. Calculate a few cells of the χ^2 test of the null hypothesis (H_0: births are equally likely to occur on all days of the year).

b. Analyze a few cells of the data graphically, as in Figure 17-1.

c. What are the advantages and disadvantages of using monthly data instead of seasonal data?

17-2 A random sample of one thousand adult Americans in 1980 were classified by education and sex as follows:

Education (last	sex	
completed school)	male	females
none	40	50
primary	100	120
secondary	230	290
college	100	70

(reconstructed from the same source as Problem 5-20 in the text)

a. State H_0 in words

b. Calculate χ^2 and the p-value for H_0

c. Can you reject H_0 at level $\alpha = 5\%$?

d. Compared to the analysis in Problem 5-21(d) in the text, is this χ^2 analysis
   i)   easier?
   ii) more insightful?

17-3 A Gallup poll of 1500 Americans just before the 1988 Presidential election showed the following approximate breakdown by age (Reconstructed roughly from the Gallup Report, Nov. 1988, p. 7):

vote	under 30	over 30	totals
Bush (R)	140	670	810
Dukakis (D)	80	610	690
totals	220	1280	1500

a.   State H_0 in words.

b.   Calculate χ^2 and the p-value for H_0

c.   Calculate an appropriate 95% confidence interval instead.

d.   Which do you think is the more meaningful analysis, (b) or (c)?

17-4 a.   Continuing Problem 17-3 (c), calculate the p-value (2-sided) for H_0. Use the appropriate t-ratio (or in this large-sample case with so many d.f., it is a z ratio). Is the p-value consistent with Problem 17-3(b)?

b.   Underline the correct choice in each bracket:
The p-value of χ^2 calculated in Problem 17-3(b) is [larger, smaller, about the same]. Thus χ^2 [can, cannot] be considered an extension of the test for independence in 2 x 2 tables, to larger tables in general.

17-5 The change in the male/female birth ratio over a generation can be estimated from the following U.S. data:

U.S. births, by year and sex (millions)

	1960	1980
male	2.180	1.853
female	2.078	1.760

(Stat. Abst. of U.S. 1987, p. 59)

Using this new data, repeat Problems 17-3 and 17-4.

17-6 Did Russian arms exports follow a 5-year cycle patterned after their 5-year plans? To test this, the yearly rises (R) and falls (F) of arms exports were recorded for 20 years (Abouchar, 1981).

plan number		year of plan				
		1	2	3	4	5
1	(1951-55)	R	F	R	F	R
2	(1956-60)	R	R	F	F	R
3	(1961-65)	R	R	F	F	R
4	(1966-70)	R	R	F	F	F

a.   Calculate the p-value for the null hypothesis (that R and F are random, without pattern). To do this, you will need to count the data in a two-way frequency table:

	year of plan				
	1	2	3	4	5
R	4	3	.	.	.
F	0	1	.	.	.

b.   Show the information graphically.

17-7   A large corporation wants to test whether each of its divisions has equally satisfactory quality control over its output. Suppose output of each division, along with the number of units rejected and returned by dealers, is as follows:

	Division		
	A	B	C
Output	600	400	1000
Rejected	52	60	88

Assuming this output can be regarded as a random sample, calculate the p-value for H_0: no difference in divisions. (Hint: Since χ^2 requires "pigeonholing" into mutually exclusive cells, the data will first have to be retabulated into "Accepted" and "Rejected" rows.)

17-8   For another useful interpretation of d.f., prove that the expected value of χ^2 in equation (17-2) of the text is $(r - 1)$. [Hint: Use equations (5-17) and (4-13).]

*CHAPTER 18 - MAXIMUM LIKELIHOOD ESTIMATION

He uses statistics as a drunken man uses lampposts - for support rather than
for illumination.

Andrew Lang

18-1 In each of the following cases, find the MLE and the MME. Is the MME different from
the MLE? If so, which is better? Why?

a. For the proportion of defectives in a population of TV tubes from which a sample
of 6 defectives out of 500 was drawn.

b. For the slope in a normal regression model, based on the following sample
statistics:

Range of X: 7 to 19   Range of Y: 58 to 73

$$\bar{X} = 12 \qquad \bar{Y} = 65 \qquad n = 25$$
$$\Sigma(X-\bar{X})^2 = 220 \qquad \Sigma(Y-\bar{Y})^2 = 516 \qquad \Sigma(X-\bar{X})(Y-\bar{Y}) = 294$$

18-2 A random sampling of three Variety stores found that one was open all night. To
estimate π, the proportion in the whole population,

a. What is the MLE?

b. To get an idea of the range of the accuracy of the MLE in (a), graph the
likelihood function. Is it vague or precise?

18-3 Repeat Problem 18-2 if a sample of 12 stores showed 4 open all night. When the sample
size was quadrupled, what happened to the accuracy of the estimate of π?

All virtue is a compromise.

William Godwin

19-1 Your firm has just purchased a two million dollar piece of machinery, and your engineers have found it to be substandard. You found out that the manufacturer that produced it substitutes cheaper components 25% of the time. You also found out that such a substitution doubles the probability that the machine will be substandard, from .10 to .20.

If your machine has cheaper components, you could win a lawsuit against the manufacturer. What are the odds of this? And what is the probability?

19-2 Suppose it rains 15% of the days and shines 85% of the days. A barometer manufacturer in testing his instrument has found that although it is fairly reliable, it sometimes errs: on rainy days it erroneously predicts "shine" 10 % of the time, and on shiny days it erroneously predicts "rain" 20% of the time.

a. Before looking at the barometer, what is the probability of rain?

b. If the barometer says "rain", will the probability go up or down? Verify, by calculating the probability.

c. If the barometer says "shine", repeat (b).

19-3 To help determine what makes schools good, 2500 elementary schools in Michigan were studied (Klitgaard and Hall, 1977). The grade 4 reading score X in each school had a mean μ, and the 2500 values of μ formed an approximately normal distribution, centered at $\mu_0 = 50$ with standard deviation $\sigma_0 = 3.3$. Within each school, the individual values of X varied around μ with a standard deviation $\sigma = 8$ approximately.

Suppose a school was picked from the records, and from it 10 reading scores X were randomly sampled, giving $\bar{X} = 54$. What would you estimate is the mean score μ for the whole school? Include a 95% confidence interval.

19-4 Continuing Problem 19-3, the proportion π of students who attained a high level of reading skill ($X \geq 60$) was also recorded in each school. The 2500 values of π had approximately a beta distribution given by

$$p(\pi) = \pi^3(1-\pi)^{22}$$

In the same school that was picked in Problem 19-3, the sample proportion of students who attained a high level of reading skill was P = 2/10 = 20%. What would you estimate is the proportion π for the whole school? Include a 95% confidence interval.

19-5 A sample of n = 3 was taken from each of four yarn types. The four sample means were: 36, 39, 42, and 35. The grand mean was 38, and the F statistic for H_0 (no difference in the four yarn types) was F = 2.73.

a. Calculate the Bayesian shrinkage estimates for the four population means.

b. On a graph, contrast the Bayesian shrinkage and classical estimates.

19-6 Repeat Problem 19-5, with the data slightly changed: Suppose the four sample means are now 36, 39, 37, and 36. The grand mean is then 37, and the F statistic is .55.

19-7 In Problem 18-12 (d) in the text, we graphically found a 95% confidence interval (CI) for π by cutting off $2\frac{1}{2}$% under each tail of the likelihood function.

a. For this to be a 95% Bayesian CI, what did we implicitly assume about the prior distribution of π?

b. Using this same assumption, use the formula (19-19) to calculate the 95% Bayesian CI.

c. Does your CI in (b) roughly agree with the CI found graphically in Problem 18-12(d) (namely, $.38 < \pi < .92$)?

d. Is your CI in (b) a little narrower than the classical CI found in Problem 18-12(e) (namely, $.35 < \pi < .94$)? Why?

O God, give us serenity to accept what cannot be changed, courage to change what should be changed, and wisdom to distinguish one from the other.

Reinhold Niebuhr

PART A - STANDARD PROBLEMS (EASIEST FIRST)

20-1 A TV manufacturer has a choice of three kinds of components to fill a crucial position in their TV sets: ordinary, at $2.00 each; reliable, at $2.50 each; or very reliable, at $3.00 each. The two better kinds have a smaller chance of breaking if the TV set is badly jarred: Past records show that the three kinds of components break 4%, 2% and 1% of the time, respectively.

If such a break costs $40 to repair, what kind of component should be used?

20-2 Assume that the loss function is quadratic, that the prior distribution of μ is normal, and that the observations X_i are drawn from a normal population with mean μ and variance 150. Then in each case calculate the best (Bayesian) estimate of μ. Also calculate the MLE estimate for comparison.

Prior Parameters		Sample Data		Estimate of μ	
μ_0	σ_0^2		n	Bayesian	MLE
100	25	200	6		
100	250	200	6		
100	2500	200	6		
100	25	200	6		
100	25	200	60		
100	25	200	600		

c. Underline the correct choice:

As the prior distribution becomes more vague, that is, as σ_0^2 becomes [smaller, larger], the optimal estimate of μ gets [closer to, farther from] the MLE estimate.

This also occurs as the sample size gets bigger. In both cases, it is because the likelihood function [overwhelms, is overwhelmed by] the prior distribution.

20-3 A poll is to be taken of your statistics class, to determine the proportion π who voted for the Republican candidate (or would have, if they had had the opportunity to vote) in the last presidential election.

a. Since we (the authors) do not know your class at all, if we had to guess π we would be very unsure. To capture this uncertainty, we have a prior distribution for π roughly given by $p(\pi) = \sqrt{\pi}$ for $0 \leq \pi \leq 1$. We can also write this as a beta function, $p(\pi) = \pi^{\frac{1}{2}}(1-\pi)^0$.

Graph this prior. Is it indeed vague?

b. The next time your class meets, get your instructor to take a random sample of 4 students. Suppose that S of these students voted Republican. Then the classical MLE estimate for π is just the sample proportion $P = S/n = S/4$. What is the Bayesian estimate, assuming a quadratic loss function, and the prior distribution given in (a)?

c. Now poll the whole class to find out what π actually is. Which estimate in (b) is closer -- the Bayesian or MLE?

d. Repeat the sampling experiment (drawing n = 4 students) in (b) several times, to average out the "luck of the draw". Which estimate would you tentatively conclude is on the whole closer to the true π -- the Bayesian or MLE estimate?

20-4 a. Continuing Problem 20-3, if the sampling experiment in part (b) were repeated millions of times, what would be the sampling distribution of S? (Don't forget that you are "omniscient", and know what π actually is from part (c).)

b. Now tabulate this distribution of S below, and use it to fill in the rest of the table to get a solid comparison of the Bayesian and MLE estimates, using the mean squared error (MSE):

s	p(s)	Bayesian estimate P*				MLE estimate P			
		P*	$(P*-\pi)$	$(P*-\pi)^2$	$(P*-\pi)^2 p(s)$	P	$(P-\pi)$	$(P-\pi)^2$	$(P-\pi)^2 p(s)$
0									
1									
.									
.									
					MSE = sum =				MSE = sum =

So which is better (in the sense of minimizing MSE) -- the Bayesian or MLE estimate?

20-5 a. Continuing Problem 20-3(a), you (the reader) of course know your own class better than we do (the authors). How would your personal prior distribution differ from ours?

b. More specifically, graph your personal prior distribution very roughly. Then find a beta distribution that crudely approximates it. (For example, how about the prior in Figure 19-3 or 19-4 of the text? If not, continue to look for a crudely matching prior by reading across the Binomial Table III(b), under n = 4 still. If this doesn't give a crude match yet, try other n: For a vaguer prior, try n < 4; for a tighter prior, try n > 4.)

c. Now use your own personal prior to determine what your Bayesian estimate P* would be.

d. Use this new Bayesian estimate P* to fill in the table (third column) in Problem 20-4(b). Continue with the table until you get a new bottom line. Is this a smaller MSE than the MLE has?

20-6 In Example 20-3 in the text we saw how an asymmetric loss function produces an asymmetric estimate of Θ. To be specific, when an estimate was too low each unit of undershooting cost 4 times as much as each unit of overshooting when the estimate was too high. Then the optimal estimate was the 80th percentile of the distribution of Θ -- where there is 4 times as much probability below as above (80% = 4 x 20%).

This can be proved generally true. For example, if each unit of undershooting costs 10 times as much (instead of 4), the optimal estimate is where there is 10 times as much probability below as above.

a.   Referring to the distribution $p(\Theta)$ in Table 20-5 of the text, what is the optimal estimate when each unit of undershooting costs 10 times as much (as mentioned above)?

b.   Verify that your answer in (a) is indeed optimal, by working through a table like Table 20-5.

20-7 Continuing Problem 20-6, now suppose the distribution $p(\Theta)$ is normal, with mean 60 and standard deviation 10. Find the least costly estimate of Θ if each unit of undershooting costs

a.   10 times as much (as each unit of overshooting)

b.   equally as much

c.   5 times as much

d.   1/3 as much

20-8 An economist constructed a 95% confidence interval for a marginal propensity to save, based on the best available data and prior (all normally distributed):

$$.02 < \beta < .10$$

a.   This estimate proved too much for his client to digest. He insisted instead on a single number. What is the best point estimate of β if, on careful probing he felt it would be equally serious to underestimate as to overestimate?

b.   Now find the best point estimate if he felt that each unit of undershooting costs twice as much as each unit of overshooting. (Hint: Problem 20-6 and 7)

CHAPTER 21 - DECISION TREES

Models don't make decisions. People do.

Austin's law.

PART A - STANDARD PROBLEMS (EASIEST FIRST)

21-1   Jack Collins, VP (Research and Development) of National Robotics, has to decide whether a promising new idea for a swimming-pool cleaner warrants the anticipated cost of 3 million dollars for development and marketing. It is a high risk project, with a 10% chance of being a complete flop with essentially no returns to defray this large expense. On the other hand, there is a 70% chance it will nearly break even, with a return of 2 million, and a 20% chance it will be very successful, with a return of 9 million. He realizes, of course, that there are hundreds of possibilities, but feels this crude grouping into three possible returns captures the main features of the risk.

His company's 86 million dollar profit last year put them in a comfortable enough position that Jack doesn't worry about this one project making or breaking them. Nevertheless their future depends crucially on selecting wisely among the dozens of projects like this that are considered each year.

Should Jack recommend that National Robotics proceed with this cleaner, or drop it?

21-1   Suppose National Robotics in Problem 21-1 has fallen on hard times. After a big shake-up, Jack has become the president and sole owner of a much smaller and wiser company -- still facing the decision on the swimming-pool cleaner. Now Jack is worried that the potential 3 million dollar loss might bankrupt him. On the other hand, he is very excited about what the net return of 6 million could do to revitalize his company. As he agonizes between these extremes, what could he do to proceed rationally?

21-3   After some very careful introspection, Jack comes up with this "utility function" or "preference curve" to capture his feelings about risk in Problem 21-2. Now what is the best decision about the cleaner?

net return ($ millions)	-3	-2	-1	0	1	2	3	4	5	6	7	8
utility	0	.14	.27	.39	.50	.60	.69	.77	.84	.90	.95	1.00

21-4   Go back to the prosperous company of Problem 21-1. Suppose an additional option is suggested, as a way to lessen the risk: For 1.3 million dollars, Jack could build and test a prototype that would predict quite well which of the three possible returns would occur (0, 2, or 9 million dollars, gross).

Without knowing the details of the test yet, what could we say about whether or not it could pay its way?

21-5   Spurred on by the answer in Problem 21-4, Jack comes up with a less expensive test. Its outcomes could be broadly classified as failure (F), bare pass (P), successful (S), and wildly successful (W). After many hours of considering his company's past experience, he comes up with this table of how likely the outcomes would be:

If the final product is good enough to produce a gross return of:	... then the chances of various test results are as follows:				
	F	P	S	W	total
0 million	.80	.20			1.00
2 million	.20	.30	.40	.10	1.00
9 million			.30	.50	.20	1.00

Jack hopes he could bring the cost of this test down from 1.3 million to about 0.5 million. Would the test pay its way now?

21-6 What is the breakeven value for the test in Problem 21-5, where it would just barely pay its way?

PART B - DEVELOPING THEMES

B-1 A PERSONAL MEDICAL DECISION

The following dilemma, communicated from the actual experience of a friend, is especially interesting because the standard medical advice ran counter to what the couple themselves felt was in their best interest.

21-7 A couple have decided it's the right time to have their first child. Their doctor, however, points out that the woman has not had the measles (German measles) and if she catches them during the first 3 months of pregnancy, there is a 30% chance the baby would suffer a severe birth defect (such as deafness or blindness). So the doctor recommends a vaccination, which would require a 2 year delay in starting a family -- the time required for the effect of the vaccine to wear off safely. (Not really true, but Problem 21-8 will give a more realistic version.)

The couple are particularly distressed by this prospective delay, because they are already 29 years old, and would like to have 4 children -- spaced every two years at age 30, 32, 34 and 36 (assuming no problem of infertility). The two-year delay would mean the children would be bumped to age 32, 34, 36, and 38.

This delay would not only be a severe strain on their patience, it would itself introduce a new risk of birth defect: Down's syndrome (a rare form of retardation just as tragic as a measles' defect) is a little more common for older mothers. In fact, statistics show that for mothers aged 38, it occurs about every 200 births; for mothers aged 30, it occurs only once every 1000 births.

A friend suggested a way out of the dilemma: postpone the vaccination until just after the first birth; since a 2 year resting period is planned in any case, the 2 year wait for the effect of the vaccine to wear off would then be absorbed at no cost.

The doctor was quick to point out the cost of <u>this</u> solution: the wife might catch measles during the first pregnancy, and live a lifetime of regret. When asked how likely this is, the doctor estimated that of all adults who failed to catch measles before 18, about 5% eventually caught measles in their adult life, so that he calculated the risk to be about .01% per month. For the crucial first 3 months of pregnancy, therefore, the risk would be about .03%.

The couple have come to you, a genetics counsellor, for advice. What would you say?

21-8 Continuing Problem 21-7, assume more realistically that the measles vaccine required not a full 24 months, but only a 3 month wait. This represents only 3/24 = 12% of the previous delay, and so means only 12% as much additional risk of Down's syndrome. Now what would you advise?

21-9   To clarify the answers in Problem 21-8, we can restate it in very concrete language. To simplify matters, suppose there were a million couples facing this decision. If they all took the option of immediate vaccination, about how many excess birth defects would occur? And if they all took the option of postponing the vaccination? ("excess" means relative to the ideal situation -- no longer attainable -- of having the measles vaccination long before marriage, which doctors of course recommend if possible).

21-10 a.   When a decision is actually your own, it sometimes has a strong emotional component that is missing from a text-book exercise. For example, if Problem 21-8 was your problem that you had to decide with your partner, which choice do you think you would favor? Why?

      b.   Many doctors would recommend the measles vaccine be taken immediately, rather than postponed. Suggest some reasons why they might give this advice.

21-11 In Problem 21-8, are there other options you can suggest? Work through your revised version of the tree to see what decision they might lead to.

21-12 At the end of Problem 21-7, recall that the doctor calculated the monthly risk of measles to be about .01%. Verify this from the earlier data ("... about 5% eventually caught measles in their adult life".)

B-2   ECONOMIC AND SOCIAL JUSTICE

     The tools of this chapter -- or more formally, Bayesian Decision Theory (BDT) -- were developed originally to help individuals make wiser decisions, that is, maximize their long-run (expected) profit. But we soon went far beyond that, to maximizing personal satisfaction (or more precisely, maximizing utility means maximizing whatever it is that the person cherishes most.)
     In this section we will extend BDT much further yet, to maximizing the satisfaction or well being of everyone altogether -- that is, to ethics.

21-13 You have to choose the best of several possible job offers, A, B, C or D. Each one has risky prospects. Specifically, suppose each offer may lead to one of five equally likely positions, whose salaries (real income, $000 annually) vary widely as follows:

Offer A	Offer B	Offer C	Offer D
10	20	20	25
10	40	50	25
10	40	50	25
10	40	50	25
300	250	200	25

Let us make all the simplifying assumptions necessary to make these salaries the whole story. For example, suppose there are no welfare payments or income taxes to change these figures. And suppose all jobs are lifetime jobs, equal in all respects except real income. To evaluate the salary differences, suppose your utility curve is as follows:

Salary	Utility	Salary	Utility
0	.00	50	.47
10	.18	100	.64
20	.29	150	.76
25	.33	200	.86
30	.36	250	.94
40	.42	300	1.00

a. Graph the utility function. Does it show increasing, constant, or decreasing marginal utility of money?
   Is your own utility curved this same way? State briefly why, or why not, in terms of what money means to you.

b. Which is the best offer to take? And the worst? What criterion did you use?

21-14 To make sure that the answer to Problem 21-13 is clear, underline the correct choice in each bracket:

a. The appropriate criterion is to maximize expected [monetary value, utility]. Intuitively, this is because it is not really relevant to add up all the dollars -- and then divide by 5 to get an average -- since dollars are not all comparable or equal. A dollar can buy much more happiness when I am [rich, poor].
   On the other hand, it does make sense to add up all the units of utility, since by their very definition, they all measure equal amounts of happiness.

b. The criterion of expected utility is remarkably powerful and simple. It summarizes a complex pattern or distribution of utilities with a single number -- the average or expected value. Other parameters of the utility distribution -- like variance or skewness -- may be of some interest to statisticians, but they are absolutely [crucial, irrelevant] to decision making. For decision making, the only thing that [matters, is completely irrelevant] is the total or average utility.

c. Why is the variance of utility irrelevant? Let us answer it another way: The variance or inequality of money is indeed important, so important that we developed the concept of utility to deal with it. For example, a huge amount of money is measured with a utility [even greater, not nearly so huge]. And this discounting once is precisely enough. Any attempt to discount again would be overcompensating; to the extent it produced a decision different from the decision that maximizes expected utility, it would produce [less, possibly more] overall satisfaction for the decision maker.

21-15 Now we are ready for the switch from maximizing what is best for the individual, to maximizing what is best for everyone altogether.
   To start informally, why do we regard as so undesirable a tyranny with a very small but rich aristocracy oppressing the great mass of citizens? Don't the citizens of our own country also vary from the ecstatic to the miserable - and even to the utterly wretched (as evidenced by a suicide rate that seems impossible to eradicate completely)? The difference seems to be that there are so few happy people in the tyranny, and so many who are wretched. To formalize this into a guiding principle or ethic, one of the earliest writers (Harsanyi, 1976, p. 195) invoked the following "principle of randomization":
   To determine how good a society of N people is, I imagine myself assigned at random to one of the N positions in it, in some sort of cosmic gamble -- I cannot count on being the ruler, nor the most unfortunate wretch either, but instead must take my chances. The social problem of how to choose between four different societies

is thus transformed into a personal decision -- choosing between four cosmic gambles. And the criterion for personal choice between different gambles is already well established, as emphasized in Problem 21-14: maximize total or average utility.[1]

a. Harsanyi's principle (maximize total utility) is a modern restatement of a very famous ethic called utilitarianism (popularly known as "the most happiness for the most people"). Use it to judge which of the following societies is most desirable.

Table of salaries ($000, annually) in each of four societies

Society A	Society B	Society C	Society D
10	20	20	25
10	40	50	25
10	40	50	25
10	40	50	25
300	250	200	25

Note that each society has 5 members (or if you want, you can imagine 5 million), and the table is just like Problem 21-13. To make the analogy complete, let us further assume each member has the utility function given in Problem 21-13, and assume the societies are equal in all respects other than real income. (In particular, we assume people neither envy nor rejoice in their neighbor's better fortune, which would lower or raise their happiness as a whole.)

b. As an alternative to maximizing total utility, Rawls (1971) proposed maximizing minimum utility. That is, within each society, circle the one individual with the least utility. Where this circled utility is greatest, there is the most "just" society. Now rank the four societies above according to Rawls' criterion.

c. Which do you think is more appropriate, Harsanyi's or Rawls' theory of social justice? Why? Can you suggest something better?

---

[1]Since the average and total are closely related by the population size N (average=total/N), whatever choice maximizes one will maximize the other. The one exception is when N itself is also a decision variable, to be chosen by an appropriate population policy for example. In this case, it turns out that total utility in many ways is a better criterion than average utility -- since total utility counts all human happiness equally, no matter what its source.

CHAPTER 22 - INDEX NUMBERS

This summer one-third of the nation will be ill-housed, ill-nourished, and ill-clad. Only they call it vacation.

Joseph Salak

PART A - STANDARD PROBLEMS (EASIEST FIRST)

22-1 The prices (per unit) and quantities (per person, annually) of various goods making up the price index in Ruritania changed over the 1980's, as follows:

	1980		1990	
item	P_0	Q_0	P_t	Q_t
bread (lb.)	$ .40	60	$ 1.00	60
shoes (pr.)	$18.00	3	$36.00	4
heating oil (gal.)	$ .40	100	$ 2.40	80

    a. Of the Laspeyres, Paasche, and Fisher price indexes, which do you expect to be biggest? And smallest? Why?

    b. Confirm your answer in part (a) by actually calculating the three price indexes.

22-2 Repeat Problem 22-1 for the <u>quantity</u> indexes.

22-3 Which of the three indexes satisfies the "factor reversal test" (i.e., makes the price index x cost index = total cost index)?
       Illustrate your answer using the data in Problem 22-1.

22-4 Is the U.S. CPI a form of Laspeyres, Paasche, or Fisher index? Give some practical advantages, and disadvantages.

22-5 What would happen to inflation if there were no gains in productivity over the years, and all wages were indexed to keep up with the Laspeyres price index? The Paasche price index?

PART B DEVELOPING THEMES

B-1 GRAPHICAL COMPARISON OF INFLATION RATES

22-6 a. The graph below shows the U.S. CPI for nearly 200 years. The major wars over that period were: the Civil War 1861-65, First World War 1917-18, and the Second World War 1941-45. What's happening to the CPI then? Why?

    b. The minor wars were the War of 1812-14, Korean War 1950-52, and the Vietnamese War 1963 to 1973 roughly. Is the CPI behaving the same way then too?

    c. What 20 year period has had more inflation than any other?

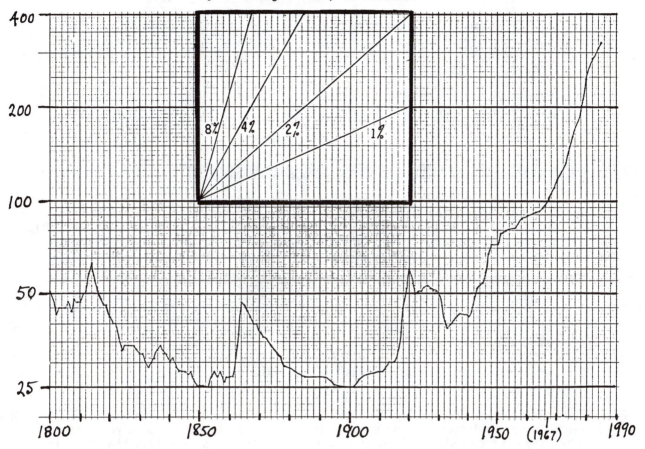

Constant inflation represented
by a straight line, as follows:

U.S. CPI 1800-1985 (1967 = 100). Doubling is marked by heavy lines.
(Stat. Abst. of U.S. 1987, and Historical Statistics of U.S., Bureau of Census, p. 210)

22-7 Note that the CPI is plotted on a ratio scale, which makes it easy to answer some questions of comparison:

a. Is inflation as measured by the CPI roughly the same as measured by the GNP deflator in Figure 22-1 of the text?

b. At 2% per year, how much would the CPI increase after 50 years? After 35 years?

c. At 4%, how long would it take the CPI to double? To quadruple?

d. Find your answers to (b) and (c) on the legend of the Figure.

22-8 Instead of a ratio scale, suppose we had used an ordinary scale for the CPI, ranging from 0 to 100 to 200 to 300 etc. in equal lengths on the Y-axis.

    a.   Very roughly, sketch what the graph would now look like.

    b.   In particular, which would look more serious at a glance, the inflation from 1915-20, or 1980-85?
        In which period was inflation actually higher (nearly doubling the CPI)?

    c.   In a sentence or two, which is appropriate for the CPI -- a ratio scale or an ordinary scale?

B-2   AGE-ADJUSTMENTS, LIKE INDEX NUMBERS, GIVE FAIR COMPARISONS

22-9 To measure how healthy a population is, the mortality rate is a common indicator. For example, to compare two states such as Maine and Louisiana, in 1978 the following statistics were supplied (U.S. Bureau of the Census microfiche):

Maine		Louisiana	
population	deaths	population	deaths
1,093,000	10,169	3,977,000	35,224

    a.   Which state has the lower overall (crude) death rate? (Express it in deaths per thousand, for convenience).

    b.   Which state does it seem healthier to live in?

22-10 The answer above may be comparing apples and oranges: If the population of Louisiana tends to have a lot more young people with low mortality rates, then youth (rather than a healthy environment) may be what is keeping Louisiana's overall mortality rate lower.
    To investigate this possibility, here is the breakdown of deaths during 1978 by age groups:

age	Maine population	deaths	death rate	Louisiana population	deaths	death rate
0- 5	76,000	188		334,000	1,514	
5-20	291,000	167		1,135,000	814	
20-45	369,000	528		1,415,000	3,034	
45-65	224,000	2,102		723,000	8,606	
65-	133,000	7,184		370,000	21,256	
Total	1,093,000	10,169		3,977,000	35,224	

    a.   Now which state has the lower mortality rate for the youngest age group (0-5 years)? And for each successive age group?

    b.   Which state therefore seems healthier, from this more careful perspective?

22-11 We have seen that all five of Main's age-specific mortality rates were an improvement on Louisiana's, to varying degrees. Now let us develop a <u>single</u> overall measure of how much better Maine is.
    We could take simply the <u>average</u> improvement. But that would fail to give the large middle category its due weight. So here is a better weighted version:

a. Suppose Louisiana's age mix was the same as Maine's. But continue to use the age specific mortality rates of Louisiana. Then what would be Louisiana's total number of deaths (called "mortality <u>adjusted</u> to Maine's population")

b. To compare with Maine, calculate the ratio of Louisiana's adjusted mortality to Maine's mortality.

22-12 The above comparison of overall mortality rates in two states is very similar to the comparison of overall prices in two time periods, that is, index numbers.

Specifically, recall that a price index compared the total cost of a fixed "basket of goods" (quantities Q_0) for two different lists of prices (P_t and P_0). More specifically, the Laspeyres Price Index (22-4) compared $\Sigma P_t Q_0$ with $\Sigma P_0 Q_0$.

Similarly, in Problem 22-11 we found the total deaths in a fixed "basket of population" (quantities Q_0) for two different lists of mortality rates (R_t and R_0). Specifically, we compared $\Sigma R_t Q_0$ with $\Sigma R_0 Q_0$.

a. If Problem 22-11 corresponds to the Laspeyres Price Index, calculate the mortality index corresponding to the Paasche Price Index. Is it nearly the same?

b. As a compromise, calculate the mortality index corresponding to Fisher's Ideal Price Index.

c. For an alternative to the Fisher-type compromise in (b), for the fixed reference population quantities (Q_0) we could <u>sum</u> the population of Maine and Louisiana, age by age. Calculate this mortality index.

22-13 If all 50 states are to be compared, not just two, then the natural fixed reference population to use is the sum of all 50 states, that is, the population of the whole country. In 1978, this is what it was:

age	population (Q_*)
0- 5	16,000,000
2-20	55,000,000
20-45	81,000,000
45-65	43,000,000
65-	25,000,000
Total	220,000,000

a. For this reference population, calculate the mortality index comparing Louisiana with Maine. That is, calculate $\Sigma R_t Q_* / \Sigma R_0 Q_*$, where R_t and R_0 are the mortality rates of Louisiana and Maine, respectively, and Q_* are the U.S. sub-populations by age tabled above.

b. To compare two states, such as Louisiana and Maine, the ratio of the two in (a) makes good sense. But what if we want to compare all 50 states? Since we can't take ratios any more, we need a single summary number for each state, such as this:

$$\lambda \equiv \frac{\text{Adjusted total mortality}}{\text{total population}} = \frac{\Sigma R_t Q_*}{\Sigma Q_*}$$

Then λ is called the "mortality rate, age-adjusted to the U.S. Population", and it is a very common yardstick of mortality. Calculate this for Louisiana (λ_L), and then for Maine (λ_M)

c. Calculate the ratio λ_L/λ_M. How does it compare to the answer in (a)?

22-14 Now for a neat twist to our story that will finally link age-adjustment to multiple regression.

a. Instead of the ratio λ_L/λ_M calculated in part (c) above, calculate the difference $\Delta = \lambda_L - \lambda_M$.

b. If Louisiana's mortality rates (age-specific) could be brought down to Maine's, and if the age composition of Louisiana was like the whole U.S., how many fewer deaths would there be in Louisiana (per thousand people, annually)? Calculate your answer in terms of Δ found in (a).

c. The difference in mortality rates Δ has another interpretation: It is about the same answer that multiple regression would give. Specifically, multiple regression would distinguish the two states by a dummy regressor, whose coefficient would measure the difference in mortality rates and turn out to be approximately Δ. (The computed regression actually had a coefficient of .00133 which is indeed close to Δ.)
    In this multiple regression, the confounding factor of age would be handled with dummy regressors (variables). How many dummy regressors would be required for the 5 age categories?

d. Although multiple regression is not quite so clean as using age-specific mortality rates, multiple regression nevertheless offers two advantages: (1) It is a standard routine already available and understood. (2) Even more important, it easily allows other confounding factors besides age to be controlled, by including them as regressors too.
    What are some of these other confounding factors? (What factors affect mortality rate, and differ considerably between Louisiana and Maine?)

22-15 To tie this all together, a familiar example will help. In Problem 1-18 of the text we saw how deceptive the crude admission rates were, because of the confounding effect of faculty. (The arts faculty at Berkeley was harder to get into, and had more female applicants.)

a. To get a fairer comparison, calculate the admission rates of females(λ_F) and males (λ_M) , adjusted to the total of 12,600 applicants as the standard. Then how big is the difference $\lambda_F - \lambda_M$?

b. In the multiple regression analysis of this data in Problem 14-7 of the text, where will you find roughly the same answer as in (a)? How close is it?

CHAPTER 23 - SAMPLING DESIGNS

Reconnaissance is as important in the art of politics as it is in the art of war --' or the art of love.

Henry Durant

23-1 To determine the mean (and hence the total) volume of wood in a 5000 acre forest, stratified sampling was used. On aerial photographs the forest was first divided up between pine and hardwood. Then from the 1400 acres designated "pine", a random sample of 28 one-acre plots gave an average volume $\bar{X}$ = 580 (cubic feet), and s = 120. From the remaining 3600 acres designated "hardwood", a random sample of 72 acres gave $\bar{X}$ = 340, and s = 80.

Find a 95% confidence interval for the mean volume per acre, and hence the total volume in the whole 5000 acres.

23-2 In Problem 23-1, suppose a complete count of all 5000 acres would have given μ = 410 and σ = 140. And suppose the hardwood acres were more inaccessible, so they each cost twice as much to measure as pine. Compared to the stratified sample in Problem 23-1,

a. How much more (or less) would a <u>simple</u> random sample of 100 acres cost? How much more (or less) accurate would it be?

b. Could they have allocated their effort between the two strata better? Justify your answer fully.

23-3 In the forest of Problem 23-1, pine <u>gradually</u> merges with hardwood of course, so that the 1400 acres designated "pine" had a few hardwood trees in it, and vice versa.

If a randomly sampled acre of pine had some hardwood trees in it, should it have been (i) thrown out or (ii) counted as part of the volume for a pine acre anyhow, or (iii) counted as part of the volume for a hardwood acre instead?

23-4 Referring to an earlier ingenious sampling design for sample surveys discussed in Problem 3-46 in the text, answer True of False; if False, correct it:

a. Randomized response is an ingenious way to obtain reliable statistics for a population, while protecting the individual's confidentiality.

b. This protection is absolutely airtight. There is no way the interviewer, or the courts, or a computer bandit, or anyone, can know about any given individual.

23-5 A random sample of young single adults in a market survey was asked "Do you intend to buy a VCR within the next 12 months? Suppose the population would give the following breakdown by sex:

stratum	stratum size	proportion answering yes
male	55%	43%
female	45%	23%
total	100%	

Using the idea of a 0-1 variable (as in Section 6-4), first verify that in the whole population, the proportion who would answer yes is π = 34%. Then find the SE of the estimate of π based on a sample of n = 100 observations,

287

a. For a simple random sample.

b. For a proportional stratified sample.

c. For an optimally stratified sample, assuming all costs are equal. Can you suggest why stratification helps so little?

CHAPTER 24 - TIME SERIES

There's nothing constant in the universe,
All ebb and flow; and every shape that's born
Bears in its womb the seeds of change.   Ovid

24-1   To forecast a time series, does simple regression usually work well? Does multiple regression? Explain.

24-2   Personal disposable income (Canadian, 1974-1977, hundreds of millions of dollars)

	quarter			
year	1	2	3	4
1974	245	267	315	284
1975	281	311	346	317
1976	306	344	381	350
1977	347	386	423	390

This data was fitted with a regression equation (using the usual quarterly dummies Q_i as in equation (24-1), and quarterly time T = 1, 2, 3, ... 16):

$$\hat{Y} = 232 + 8.9T + 24\ Q_2 + 54\ Q_3 + 14\ Q_4$$

Use the given equation to forecast the series for the next 4 quarters, in 1978.

24-3   If the residuals $\hat{e}$ showed serial correlation, outline how that could be used to improve the forecasts in Problem 24-2.

24-4   Tabulate the seasonally adjusted series in Problem 24-2 (Hint: Problem 24-4 in the text).

24-5   For the data in Problem 24-2, calculate

   a.   The centered moving averages M

   b.   The ratio-to-moving-average Y/M

   c.   The seasonal S (by averaging over the four years found in part b)

   d.   The seasonally adjusted series. Does it roughly agree with Problem 24-4?

*CHAPTER 25 - SIMULTANEOUS EQUATIONS

Whatever moves is moved by another.

St. Thomas Aquinas

25-1 In the simple consumption model shown in Figure 25-1 in the text, suppose the true consumption function is Y = 10 + .8X, and the following 5 rows of data have been observed:

Y	X	I
68	75	7
64	65	1
88	95	7
44	45	1
66	70	4

    a. Graph the true consumption function. Plot the scatter of 5 points, and shade in the parallelogram they outline (hypothetical data, contrived to make a small sample as good as a large one.)

    b. Regress Y on X using OLS. Graph it. Is it unbiased?

25-2 Using I as the instrumental variable in Problem 25-1, calculate an unbiased estimate of the consumption slope β. Is it closer to β than is the OLS estimate?

25-3   a. What is wrong with OLS estimation of a simultaneous system in general?

    b. What is the solution?

These brief answers were not verified as thoroughly as the ones in the textbook, so that an occasional numerical mistake may occur. The authors would greatly appreciate hearing of any you have tracked down - T.H.W., R.J.W.

1-1   Created equal by randomized assignment, kept equal and evaluated fairly by keeping everybody "blind".

1-2   58% ± 4.6%   64% ± 6.3%
      52% ± 3.0%   52% ± 2.7%

1-3   This observational study does not permit such naive conclusions because of confounding factors. And maybe causation is the other way (crime producing low density, as people flee the core).

1-6   95% CI for long-run proportion:
      π = .1720 ± .0074
      i.e., .1646 < π < .1794
      Since this interval includes the "fair" value of .1667, it may well be just a fair die randomly fluctuating.

1-7   We can't draw any conclusion at all from this data done. For example, if smallpox were absolutely no threat, this vaccination program would have foolishly wasted 100 lives. But if smallpox were a very serious threat, then this program would have saved many thousands of lives.

      So we need to additionally know how serious a threat smallpox was. [In fact, by 1975 smallpox had become practically <u>extinct</u>, and so the program was wisely discontinued then.]

1-8   b.   Not very evenly. As well as 5-5, they will often be split 6-4 or even 7-3.
      c.   More evenly, rarely as lopsided as 60-40.
      d.   It does indeed show how randomization tends to even out in the long run.

1-9   a.   are drawn randomly
      b.   randomly

1-10 a.   Absolutely. And good science too, since reluctant subjects are not reliable.
      b.   It <u>is</u> possible to largely achieve both. First ask for volunteers for the experiment, then assign them randomly to the treatment or control.

1-11 a.   Yes, as explained in (b)
      b.   Yes, multiple regression would be an analysis as close as possible to the desired short-run "matching" of the measured variables.

1-12 a.   Expert judgement may still have bias, which is particularly troublesome in large scale samples or experiments.

      b.   Yes.   Use expert judgement to determine which are the potentially confounding factors to be matched for perfect balance.   Then use randomization to achieve the best feasible balance for the remaining variables (including those not even thought of) -- as in Problem 1-14(b).

2-1   a.   f = 19, 19, 8, 2, 2
      b.   .98
      c.   1.08, 1.04

2-2   Area = 3,620,000 mi^2

2-3   a.

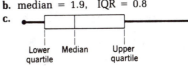

      b. median = 1.9, IQR = 0.8
      c.

      Lower   Median   Upper
      quartile   quartile

2-4   a.   1.5   ***********
           2.0   ****************
           2.5   *******
           3.0   ****

      b.   2.04, .47, 23%

      c.   24.5, 5.6, 23%

      d.   1398 ft.^{3} (or roughly, 1332 ft.^{3})

2-5   Yes: For n = 25, for example, the median is #13. The lower quartile is then the median of the lowest 13, which means it is #7 -- cutting off the lowest six.

2-6   a. $\bar{X}$ = 5.5, Q_U = 19, Q_1 = 3

c. Very skewed, with $\bar{X}$ far above $\overset{\shortmid}{X}$

d. $\bar{X} = 388/20 = 19.4$, which is even higher than Q_U

2-7 a. $\overset{\shortmid}{X} = 10$, $Q_U = 25$, $Q_L = 5$
     c. Very skewed, with $\overset{\shortmid}{X}$ far above $\overset{\shortmid}{X}$
     d. $\bar{X} = 381/15 = 25.4$, which is even higher than Q_U

2-8 a.

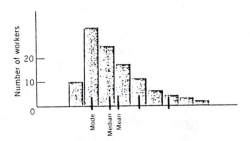

     b.

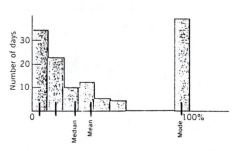

2-9 a. mean
     b. median, median, median

2-10 The mode lacks resistance.

2-11 a. 2.0   b. 1.4

2-12 2.0

2-13 a. Like the "Giant Oil Drum", the Giant Person appears 2.5^3 times as big. Lie factor $= (2.5)^2 = 6.2$. Instead, draw $2\frac{1}{2}$ people of the same size as the first.

     b. The black graph switches from imports to exports. And the y-scale doubles.

2-14 a. 1/3, nearly 1/2
     b. more than doubled in acreage
     c. 31%, 45%, so the average farm was 2.2 times as big.
     d. Graphs seem to level off because the

last years of course show less change than earlier decades. So exclude 1972 and 1973, or else mark them off clearly.

2-15 a. Canada, about 9%; Mexico, about 6%.
     b. Brazil is a little bigger (about 10%)
     c. about 25% by the U.S.; 2% or 3% by Brazil.

2-16 a. Midnight to 3 a.m., because there is less traffic and industry.
     b. Riverside
     c. In the west-central part of San Bernardino County. It also produces more of the other two pollutants than all the rest of the county at that time.

2-17 a. It doesn't say. For all we know, it might be appropriate amount of grief.

     b. We should first compare abortion to the alternative, as a base or control.

     c. This statistic also lacks a base for comparison. It might only mean, for example, that it takes rare courage to admit making a mistake.

     d. We agree.

2-18 a. Apparently from 1 in 10,000 to 1 in 135, which is about 75 fold.

     b. .000085 = 1 in 11,800. Compared to 1 in 10,000, it has <u>decreased</u> slightly. So the answer in (a) may be crazy. WARNING: These answers (and in 2-19) are based on Maclean's figures, which have shown themselves to be hardly trustworthy.

2-19 a. About 75 times (since the average life lasts about 75 years), which gives a lifetime risk of about .0064, or .1 in 155.
     b. In the same ballpark (but slightly lower).
     c. 75, 75, skulduggery

3-1 a. .50, .30, .65, .15
     b. .50, .70, .85, .35

3-2 a. no   b. no

3-3 a. yes   b. no

3-4 a. $1/15 = .066$ b. $7/15 = .467$
     c. $7/15 = .467$

3-5 a. 49 b. .01 c. .32

3-6 .40, .44, .16

3-7 a. F b. T
     c. F d. T

3-8 a. 28% b. 29%, 83%, 8%
     c. All Canadians are equally likely to be in Hong Kong.

3-9 .973

3-10 a. .0000037 b. .0000037
     c. .0000185 d. .00024

3-11 The actuary may be calculating the wrong odds. How many material witnesses were there in that huge crowd? 15? Or 1500?

3-12 Even the richest man has finite wealth, and risks losing it all. Why should he take even a tiny risk, just to win peanuts?

4-1 a. .001 b. .159 c. .840

4-2 a. .261 b. .550
     c. 390 d. 160

4-3 a. i)   13, 20
        ii)   1.3, 4
        iii) 4.5, 10
     b. 0, 1
     c. Normal

4-4 a. .055 b. .930
     c. Be kept blind, to avoid bias

4-5 a. 7.6, 2.04
     b. 1.50 biscuits c. 59.8

4-6 a. .648 b. .733

4-7 a. .047 b. .0022
     c. No. If this claim is true, a near miracle has occurred.

4-8 a. .001, 3.2 b. .406
     c. capacity of 5 workers

4-9 a. 1.0 b. 1.0 c. 1.0

4-10 a. .121 b. 2.00
     c. 1.84 d. $3.68
     e. trials are independent, with a

constant $\pi = .20$

4-11 a. $E(X) = 440$
     c. $E(C) = \$1,350$ $\sigma = \$910$

4-12 a. Yes, $E(C) = \$950$
     b. 300 is best, then $E(C) = \$850$
     c. The optimal number is less than the expected sales (300 vs. 440) because undershooting is only half as expensive as overshooting ($5 vs. $10).

4-13 a. No, No. Being blind prevents bias
     b. .006 c. (i) True
     c. ii) All wrong and backwards too. Corrected version (like b): If he is innocent, then the chance he shows guilty knowledge in 6 or more out of 10 questions is only 6 in 1000.

4-14 a. $4000, $E(G) = \$1200$
     b. $E(G)$ is a maximum of $1500 for B = $44,000

4-15 a. $B_0 = \$43,000$
     b. Because $P(B)$ is only approximately a straight line.

4-16 a. high, low
     b. peace treaties, bitterness

4-17 a. Failure to achieve agreement with the enemy until the eleventh hour was tragic.
     b. By contrast, this showed remarkable enlightenment, that in the long run benefitted the U.S. as well as her former enemies.

5-1 a. .65 b. 70, 15.6
     c. 30, 26.5

5-2 i. a. .65, 10 b. 70, 15.6
        c. 30, 26.5
        The Negative covariance means that students who did well in the first exam tended to do poorly in the second, and vice versa. This produces less variance in the total or average grade, but more variance in the difference I.

     ii. a. 65, 14.1 b. 70, 14.9
         c. 30, 28.3

5-3 .52

5-4 a.   .532   b.   .841   c.   .898

5-5 a.   .981
     b. $Cov(D,X) = -48$. Therefore students who start out weakest tend to show the most improvement.

5-6 a. $p(x_1, x_2) = 1/9$
     b.   Both distributions are $p(x) = 1/3$
     c.   independent, cov = 0
     d.   both means are 5, both variances are 4.67
     e. $E(\bar{X}) = 5$, var $(\bar{X}) = 2.33$
     f.   No difference at all
     g.   True.

5-7 $E(\bar{X}) = 5$, var $(\bar{X}) = .467$

5-8 a. $p(x_1, x_2) = 1/6$ off the diagonal
     b.   Both distributions are $p(x) = 1/3$
     c.   not independent, cov = -2.33
     d.   Both means are 5, both variances are 4.67
     e. $E(\bar{X}) = 5$, var $(\bar{X}) = 1.17$
     f.   For sampling without replacement, the absolute frequencies are important (unless the population is large compared to the sample size).

5-9 a.   X beats Y 54% of the time
     b.   Y beats Z 54% of the time

5-19 a.   The statement seemed right, and so X seems the strongest team, and Z the weakest.
     b.   We suppose X will usually beat Z, of course.
     c.   X beats Z only 36% of the time! (A direct contradiction to our conjecture in (b)).

5-11 a.   Z is the winner, winning 55% of their games (vs. 45% and 50%)
     b.   Y is now the winner, with average score 20,000 (vs.19,200 and 19,000)

5-12 a.   Tough decision, but we favor the second rule - for reasons given in part (b).
     b.   We agree.

6-1 a.   population mean, normal
     b.   standard error SE, less, σ

6-2 .54

6-3 .046 (wcc, .029)

6-4 a.   Not a random sample, because the single student in the front row, for example, is 4 times likelier to be picked than each of the 4 students in the back row.
     b.   No, because it is not random.

6-5 .161

6-6 .918

6-7 a. $\bar{X}$ may tend to be below μ (negative bias) since stay-at-homes may tend to eat less fast-food.
     b. $\bar{X}$ now has no bias, and so will be closer to μ on average.

6-8 .992

6-9 a.   .203   b.   .047
     c.   .0017 -- smallest of course

6-10 .082 (wcc,.136)   Or, by interpreting Table III c, .149. Correct value = .134.

6-11 a.   .002
     b.   Assumed all skiers were equally often on the tram (equally fast up and down the mountain). And assumed independence (no bunching, as in a ski class of mostly light kids).

6-12 b.   Normal, centered at 31, with SE = 2.65
     c.   .000337 $\approx$ .03%

6-13 a. $\mu = 1.10$, $\sigma = 0.83$ b.   .004
     c.   If the dean is right, a near-miracle has occurred.

6-14 a.   .064   b.   .123   c.   True

6-15 .988

6-16 .990

6-17 a. $\mu = .70$ = the population propor-tion
     b.   .985 (just a little less than in Problem 6-19)

7-1 a.   .114 mm b.   -.004 mm

7-2 a   .error = $18,000
         squared error = 324,000,000
     b.   198,500, which is much much better than (a).
     c.   I wouldn't trust it as far as I could throw it.

7-3 b. $\bar{X}$ usually is closer to $\mu = 0$ than is $\overset{!}{X}$ (rel. eff. $\simeq$ 157%)

7-4 b. Now $\overset{\downarrow}{X}$ usually is closer to $\mu = 0$ than is $\bar{X}$.

7-5 a. 0 b. $\pi(1-\pi)/n$ c. $-\pi(1-\pi)/n^2$

7-6 314

7-7 Bias = 61% - 43% = 18% (in favor of R). So this bias causes the average sample to "elect" the wrong candidate R.

7-8 59.6% [= .80(210/301) + .20(80/398)]

7-9 Sampling without replacement is better (rel. eff. = 125%)

7-10 b. MAE   .34   .29$\checkmark$
         MSE   .17$\checkmark$ .29

7-11 MAE(n=4)   .33   .25$\checkmark$
     MSE(n=4)   .19$\checkmark$ .25
     MAE(n large) .28   .17$\checkmark$
     MSE(n large) .14$\checkmark$ .17

7-12 a. True
     b. The new system forecasts better (MSE = .11 vs. .14)

7-13 a. 0 b. $2\sqrt{\pi_Y(1-\pi_Y)/n}$
     c. rel. eff. of P_A = .0215n + .062, which gives (i) 221% (ii) 1081%
     d. $.180 \pm .054 \simeq 18\% \pm 5\%$

8-1 a. $1.32 \pm .055 \simeq 1.32 \pm .06$
     b. $.11 \pm .022 \simeq 11\% \pm 2\%$

8-2 a. $\pi = .523 \pm .148 \simeq 52\% \pm 15\%$
     b. We agree

8-3 a. $\pi_2 - \pi_1 = -.050 \pm .034$

     b. $\pi_2 - \pi_1 = -.085 \pm .036$

     c. As (a) and (b) show, the wording does make a difference (or is it the week's time delay?) As to which wording is appropriate, this is not a matter of logic, but of value judgement.

8-4 7.0 ± 5.1

8-5 a. $.540 \pm .025 \simeq 54\% \pm 3\%$
         $.636 \pm .064 \simeq 64\% \pm 6\%$

$.523 \pm .027 \simeq 52\% \pm 3\%$
$.113 \pm .069 \simeq 11\% \pm 7\%$

b. Most precise is (i) because it is based on the largest sample.
    Least precise is (iv) because it has two component sources of error.

8-6 b. $\bar{X} = 4.0, 3.2$ s = .76, 1.22
     c. $\mu_1 - \mu_2 = .80 \pm .68$

8-7 a. 1989 mean = $3.27 \pm .28$ days
         decrease = $.29 \pm .41$ days
     b. 1989 chance = $.06 \pm .047 \simeq 6\% \pm 5\%$
         decrease = $.08 \pm .082 \simeq 8\% \pm 8\%$

8-8 c. .95
     d. False: ... are wider <u>on average</u> than ...

8-9 a. .050
     b. 3.34
     c. $.050 \pm .018$

8-10 a. 70,000 (.04) = 2800 lives
     b. 12,000 (3.0) = 36,000

8-11 b. $\mu_M - \mu_W = -.08 \pm .11$

8-12 a. less than 95%
     b. 95%
     c. much less than 95%
     d. very likely more than 95%

8-13 a. mean improvement = $.150 \pm .069$
     b. There are many reservations. For example, the 150 boys might be a biased sample of the whole 453. Also, whatever changes occurred in the boys may be due to confounding factors such as simply growing up, rather than the detention home itself.

8-14 a. $4.2 \pm .1$
     b. Michigan is relatively clean, but we cannot count on pH > 4.4 (but pH 4.3 we <u>can</u> count on)
     c. Seems true.

9-1 a. $.25 \pm .022 \simeq 25\% \pm 2\%$
         $.52 \pm .025 \simeq 52\% \pm 3\%$
     b. $.27 \pm .033 \simeq 27\% \pm 3\%$
         Is discernible.

9-2 a. $H_0: \pi = .40$, $H_A: \pi > .40$
     b. $S \geq 6$ c. .050
     d. .448, called β

9-1 a. $.25 \pm .022 \simeq 25\% \pm 2\%$
          $.52 \pm .025 \simeq .52\% \pm 3\%$
     b. $.27 \pm .033 \simeq 27\% \pm 3\%$
          Is discernible.

9-2 a. H_0: $\pi = .40$, H_A: $\pi > .40$
     b. $S \geq 6$ c. $.050$
     d. $.448$, called β

9-3 $\mu \geq \$6.90$

9-4 For H_0: $\mu = 1200$
     a. $\mu > 1216$, discernible
     b. $\mu > 1195$, indiscernible
     c. $\mu > 1172$, indiscernible
     d.   Between $\alpha = 5\%$ and 1%, but closer
          to 1%. About 2%.
     e.   True.

9-5 b.   like 95% confidence, $\mu_1 - \mu_2 = .23 \pm$
          $.20$ (which is discernible)

9-6 a. $p \simeq 0$ ($z = -6.0$)
     b.   If you can believe the problem as
          stated, discrimination has
          certainly occurred . However, it
          is important to look deeper as in
          Problem 9-7.
9-7 a.   16.2%
     b. $p \simeq .76$ or $p = .73$ (one-sided!)
     c.   Given the eligibility rule, there
          is no evidence whatsoever that the
          grand jury discriminated against
          blacks.
     d.   The major problem may be the racial
          discrimination in the past, which
          has left so many blacks illiterate.
          Or possibly the literacy
          restriction was unfair.

9-8 Quite possible that people tended to
     give themselves "the benefit of the
     doubt". This bias would require us to
     revise both answers in (a) downwards,
     with less subsequent change in (b).

9-9 a. $36.3\% = \alpha$
     b. $36.3\% = \beta$
     c. $\$1,017,000$, $\$1017$

9-10 a. $C = 360$ (disastrous)
     b. $\beta = .826$
     c. $\$1,549,000$
          $\$1549$ which is much worse.

9-11 We could reduce the cost to $900 per
     batch by simply omitting the test, and
     cleaning every batch. (It would save
     the cost of the test, too). This
     corresponds to $C = -\infty$, $\alpha = 1.00$, and
     $\beta = 0$.

better yet. The very best critical
value turns out to be $C = 156$ (provided
by advanced Bayesian Decision Theory).
Then
     a. $\alpha = .773$
     b. $\beta = .072$
     c. $\$846,000$, $\$846$ which is indeed
          better than $\$900$. If your guess
          for C gave an average cost less
          than $\$900$ too, congratulations.

9-12 a. $.83 \pm .04$, discernibility different
          from $.50$.
     b. $.05 \pm .15$, not discernibly
          different
     c.   See Problem 9-13.

9-13 a. $\mu_1 - \mu_2 = 54 \pm 26$
     b.   Is discernible (H_0 rejected)

9-14 There is a conceptual population of all
     babies in this culture and gene pool,
     from which the 90 babies may be regarded
     as a random sample. Then the CI and p-
     value are "screening devices" to screen
     out experiments with too little
     evidence.

10-1

Source	SS	df	MS	F
industries	553	2	276.5	114
residual	355	147	2.41	(p <<.001)
total	908	149		

     b. $\mu_1 - \mu_2 = 2.50 \pm .77$
          $\mu_1 - \mu_3 = 4.70 \pm .77$
          $\mu_2 - \mu_3 = 2.20 \pm .77$

10-2

Source	SS	df	MS	F
industries	495	2	247	82
residual	355	117	3.03	(p <<.001)
total	850	119		

10-3

Source	SS	df	MS	F	p
stores	104	2	52	19.5	<.01
bakeries	222	3	74	27.7	<<.001
residual	16	6	2.67		
total	342	11			

10-4 $\mu_1 - \mu_2 = 7.0 \pm 5.0$
      $\mu_1 - \mu_3 = 10.0 \pm 5.0$
          etc.

10-5 It would now be one-factor ANOVA, with
     greater residual variance, a weaker
     test, and wider confidence intervals.

10-6 a.

Source	SS	df	MS	F
camp.	534	2	267	3.76
resid.	853	12	71.1	(p<.10)
total	1387	14		

b.

Source	SS	df	MS	F
camp.	310	2	155	22.7
resid.	82	12	6.83	(p<<.001)
total	392	14		

c. Using the difference y-x is better. Then each store serves as its own "match", so the residual variance is reduced (from 71.1 to 6.83).

10-7 $\mu_1 - \mu_2 = -7.0 \pm 4.6$
$\mu_1 - \mu_3 = 4.0 \pm 4.6$
$\mu_2 - \mu_3 = 11.0 \pm 4.6$

10-8 a. Yes, if the class is large.
b. About 5%, if the class is large.

10-9 a. No, it is distributed around a much higher mean.
b. Many more than 5%, called the power of the test $(1-\beta)$.

11-1 b. 13.43°

11-2 $\hat{P} = 13.3 + .033 I$

11-3 b. $\hat{V} = 3.08 + 16.0C$
c. 57.1 ft^3

11-4 $\hat{V} = 4.8 + 9.67(1.3)^3 = 26.0 \text{ ft}^3$

12-1 For 11-1, $\beta = .0057 \pm .0038$, which is discernibly positive
For 11-2, $\beta = .033 \pm .162$, which is not discernibly positive.

12-2 $13.43 \pm 3.43 \simeq 10.0 \text{ to } 16.9$

12-3 a. $\hat{Y} = 7.5 - 0.050X$
c. $\beta = -.050 \pm .046$
d. Not fair, because this observational study is confounded by factors such as diet, alcohol, etc.

12-4 a. $\beta = 1.71 \pm 0.77$
b. yes

12-5 a. 87.4 ± 3.54
b. 88.5 ± 2.61

12-6 a. 87.4 ± 18.1
b. 88.5 ± 13.1
c. (a) is wider, because there is an additional source of uncertainty -- the worker's experience.

13-1 a. $\hat{S} = -2.0 + 0.20X$
c. The simple correlation is the effect of income confounded with assets.

d. 4.48 thousand
e. .48 thousand more
f. 1.86 thousand more

13-2 $\beta_1 = .162 \pm .027$, which is discernibly positive.
$\beta_2 = -.532 \pm .091$, which is discernibly negative.

13-3 a. Both admitted ($\hat{Y} = 3.55, 3.14$)
b. Chris would likely do better, because he had a higher $\hat{Y}$(by .21 units)

13-4 a. Other things (GRE and QI) being equal, a student with a GPA that is one unit higher can be expected to have a graduate performance Y that is .76 units higher.
b. For QI = 1, 2, 3, we get three lines:
$\hat{Y} = .14 + .76 \text{ GPA}$
$\hat{Y} = .39 + .76 \text{ GPA}$
$\hat{Y} = .64 + .76 \text{ GPA}$

13-5 a. Not necessarily, because of confounding (Part (b) in fact shows Y against R has a negative coefficient).

13-6 a. increase, 1.00
b. 6, above
c. 14.4, above
d. 23.0, above

13-7 a. $b_r = b_1 + bb_2$ (13-41)
$= .50 + (-.31)(8.0) = -2.0 \checkmark$
b. No. Rainfall itself helps, as shown by the multiple regression coefficient (+.50). But high rainfall tends to occur with low temperature, which has an overwhelming negative effect.

14-1 a. up 5.8¢, down 8.2¢, up 0.5¢
b. suburban, young, indoor

14-2 a.

CI	$t \simeq z$	p	
.41 ± .03	29	$\simeq 0$	*
-0.8 ± 0.4	-3.6	$\simeq .0001$	*
0.2 ± 0.5	0.8	$\simeq .2$	
-0.8 ± 0.4	-4.2	$\simeq .00001$	*
0.1 ± 0.4	0.5	$\simeq .3$	

b. Yes: C_1 and C_4 (urban core and fringe) form a lower cluster than the others.
c. The two clusters are real (not merely sampling flukes)

14-3 b. Yes, they confirm just what we expect.

14-4 a. Yes. More money and more people should mean more roads.

     b. Yes, because CI have relatively little fog:
$$\beta_1 = 1.17 \pm .10$$
$$\beta_2 = 1.10 \pm .14$$

     c. 6% higher R, 5% lower R

14-5 a. 4.6%   b. 17%
     c. 2.0%   d. 14% less

14-6 17% ± 10%, 2.0% ± 1.6%

14-7 a. Correct arithmetic, but don't forget that new vans tend to be F, which confounds the conclusions. See part (b) for clarification.

     b. Older cars <u>of the same make</u> on average cost more ($218 per year of age). And F vans cost $120 more than G vans <u>of the same age</u>.

14-9 b. For temperature, no real pattern. But for rainfall, the graph shows high rainfall and unusually high yield occur together:

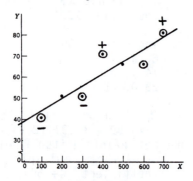

     c. Include rainfall as well as fertilizer in a multiple regression. It would reduce confounding as well as prediction error.

14-10 Rainfall of course, and its multiple regression coefficient would be positive.

14-11 a. 4   b. 2   c. 8
     d. 4 + 2 + 8 + 45 = 59 ✓

14-12

Source	SS	df	MS	F	p
regions	464	4	116	4.40	<.01*
urb.	102	2	51	1.93	<.25
inter.	109	8	13.6	0.52	>.25
resid.	1187	45	26.4		
total	1862	59			

14-13 Yes, and the multiple regression would now be called ANOCOVA (Analysis of Covariance).

15-1 b. r = .34
     c. $\hat{Y} = .191 + .32\,X$

15-2 Worst two will likely improve, while the best two will likely deteriorate (regression to the mean).
     This indeed happens. For example, the worst player improved from .220 to .260

15-3 a. $\hat{Y} = .191 + .32\,X = .284$
     b. $\hat{X} = .167 + .37\,Y = .255$

15-4 a. Approx. $-.36 < \rho < .78$
     b. $\beta = .32 \pm .71$
     c. Both say "not discernible" because zero is in the CI.

15-5 a. Y = .284 ± .062
     b. X = .255 ± .072

15-6 a. smaller, because there is less "leverage" in each half. (See (c) for details)
     b. r = .26 and .08
     c. True

15-7 a. r = .51, .073, .016, .084, .011
     b. r = .44, the very same

15-8 a. 19%, 52% which is 33% more
     b. 3.8, 2.9
     c. Y = 47.7 ± 7.4
     d. Y = 47.55 ± 5.7

15-9 a. Different salaries on average, because of different productivity. So there is no discrimination.
     b. Men's line coincides with women's.
     c. coefficient of M is 0, which would be correctly interpreted. Specifically, it shows zero extra salary for men compared to women <u>with the same productivity</u>.

15-10 Exactly the same answers as in 15-9.

15-11 a. Same answer still: different salaries on average because actual productivity is different. So there is no discrimination.
     b.

In this Figure, once more note that each regression line was correctly fitted to its ellipse by splitting in half the little vertical lines that indicate the range of vertical spread (as in Fig. 15-7 in the text).
     Since each ellipse has been "spread out" horizontally, this makes each

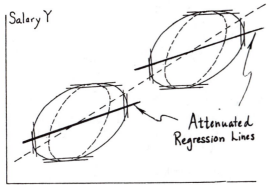

Salary Y

Attenuated Regression Lines

Measured Productivity X

regression line also more horizontal, with less slope. This is called "attenuation", and makes the men's line higher than the women's!

   c. Thus the coefficient of M is now positive. If this is given the usual interpretation of discrimination, it is clearly wrong. It is only evidence of attenuation.

15-12 a. man, woman, sex discrimination against women.
      b. X, satisfy the regression model (13-3)

15-13 a. How much more productive men are than women earning the same salary.
      b. It would be positive, since the <u>reverse</u> regression lines would be more steeply sloped (as in Figure 15-8 of the text).
          That is, men seem to have greater productivity than women <u>earning the same salary</u>, so now men seem discriminated against.
      c. women, men; neither

16-1 a. Very little credibility: p = .035
      b. p = .145

16-2 a. 93% CI: $-2 \leq \nu \leq 4$
      b. Assumed that the differences are due to policy alone, and not to confounding factors such as more flu epidemics in the second year, etc.
          Very important assumptions, also made in Problem 16-1.

16-3 a. H_0: The core and suburban populations are the same.
      b. p = .048 (W = 19)

16-4 a. One that is reasonably close to its target, even if the population is very non-normal (long-tailed, especially).
      b. Delete some of the observations from both ends, then average the rest. More robust than $\bar{X}$. Better than $\bar{X}$ for populations with long thick tails, a little worse for normal populations or populations with shorter tails than the normal (rare in practice.)

16-5 a. The biweighted mean doesn't cleanly cut off the end observations (as does the trimmed mean). Instead, it just weights them gradually less and less.
          Compared to the trimmed mean, it is a little more robust but requires more computing.
      b. It uses the same weighting function to discount y-outliers in regression.

16-6 a. higher, more, skewed
      b. 15, half

16-7 $p \simeq .00001$, since z = -4.24 (wcc, $p \simeq .00002$ since z = -4.07) (Based on 4 out of 32 differences being negative, discarding one occurrence of zero difference)

16-8 p << .0005 (t = 6.10)

16-9 We feel the t test is more appropriate for two reasons: (i) it fully counts the extreme lead levels, which are medically very serious. (ii) As mentioned on p. 262 of the text in a footnote, it is quite robust for n as large as 33.
      As a bonus, t routinely gives a 95% CI to express <u>how large</u> the average lead effect is: 17.0 ± 5.7.
<u>Remarks</u> This example shows why classical statistics remain important and deserve first place in any basic text.

16-11 a. Good matching keeps important extraneous factors constant, and would show up in the graph as high correlation in the x and y levels (data in a narrow ellipse tilted at 45°, which finally would project to a precise and narrow range on the dotted diagonal axis of differences.)
      b. We see no evidence at all of such an ellipse tilted at 45°, so matching did not help in this case (apparently child's age and

neighbourhood were not important factors).

As final evidence, note that the differences have a disappointingly large spread (IQR = 21, which exceeds the IQR = 18 for the exposed children.)

17-1 a. $\chi^2 = (7280-7497)^2/7497 + ... = 6.3 + ...$

c. With huge n, monthly data provides appropriate detail. But it is more work, and if n were small, it might not achieve discernability.

17-2 a. Education is independent of sex
b. $\chi^2 = 11.6$, p < .01
c. Yes, since p < α
d. Easier, but less insightful. This explains the popularity of χ^2: it's easy, even if it isn't very deep.

17-3 a. Voting pattern is independent of age.
b. $\chi^2 = 9.64$, p < .005
c. The under 30 support Bush by 11 percentage points more than do the over 30. (11% ± 7%, with 95% confidence)
d. We prefer (c) because it states not merely that there is a difference, but <u>how large</u> the difference is.

17-4 a. p ≃ .0014 (z = 3.2). This agrees with 17-3 (b), but is more precise.
b. about the same, can
   Remarks: $z^2 \approx \chi^2$, just like $t^2 = F$ in Chapter 10

17-5 a. Sex ratio doesn't change
b. χ^2, p < .025
c. Very slight change: boys rose by 0.09 percentage points (.09% ± .07%, with 95% confidence)
d. (c), because it emphasizes the change is trivial.
a. p ≃ .023 (z = 2.49) This agrees with 17-3(b).
b. About the same, can

17-6 a. $\chi^2 = 10.9$, p < .05

17-7 $\chi^2 = 13.9$, p < .001

18-1 a. MLE = MME = 6/500 = .012
b. MLE = MME = b = 294/220 = 1.34

18-2 a. .333
b. L(π) is very vague:

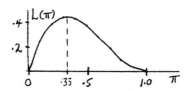

18-3 a. .333
b. L(π) is now only about half as wide, i.e., the accuracy about doubles (Just as in CI):

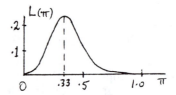

19-1 odds = .67 (2 to 3), probability = .40

19-2 a. .15   b. up: .44
c. down: .02

19-3 $\mu = 52.5 ± 3.9$

19-4 $\pi = .162 ± .119 \simeq 16\% ± 12\%$

19-5 36.7, 38.6, 40.5, 36.1

19-6 37, 37, 37, 37

19-7 a. Prior is flat, so that posterior = likelihood.
b. $\pi = .67 ± .27 = .40$ to .94
c. Very close agreement
d. Is indeed a little narrower, because it is based on more information.

20-1 Reliable at $2.50 each, to minimize the expected total cost at $3.30

20-2 a. 150, 200   b. 150, 200
    191, 200   191, 200
    199, 200   199, 200
c. larger, closer to; overwhelms

20-3 a. It is indeed vague, giving higher likelihood to higher values of π.

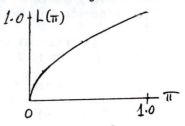

b. P* = (S + 1.5)/(n + 2.5). For example, if S = 1, P* = .38

20-4 a. S has a binomial distribution, with n = 4 and π = the value in Problem 20-3(c).

   b. Here is an example, if π = .40. Then p(s) = .130, .246, .346, .154, .026 from Table III b. Correspondingly, P* = .23, .38, .54, .69, .85, and eventually MSE = .042. Correspondingly, P = 0, .25, .50, .75, 1.00, and eventually MSE = .060. So in this case, P* is better.

      Of course,, if π = .60 or .80, then P* is much better. But if π is near 0, P* is worse.

20-5 We expect most students would obtain a Bayesian estimator P* that was better than P. But if the prior is centered badly and is very narrow, the Bayesian estimator P* will be worse.

20-6 a. The 91st percentile, which is 80.

   b. For 80 texts ordered, the expected loss is $40; while for 70 or 60 texts, the expected loss is $42 or $88 -- getting worse.

20-7 a. 73 (91st percentile)
   b. 60 (median)
   c. 70 (83rd percentile)
   d. 53 (25th percentile)

20-8 a. β = .06
   b. β = .0688 $\simeq$ .07

21-1 Proceed, for an expected net return of 0.2 million.

21-2 Carefully think through his utility function, and then maximize expected utility (EU).

21-3 Drop it (EU = .390 vs .369)

21-4 A _perfect_ prediction would only be worth 1.2 million (EVPI). So this option could not possibly pay its way.

21-5 No. Using it would only net 0.08 million on average, which isn't as good as proceeding without it.

21-6 .38 million

21-7 "Postponing" (postponing the vaccination until after the first child) means much less extra risk (.000090 vs. .004000)

21-8 "Postponing" still means less extra risk (.000090 vs. .000500)

21-9 Immediate vaccination means 500 excess birth defects, while "postponing" means only 90.

21-10 b. They can't easily be sued if this advice turns out badly. (If Down's syndrome occurs a long time later, they could argue "it might have happened anyhow").

21-12 After age 18, there are about 50 years of life left, or 600 months. Therefore the monthly risk $\simeq$ 5%/600 $\simeq$ .01%.

21-3 a. Decreasing marginal utility of money (i.e, money is worth less and less.) Nearly everybody's utility is curved like this, because we purchase first what is most important to us, so that later purchases are not so satisfying (per dollar).

   b. C is best, D is worst (The four expected utilities are .344, .498, .513, and .330, respectively)

21-14 a. utility, poor
   b. irrelevant, matters
   c. not nearly so huge, less

21-15 a. C is best, D is worst (exactly as in Problem 21-13(b).)

   b. Now D is judged best (maximum is 25), A is worst (minimum is 10)

   c. Rawls' criterion completely ignores everyone except the single most miserable person in the society. If Society E had one person at income 24.99, and five million at income 300, Rawls' would still judge it inferior to D. How peculiar.

      On the other hand, Harsanyi's utilitarianism seems very sound. It has withstood the test of time over centuries in one form or another, and we haven't seen anything that looks any better. (However, we have seen lots of attempts to take the distribution of utility into account, which overcompensate as described in Problem 21-14(c). The most bizarre example is Rawls' attempt.)

22-1 a. PPI < FPI < LPI, for reasons given on p. 669-670 of the text (The PPI allows for people partially escaping inflation by substituting goods whose prices have risen least.)

   b. LPI = 346, PPI = 309, FPI = 327

22-2 a. PQI < FQI < LQI, for similar reasons.
      b. LQI = 108.5, PQI = 97.1, FQI = 102.6

22-3 Fisher's only. Since total cost index = 336, we verify: 327 x 102.6 = 336./

22-4 A form of Laspeyres. It is easy to work out, but exaggerates inflation. To the extent that payments such as wages and social security are indexed to inflation, this tends to produce an inflationary spiral.

22-5 LPI would tend to wind the inflationary spiral up, while the PPI would tend to wind it down.

22-6 a. CPI sharply rises, as the Government tries to suddenly pay for a huge emergency by the simplest means: printing more money.
      b. Also rising, but less sharply.
      c. The last 20 years, 1965-85. (US inflation is a modern problem)

22-7 a. Yes. If we allow for the wider scale on the CPI, it has the same shape as the GNP deflator.
      b. 169%, since $(1.02)^{50}$ = 2.69. 100%, since $(1.02)^{35}$ = 2.00
      c. About half as long to double as in (b), that is, 18 years. Then 35 years to double and redouble (quadruple).
      d. To rise from 100 to 200, the legend shows it takes 35 years at 2%, for example.

22-8 a.

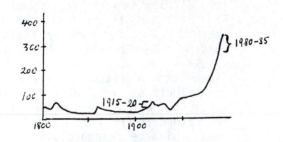

      b. The later inflation from 1980-85 looks twice as serious, but in fact it's only half as serious.
      c. A ratio scale is more appropriate, because it allows us to judge relative inflation at a glance.

22-9 a. Louisiana is lower (8.9 vs. 9.3)
      b. Louisiana, because of (a)

22-10 a. Maine is lower for age 0-5 (2.5 vs. 4.5) and also for every other age :

2.5	vs	4.5
0.57		0.72
1.43		2.14
9.38		11.90
54.0		57.4

      b. Now Maine seems healthier. This is another example of Simpson's Paradox, as in Problem 1-18 of the text.

22-11 a. 4.5(76) + .72(291) + ... = 11,640
      b. 11,640/10,169 = 1.145

22-12 a. Now we use Louisiana's population instead of Maine's as our standard. Then mortality index = 35,224/30,267 = 1.164, which is quite close to 1.145 (Just like the two price indexes are close)
      b. Compromise = $\sqrt{(1.145)(1.164)}$ = 1.154
      c. 46,831/40,434 = 1.158, which is a second compromise.

22-13 a. 2,231,640/1,940,520 = 1.150, which is a third compromise.
      b. λ_L = .01014 = 1.014%, λ_M = 0.882%
      c. 1.014%/.882% = 1.150, same as (a)

22-14 a. Δ = 0.132% or 0.00132
      b. .132% of 1000 = 1.32 deaths per thousand
      c. 4 dummy variables
      d. race, income, etc.

22-15 a. $\lambda_F - \lambda_M$ = .4301 - .4146 = +.0155
      b. coefficient of sex dummy variable, which is + .005. This roughly agrees with (a) -- both answers show females have a trivially higher admission rate (about 1% higher).

23-1 μ = 407.2 ± 18.2
      total = 2.036 ± .091 million

23-2 a. A simple random sample would cost the same (on average), but would be less accurate (SE = 14.0 vs. 9.3). We could say 34% less accurate, or 56% less efficient.
      b. Yes, sample relatively more where it is cheaper and more variable (pine). Formula gives optimal ratio of pine/hardwood is 45/55 (vs. 28/72 formerly).

302

23-3 Count it as a pine acre (ii), to be unbiased. (Stratification requires that the strata be rigidly adhered to if their weights W_i are to be used validly.)

23-4 a. True   b. True

23-5 a. .0474   b. .0463
c. .0462, still not much better than (a). Stratified sampling helps very little in 0-1 populations in general, because it's hard to find homogeneous strata (a stratum with 0's and 1's is just about as varied as the population itself with 0's and 1's, unless π is very close to 0 or 1)

24-1 Simple regression often works badly because of seasonal variation and serial correlation. Although multiple regression can look after the seasonal variation using dummy variables, serial correlation can still be a problem if it is not specially treated.

24-2 a. Ignoring the serial correlation, $\hat{Y}$ = 383, 416, 455, 424

24-3 Simplest solution is to assume first order serial correlation, $e_t = \rho e_{t-1}$. Estimate ρ by regressing $\hat{e}_t$ against $\hat{e}_{t-1}$. Use this to forecast the dwindling residuals, which should then be included in the forecast. (See footnote 2 in Chapter 24 of the text for details.)

24-4
268	266	284	293
304	310	315	326
329	343	350	359
370	385	392	399

24-5 See text Table 24-2 for method. The seasonally adjusted series would be very similar to Problem 24-4 above.

25-1 a.

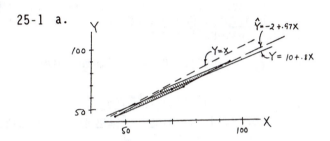

b. $\hat{Y}$ = -2 + 1.97, bias = .97 - .80 = .17.

25-2 b = .80, which is dead on target (because of the contrived data).

25-3 a. It is biased and hence will not get close to target even for huge samples (inconsistent).
b. Use instrumental variables.

REFERENCES

Abouchar, Allan (1981), Personal Communication of Some Figures from the Stockholm Peace Research Institute.

Dawes, R.M. (1971), "A Case Study of Graduate Admissions: Applications of Three Principles of Human Decision Making", <u>American Psychologist</u> 26, p. 180-188.

Diaconis, P. and B. Efron (1983), "Computer-Intensive Methods in Statistics", <u>Scientific American</u> 248, May 1983, pp. 116-130.

Fairley, W.B., and F. Mosteller, ed. (1977), <u>Statistics and Public Policy.</u> Reading, Mass: Addison-Wesley.

Finkelstein, M.O. (1980), "The Judicial Reception of Multiple Regression Studies in Race and Sex Discrimination Cases", <u>Columbia Law Review</u> 80, pp. 737-754.

Fischhoff, B., P. Slovic, and S. Lichtenstein (1986), "Knowingwith Certainty: The Appropriateness of Extreme Confidence," in <u>Judgment and Decision Making: An Interdisciplinary Reader</u>, edited by H.R. Arkes and K.R.Hammond, pp. 397-416. Cambridge: Cambridge University Press.

Fuchs, Fritz (1980), "Genetic Amniocentesis", <u>Scientific American</u> 242, June 1980, pp. 47-53.

Glover, D., and J.L. Simon (1975), "The Effects of Population Density upon Intrastructure: The Case of Road Building", <u>Economic Development and Cultural Change</u>, Vol. 23, pp. 453-468.

Griliches, Zvi, and W.M. Mason (1973), "Education, Income and Ability", in <u>Structural Equation Models in the Social Sciences</u>, edited by A.S. Goldberger and O.D. Duncan. New York: Seminar Press.

Haarman, D.J. (1985), "Letter to the Editor", <u>Journal of the American Medical Association</u> 253, p. 1878.

Harsanyi, John C. (1976), <u>Essays in Ethics, Social Behaviour, and Scientific Explanation</u>. Dordrecht: Reidel.

Kaye, David (1982), "Statistical Evidence of Discrimination", <u>Journal of the American Stastical Association</u>, 380, pp. 773-787.

Klitgaard, R.E., and G.R. Hall (1977), "A Statistical Search for Unusually Effective Schools", in Fairley and Mosteller, 1977, pp. 51-86.

Langer, W.L. (1976), "Immunization against Smallpox before Jenner", <u>Scientific American</u> 1976, pp. 112-117.

Lykken, D.T. (1975), "The Right Way to Use a Lie Detector," <u>Psychology Today</u>, March 1975, p. 60.

McFarland, L.V., J.R. Harris, J.M. Kobayaski and others (1984), "Risk Factors for Firework's Related Injury in Washington State", <u>Journal of the American Medical Association</u> 251, pp. 3251-3254.

Morton, D., Saah, A., Silberg, S., Owens, W., Roberts, M., and Saah, M. (1982), "Lead Absorption in Children of Employees in a Lead Related Industry", <u>American Journal of Epidemiology</u>, 115, pp. 549-555.

Nemenyi, P., S.K. Dixon, N.B. White Jr., and M.L. Hedstrom (1977), <u>Statistics from Scratch</u>, Pilot edition. San Francisco: Holden-Day.

304

Randolph, W.C. (1988), "Housing Depreciation and Aging Bias in the Consumer Price Index", <u>Journal of Business and Economic Statistics</u> 6, pp. 359-371.

Rawls, John (1971), <u>A Theory of Justice</u>. Cambridge, Mass: Harvard University Press.

Rosenbaum, P.R. (1989), "Exploratory Plots for Paired Data", <u>American Statistician</u> 43, pp. 108-109.

Salk, Lee (1973), "The Role of the Heartbeat in the Relation between Mother and Infant", <u>Scientific American</u>, May 1973, pp. 24-29.

Simon, J.L. (1981), <u>The Ultimate Resource</u>. Princeton, N.J.: Princeton U. Press.

Tufte, E.R. (1983), <u>The Visual Display of Quantitative Information</u>. Cheshire, Conn: Graphics Press.

Tversky, A., and D. Kahneman (1974), "Judgement under Uncertainty", <u>Science</u>. September 27, 1974, pp. 1124-1131.

Wagner, C.H., (1982), "Simpson's Paradox in real Life". <u>The American Statistician</u>, February 1982, pp. 46-48.

Wainer, H. (1984), "How to Display Data Badly". <u>American Statistician</u> 31, pp. 137-147.